MORE PRAISE FOR *THE INEFFICIENCY ASSASSIN*

"Helene Segura's vivid examples from real life and pop culture, her anxiety-dissolving humor, and her clearly presented and comprehensive wisdom make *The Inefficiency Assassin* a book that belongs on every professional's bookshelf."
— **Julie Bestry**, CPO®, president of Best Results Organizing and author of
57 Secrets for Organizing Your Small Business

"I am a big fan of managing your time as effectively as possible. Helene Segura outlines the quickest ways to make that happen. It's a must-read."
— **Jane Atkinson**, author of *The Wealthy Speaker 2.0*

"Helene Segura understands how to guide her readers in this book to improve their individual time management tracks. Her CIA framework is a step-by-step guideline for effective work–life integration. I thoroughly recommend this book for anyone who is aiming to become the master of his or her own time management."
— **Michael Brecht**, CEO of Doodle.com, author of
The Productivity Book, and productivity blogger on MichaelBrecht.com

"Using *The Inefficiency Assassin*'s CIA framework, I've made powerful changes that have allowed me more time to be present with my family while still moving forward in my business. Helene Segura's approach is simple, easy, and a wonderful resource to visit to get back on track."
— **Carol Frazey**, MS, founder of TheFitSchool.com and author of
The Fit School Diet Plan

"Helene Segura does it again with this book, now aiming her crosshairs at workplace time wasters! Her experience with clients for so many years, along with her natural strokes of genius and sharp wit, will shave off hours from your work week."
— **Lorie Marrero**, CPO®, author of the *Wall Street Journal*–bestselling book
Clutter Diet and founder of ClutterDiet.com

"Completing tasks efficiently in less time simply by processing your work and your thoughts, and using common sense? Now, that's music to my ears! *The Inefficiency Assassin* just changed my life!"
— **Kim Etheredge**, cofounder of Mixed Chicks hair products

"Helene Segura offers innovative solutions for your productivity roadblocks. She delivers her wisdom in easy-to-understand, bite-sized, and often-humorous chunks. Follow her recommendations, and you'll gain countless hours of new-found time."

— **Laura Stack**, founder of The Productivity Pro, Inc.,
and author of *Doing the Right Things Right*

"Wow, Helene Segura really gets it: time management is really about life management. She knows how to go from the big picture down to the little details and how to create the right context to not only get more done but also feel better about it. She doesn't just have great ideas; she also organizes them in a user-friendly way so you can get the most out of them. This is the book to get."

— **Ari Tuckman**, PsyD, MBA, ADHD expert, speaker,
and author of *More Attention, Less Deficit*

"*The Inefficiency Assassin* slays chaos and indecision. As a person with attention-span and follow-through issues, I was grateful to discover that Helene Segura shares the doable secrets to take my creativity from ideas to reality. And she does it in bite-sized, digestible chunks even I can handle. Everyone who wants to achieve something important needs *The Inefficiency Assassin*."

— **Jeff Anderson**, writing consultant, speaker, and author of
the Zack Delacruz series and *10 Things Every Writer Needs to Know*

"*The Inefficiency Assassin* is a concise, straightforward, and comprehensive plan that provides realistically attainable tactics to solve every major productivity problem. It details precisely how to eliminate these issues so you can have the professional and personal life you desire. With Helene Segura's help, you can say farewell to guilt and exhaustion and to being overworked and overwhelmed."

— **Erin Rooney Doland**, editor-in-chief of Unclutterer.com
and author of *Never Too Busy to Cure Clutter*

THE INEFFICIENCY ASSASSIN

THE INEFFICIENCY ASSASSIN

TIME MANAGEMENT TACTICS FOR WORKING SMARTER, NOT LONGER

HELENE SEGURA, MAEᴅ, CPO®

New World Library
Novato, California

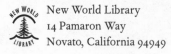 New World Library
14 Pamaron Way
Novato, California 94949

The material in this book is intended for education. It is not meant to take the place of diagnosis and treatment by a qualified medical practitioner or therapist. No expressed or implied guarantee of the effects of the use of the recommendations can be given or liability taken.

Text design by Tracy Cunningham

Library of Congress Cataloging-in-Publication Data is available.

First printing, April 2016
ISBN 978-1-60868-400-7
EISBN 978-1-60868-401-4
Printed in Canada on 100% postconsumer-waste recycled paper

 New World Library is proud to be a Gold Certified Environmentally Responsible Publisher. Publisher certification awarded by Green Press Initiative. www.greenpressinitiative.org

10   9   8   7   6   5   4   3   2   1

For
Marcus Luttrell,
Chris Kyle,
Anthony Mendez,
Dorothy Blum,
Gene Grabeel,
Jeanne Vertefeuille,
Sandy Grimes,
Dr. "Say,"
Andrew Segura,
and all the warriors and operatives —
known and unknown,
living and deceased,
past, present, and future —
who make our freedom to live the American dream possible

Contents

PART 3. ASSEMBLE YOUR TEAM

Life and Work Are Not Solo Missions

PART 4. SITUATIONAL SOLUTIONS

Introduction

Your Time Management Revolution Starts Here!

Julie is quite well known in her field and is often sought to give lectures or develop programs for large organizations and corporations. Despite her services being in such high demand, she felt she had done a great job in setting office hours. She went into her office only from 8:30 in the morning until 3:00 in the afternoon, Monday through Friday, so that she could drop her kids off at school in the morning and pick them up in the afternoon, and then take them to practices or games. She carried her smartphone with her at all times, so that she could always squeeze in a little work here and there — while waiting in a lobby, while standing in line at the grocery store, or after the kids went to bed. She could also sneak in a peek on the weekends while the kids were running around the yard or swimming.

One early evening at her son Ben's baseball game, she felt her phone vibrate in her lap. She had just received an email from one of her best (i.e., a top-dollar account) clients, who had a question about an upcoming meeting. Julie felt she needed to respond to her client's email immediately. Ben picked up a baseball bat in the dugout and tentatively walked toward the batter's box as Julie began typing her quick response.

The next thing she knew, everyone in the bleachers around her jumped up and started whooping, hollering, and whistling. The crowd was going wild!

"Oh my gosh! What's happening?" she thought as she typed frantically, as fast as her thumbs would allow.

She hit the send button and finally stood up to see what the ruckus was all about.

Julie had just missed her son's first home run. She was crushed.

And so was he.

• • •

"If I can just get this one more promotion, we'll be set..."

When I was a junior in college, I was introduced to "Dr. Say." Now retired, he'd spent his career as an agent with a law enforcement bureau. He did occasional contract work for them now. A mutual friend told him that I was interested in going to work for the DEA (Drug Enforcement Agency), and he agreed to meet with me to tell me about how to prepare for the application process, as well as the job ahead.

I was relieved to learn that my research about the application process had been quite accurate. (Keep in mind, this was in the days before the internet.) I knew what qualifications — both academic and physical — I needed to meet, and I was fully prepared to work toward them.

When we started talking about the job itself, I couldn't contain my excitement. He shared a few examples of cases and the work involved. I was in heaven! This was exactly the kind of adrenaline-filled life I wanted to live. Move over, *Adam-12*, *S.W.A.T.*, *Cagney and Lacey*, and *Miami Vice*. My lifelong dream of being an undercover cop or agent was on the verge of coming true! It was going to be my turn to bust criminals.

But then we started talking about life outside of the job. More accurately, we started talking about the lack of life. He told me to look around his condo. There were no pictures of people. There was very little decor. In my haste to pick his brain, I had neglected to realize that I was not in a happy environment.

Dr. Say asked me, "Do you know why I'm an old man sitting alone in a condo with no sounds, no life?"

"No, sir," I said.

"It's because I chose work over my family. I was afraid to say no or request an alternate assignment. I was too fearful to try to get a different job. My wife and kids made their choice, too. They left me because I was never there for them."

I was stunned and speechless. To the casual observer, he'd lived an exciting life helping capture criminals. But behind the scenes, life was far from perfect.

Dr. Say did earn every promotion he sought and every raise he wanted. He worked his tail off to have a stellar career and make a better life for his family. The painful irony of it is that the price he paid was the very thing he cherished, his family.

What he shared with me had such a profound impact that he literally changed my life forever. At that time I had no plans to get married, but I knew that I wanted to have a personal life and happiness. To this day, I still think of him and how his decisions about time had affected his life.

• • •

This next example I'd like to share with you is directed toward entrepreneurs, but given the experiences shared with me by all the dedicated, hardworking, driven employees I've worked with, I know that everyone will relate.

When you go into business, you do so because you have a passion or a calling. You have figured out the love of your life — not the person, but that thing you love to do, that thing that makes you happy to wake up every morning. And you discover a way to make money doing it. Or maybe you didn't have a passion, but you or someone you know came up with a grand plan — a surefire way to make a ton of money. In Tricia's case, it was the former.

When Tricia started her eco-friendly soap business, she didn't worry about productivity or staying organized day in and day out. She was primarily concerned about hustling after clients and generating enough revenue by the end of the month to pay the rent, pay the utilities, buy groceries, and maybe have a few bucks left to splurge on something fun. She quite often had thumb-twiddling time while she was waiting for the phone to ring, hoping the next caller would be her cash-cow client.

As Tricia learned the ropes and figured out what tasks she needed to complete in order to build her business and be more successful, she started to increase her contact base. Her reach was growing. People had heard about her. Customers started rolling in. Money finally arrived. She had tasted success and wanted more. She thought she'd figured out what she needed to do: *I need to double up on what I've done to get here!* She went into overdrive with networking, marketing, customer service, picking up even more clients, and making even more money.

Tricia, like the typical entrepreneur, never started the business saying,

"These are the systems I'll put in place in order to stay organized." Or "These are the processes I'll use in order to be productive and maximize my time throughout the day." After all, how can you already have systems when you start out if you're not sure what you're supposed to be doing, and you don't even have clients?

Her schedule got so insanely busy that she didn't know which way was up. The line between her business life and personal life got so blurred that she didn't remember when it had actually existed. Her day became so full of phone calls, emails, meetings, and to-do lists that on some days, she woke up and didn't even know where to begin.

Tricia went into business to have the freedom to do what she wanted to do, the way she wanted to do it. She no longer worked for The Boss. She could set her own schedule. She could decide her days off. She was no longer chained to someone else's desk.

But she'd lost every freedom she'd dreamed of and wanted. She was chained to her desk (and phone and computer). She never took a day off. She didn't spend more time with her friends or family. In fact, during the fleeting moments she was with them, they gave her guilt trips for not being around. She had become The Boss, that entity she had been trying to escape in the first place. She was burned out from constantly working and wondered why she'd gotten into this crazy soap business in the first place. Her passion, relationships, and entire mental state had bitten the dust.

• • •

If you relate to any of the three examples above, this book is for you! Each of them shows the price paid when our work and personal lives fall out of balance. I'm not suggesting that being a stellar employee or owning a business can be a piece of cake and that you can skip work on a whim multiple times per week. That's why the subtitle of this book contains the words "Working Smarter, Not *Longer*" instead of the more commonly used phrase "Working Smarter, Not *Harder*." We're go-getters, and we do work hard, so it's a lie to promise you that you'll never have to. However, what I am saying is that *intentional* work, combined with planning and efficient processes — along with some dashes of fun! — will yield you the same or more accomplishments and revenue in less time, which will give you the time for the freedom and balance you desire — working smarter, not longer.

> Why limit Happy to an hour?
>
> – Attributed to W. C. Fields

Hopefully, by this point you realize that you need productivity and order in your day so that your blood pressure and stress levels don't cause a stroke or heart attack or divorce or breakdown. I use the word *hopefully* because some of my consulting and coaching clients — like Tricia — seek me out *after* they have crashed and burned. They now need to pick up the pieces and put themselves and their lives back together. I am so thankful that they are turning things around, but my dream is to help more go-getting professionals create the time they need to live a fulfilling life *before* something tragic happens.

And I don't want you to miss special moments in life, like the terrible experience Julie had when she didn't get to see her son's first home run. So many times, we find ourselves chasing what we think will help our career dreams to come true, and we end up missing the highlights in life. To paraphrase attorney Arnold Zack, when folks are on their deathbed, no one ever says, "I wish I'd worked more." In fact, on many occasions, the regret is the opposite.

Whether we work in a small or large company, telecommute, or own our own business, we are all warriors and super agents in some form or fashion. We are on a crusade in constant pursuit of our target: success. We gather whatever weapons and tools we can find to bust out of containment and forge ahead. We go undercover to find out how to get a leg up on the competition. We tend not to rest until each of the cases on our lengthy list is solved. We get knocked down and bounce back. But whether we're male or female, parents or sans kids, single or married (or your Facebook relationship status is "It's complicated"), we also desire some calm in between adrenaline rushes.

> Science is organized knowledge; wisdom is organized life.
> – *Will Durant*

If you want peace and some semblance of balance in both your work life and personal life, then no matter what stage of your career you're in — your fifth month, your fifth year, or your fifth decade — it's critical to understand organization and productivity.

At this point, you might be asking yourself, "What exactly does 'being organized' or 'being productive' even mean?"

When I write about or discuss organization and productivity, I focus on these meanings:

- Arranging or planning in a particular way
- Doing or achieving a lot: working efficiently and getting good results
- Having time to do what you want to do

The first two are right out of Webster's dictionary. I threw that third definition in there because it's what busy professionals like you crave.

As much as I would love to tell you that I can wave a magic wand and your life will change for the better overnight, I'm sure you know by now that that just isn't the case. Otherwise, the last time you stressed out, you would have bought said magic wand instead of another box of chocolates or that bottle of wine.

It will be critical for you to sift through the facts of the case and determine which strategies and tactics to use to make your mission successful. Some of you may try to revolutionize everything at once, and that will work for you. Others might try implementing just one change per week or month because that's more at your comfort level.

No matter how you proceed, please realize that nothing will change if you don't do something *different*.

Are you tired of feeling overwhelmed from having so much to do?

Do you want to never miss another special moment?

Do you wish you had more time in the day?

Do you want to learn how to improve productivity, so that you can increase success and decrease stress levels?

If you answered yes to any of these questions, you're in the right place.

Welcome aboard! It's time to go on a mission...

BECOME YOUR OWN HERO

Chip is a friend of mine who works for an incredibly fast-growing tech company. He's built a bit like a linebacker, about six feet tall and almost 300 pounds. You wouldn't want to meet him in a dark alley, but he's a blast to spend time with.

This guy is such a hard worker. He is *always* working, from the time he arrives at the office (which is usually early) until the time he leaves (which is usually late). He rarely stops for lunch. He normally eats something out of a box or can at his desk.

He's super-nice. He never says no to a request. He always drops anything he's working on in order to help a coworker or client. He never asks for help. He's a big, tough guy, so he feels like he needs to carry the entire load by himself at all times.

Or he did... until one day in the middle of a meeting, he experienced excruciating chest pains. He turned shades of white and green, grabbed his chest, and sputtered, "Someone call 911!" At the hospital, the doctor said to him, "Your blood pressure is through the roof! I can't understand how you're still alive!"

Talk about an awakening!

Chip almost became a member of the "Coronary Club." Right then and there he quit his bad habits cold turkey. He was only 48 years old and had a lot more living to do. Eventually, his stress levels and blood pressure went down without surgery or medications. He worked fewer hours yet completed more work and at a higher level of quality. He even took an extended break for a long week-end getaway. How did he turn his habits around? By doing what we'll be doing here — creating a Time Management Revolution and becoming his own hero.

In any book, television show, or movie involving agents or detectives, the hero has to figure out what the dilemma is, determine the causes, and apply the solutions through strategies and tactics that fit the situation. Today, like Chip, each one of you is the hero of your own super-agent story, and you're about to receive the options to use for your strategic and tactical solutions. All of us have the capacity for a Time Management Revolution inside us. We just need to bring it out from deep cover and into our consciousness. (For dramatic effect, this is the part where you stand up, throw your cape behind your shoulders, and declare, "Oh, yes, I will be my own hero!")

> To strive, to seek, to find, and not to yield.
> — Alfred, Lord Tennyson, "Ulysses"

As I alluded to earlier, after meeting with Dr. Say, I changed my mind about becoming an undercover law enforcement agent. Instead, I started my adult career by becoming a change agent as a teacher in a Title I school. Teaching my kiddos time management skills by improving their critical-thinking skills is how I wound up starting my productivity consulting business years ago. It was then that I became an agent of change by helping clients to find work–life balance. I teach people how to be more efficient. I help them to lower their stress levels. I bring peace to people's lives — and more profit to companies' bottom lines — by slaying wasted time. I'm blessed to be able to speak all over the country as The Inefficiency Assassin. (Please know that I do not condone violence. However, I am all for battling lost time!)

I grew up reading Nancy Drew mystery novels, competing with my best friend, Amy Epman, in elementary school to see how many we could check off our reading list. You'll find that the love I still carry for agent and detective books and movies is reflected not only in my job title but also in the examples and themes that I use in my keynotes, as well as in this book.

HOW THIS BOOK IS SET UP

The beauty of what I'll teach you in this book is that anyone can do it! While I will throw in some science here and there to explain why things happen, what you as a business professional need to do to be productive is not scientific. It's a choice of mind over matter — making better decisions and implementing them.

In order for you to become an agent of change in your own personal and work life, we'll be massaging your brain at two different levels as you read this book: strategic and tactical. What most people want is to be handed tactical information — a checklist of what to do. It's catchy. "Top 5 This" and "Top 10 That." It's short and sweet. It's easy to digest. However, to successfully implement the tactical over the long term, it's important to understand the strategic — how the tactics fit into a long-term strategy — which is why I will share both strategic concepts and tactical tips with you.

Implementing organization and productivity is very similar to planning a mission. So, before you dive into action, it's important to map out the big picture. The heart of this book is set up in three parts, which contain 30 approaches for working smarter, not longer — my CIA framework for your Time Management Revolution:

Create Clarity   Part 1
Implement Structure *and* Flow   Part 2
Assemble Your Team   Part 3

Each chapter of solutions contains the following sections:

Goal: Should you choose to accept this mission, this is the lowdown on the mind-set you need to apply in order to make your life better.
Tactics: If you're limited on time and need a quick fix, and/or you're screaming, "Just tell me what to do!" implement these solutions. These are the ever-popular top five or top seven things to do — the how-to tactical solutions for the situation. They are the weapons that will get you out of your time deficit.
Strategy: When it comes to time management, thinking *is* doing. If you're saying, "Just tell me what to do!" it's important to realize that

recommending how you should think — how your brain should operate — *is* telling you what to do. Just because it's mental doesn't mean it's unimportant. In fact, it's absolutely critical that you take more mental action than physical action. If you want to truly understand how you got into your current situation, why the aforementioned tactics are recommended, and how to prevent getting into the same situation in the future, read this section too. These are the overall strategic-thinking concepts and mind games to apply. This is your protective armor and your battle plan, both of which lead you to more success on your missions.

Next Steps: To aid you in successfully completing your mission, debrief the chapter with these questions, and plot your next steps.

Those of you who feel that self-discovery and learning the reasons behind what works and doesn't work is just a bunch of hooey can simply read the "Goal" and "Tactics" portions for your how-to tips — and skip the rest of the chapter. Those of you who want to dive deeper can read the "Strategy" and "Next Steps" sections. If you're ready for deep undercover work, you can utilize the activity guide that complements this book and is available as a download at www.Helene Segura.com/30tactics.

After the chapters that explain my CIA framework, I've also included part 4, "Situational Solutions." These chapters provide "troubleshooting" assistance for the most common pitfalls that busy professionals face.

STRATEGIES AND TACTICS: NAMES AND ACRONYMS

For the best possible learning experience, I encourage you to read the chapters in order so that you can fully understand the complete CIA framework for better time management — or, should I say, *mind* management. However, I realize that because you're struggling with finding time, you may not have that luxury just yet. Therefore, the book has been formatted so that the various situations that busy professionals face are divided up into individual chapters to enable you to pick and choose which situations apply to you and hop directly over there to get the tactical tips you need. I do encourage you, though, to read the "Strategy" sections when you're ready for that information. It's mind-bending knowledge that will truly help change the way you view time.

Many of the concepts in the book are interrelated, so you'll find that I do

> If you have an important point to make, don't try to be subtle or clever. Use a pile driver. Hit the point once. Then come back and hit it again. Then hit it a third time — a tremendous whack.
>
> — *Winston S. Churchill*

repeat strategies and tactics here and there. The repetition will help those of you who decide to skip around — you won't miss anything. The repeated information will also serve as reminders and will help you learn and remember what to do. After all, humans must read or hear ideas four to seven times before we synthesize them. After all, humans must read or hear ideas four to seven times before we synthesize them. (Repetition. Get it?)

If you read the book in order, each strategy or tactic will be discussed in full at its first mention and then referred to multiple times throughout the book. Just in case you skip around from chapter to chapter — or you return to this book later for a refresher — here's a location guide for my interestingly named strategies and tactics:

NAME	OBJECTIVE	CHAPTER
3+3	Set priorities for the day	9: Get It All Done in 24 Hours
CHOP	Get rid of annoying tasks	9: Get It All Done in 24 Hours
Mind Liberations	Declutter your brain	10: Set Reminders, and Never Forget Again
Cinco P	Declutter space and papers	12: Dig Out from a Buried Office
DID	Process paper efficiently	19: Deal with Incoming Daily Paper

ONLINE RESOURCES

If you wander over to www.HeleneSegura.com/30tactics, you'll find links to time management planning templates, the activity guide for this book, research by neuroscientists and psychologists that supports what I assert in my book, a glossary, apps and software programs that might be useful tools, suggestions of helpful office supplies and great books, quote sources, videos, and more.

IF YOU DON'T HAVE TIME TO READ THIS...

Throughout my book, I'll present various case studies from my client base. Some of my clients work for big corporations. Some clients work for small businesses. Some clients telecommute. Some clients own their own companies. Some clients own their own franchises. No matter what your situation is, you can learn from others' experiences in order to improve your current personal and/or work life.

Some of you will receive tremendous affirmation because you're already doing some of what I mention. Celebrate! Others of you will slap your forehead and declare, "Brilliant! I never thought of that!" And some of you might say, "Well, duh! That's simple. There's nothing new. We should all be doing that!" So then the question for you becomes, *Are you? Every day?*

Applying just one of the concepts that I share with you in this book will save you — at a bare minimum — at least 60 minutes each workday...which is five hours per week, 20 hours per month, 240 hours per year. That's six workweeks! Who wouldn't want all that extra time?

The majority of clients I work with don't have the time to read this book in one sitting. And that's perfectly fine. If you fall into that category, I encourage you to set aside 15 minutes at the same time each day — perhaps right before or after breakfast, during lunch, or in the evening — to pick up this book and read a little each time. If you commute via train or metro, wouldn't this make a good read — and a perfect distraction from any smelly folks who plopped down near you?

It's important to understand that everything you'll be doing here is ongoing. It's not a one-shot deal. After all, we're human. We evolve. We change. Our responsibilities change. Those around us change. I encourage you to come back to revisit this handbook whenever you start to feel a little off-kilter.

The time you invest in reading this book is an investment in your career, your personal relationships, and your physical and mental well-being. If you're thinking, "I don't have time to read all this," that's exactly why I strongly encourage you *to* read it all — because the strategies and tactics in this book will give you the time to do whatever you want!

Have your pen, highlighter, sticky notes — whatever tools you need — ready to help you to interact with the text. If you're reading the digital version, hopefully your system has a bookmark and note-taking function. If not — or perhaps in addition — don't be shy about carrying around a journal or spiral-bound notebook to take notes and develop your plans; or you can utilize the companion activity guide.

MY COVER STORY

I love adventure. Every summer my husband and I travel for three weeks, completely unplugged. We journey off the beaten path to "nonnormal" destinations like Bran, Romania, and Mostar, Bosnia. What I learn about people, cultures, and political and ethnic divisions around the world helps me relate to people and become a better teacher of behavioral modifications.

I was born and raised in Los Angeles and was known for my sports prowess (four varsity sports my senior year of high school), not my smarts. I was the kid in AP class who had to study her tail off in order to make decent grades. I had my brainiac friends, jock friends, and thug friends. This mixture was my introduction to figuring out different types of people in order to get along with them.

I grew up a tomboy, rarely wearing dresses or makeup. I preferred cleats and a shaved head. As an adult, I watch Aggie football every Saturday and the Dallas Cowboys every Sunday. I've only recently learned about girlyness, and I'm still learning. My hair and makeup look good in my headshots because I paid someone to do them for me on picture day.

After graduating from high school, I made the crazy move to "Cowtown" in order to attend and play soccer for Texas A&M University, where, between my extracurricular activities and what I perceived as my lack of smarts, I struggled to make good grades. Heck, I even got kicked out of the dorms one summer because of low grades. (My soccer career ended after one season when I blew out my ankle.)

I told my parents during the first semester that I wasn't moving back to L.A. because I loved the laid-back pace. I eventually settled in San Antonio — which to me was the most relaxed large city I'd ever visited — and became a teacher.

It was not until I started studying brain research in grad school that the light-bulb came on, and I figured out how to process new information in a way that I could remember it and make adjustments in my routines as necessary. An easier way to learn and modify behavior and manage time is what I taught to my high school students in the first half of my adult life and eventually to my clients in the current second half.

Looking back on my life thus far, I realize that I've always been a teacher: as a babysitter growing up, a resident adviser in college, a teacher for 11 years in a Title I school, and an educational consultant.

I've always had an interest in business: holding summer jobs managing all the stations at a fast-food restaurant, assisting the tailors of men's suits in a national retail clothing chain, working behind the scenes in the insurance and banking industries, and studying during grad school how to run a school campus like a business.

I've also always been an entrepreneur. When I was a kid, I set up a highly profitable Kool-Aid stand and sold wood carvings to my neighbors. In high school, I unofficially ran a designated-driver service for my friends. For a while, I sold Mary Kay cosmetics so that my friends and I could get a discount on the products. After meeting many teachers who struggled during retirement, my husband and I (back in my teaching days) invested in rental houses, and we ran that "company" for several years. In 2001, I founded an online wedding accessory business after developing a bridal emergency kit.

Finally, these worlds of teaching, business, and entrepreneurialism merged in 2006, when I became a productivity consultant. At last, I'd figured out what my passions were and what I needed to do for a living to be happy. One focus. One goal. Success. Happiness.

I love helping people to become more efficient, which allows them to find peace and calm in their lives.

And time for travel, wine, and good food.

And learning how to ride a motorcycle.

It's on my bucket list!

What's on yours?

● ● ●

I share all this with you for multiple reasons:

First, it's easier to learn from people and carry on a conversation with them when you know more about them and make even the smallest connection. Since I'm not sitting across from you at a café or a bar, this is the start of our connection and our conversation. It's nice to meet you!

Second, have you ever been to a training presented by someone who hasn't actually experienced what he or she is training you in? That's annoying. That happened all the time back in my teacher days. Presenters would come in and tell us how to do things, even though they'd never been a teacher. In the business world, I've been to marketing sessions presented by people who've never had to market for themselves. What the—? In addition to all my training for and experience as a Certified Professional Organizer®, productivity trainer, and consultant, my knowledge of how entrepreneurs and business folks roll has come from being an entrepreneur and businessperson, just like you.

And third, this serves as an example for the stroll down memory lane that I'd like you to take.

Now it's your turn!

I promise we won't go too deep into self-assessments. (If you truly want to learn more about yourself and how you best operate, feel free to obtain a copy of my *ROAD MAP to Get Organized* book.) But it is important to acknowledge where you've been, what you've accomplished, and what you'd like to focus on.

You can take a shortcut and just answer the following questions mentally. But if you'd like deeper learning to happen, I highly encourage you to record your thoughts here in this book, in the activity guide download, on a digital device in the notes section, or in a separate journal.

BACKGROUND CHECK: WHAT'S *YOUR* COVER STORY?

There are no right or wrong answers; it's simply interesting to know these things about yourself. So dive on in!

- What were you like as a kid?
- What are you like now as an adult?
- What are your hobbies, passions, and/or interests?
- What do you do for a living?
- What led you to decide to start your own business or take the job you currently hold?
- Do you see anything from your past and/or anything from your interests and hobbies that ties in with what you do now?

> Who arrrrrrrrrre you?
>
> – *Caterpillar in* Alice in Wonderland, *by Lewis Carroll*

Again, there's no right or wrong; it's simply interesting to know these things about yourself and discover any patterns in your life. Sometimes we can discover that we've allowed the same types of challenges to repeatedly knock us off track. Knowing this helps us to become more aware and to avoid those downfalls in the future. And by answering the previous questions, we can discover what we love and what makes us tick, which — as we'll learn in part 1 — will help us to make better decisions about how we'll use our time.

- What hobbies, passions, or interests do you wish you had more time for?
- What are your accomplishments?
- Were the accomplishments you listed all personal, all business, or a combination?

If all the accomplishments you listed were personal, you might find that you tend to focus more on the personal part of your life, and you'll have to kick up the amount of attention you pay to the business part of your life if you want to perform at a higher level there. If all the accomplishments you listed were business related, you might need to do the opposite and pay more attention to the personal part of your life.

This book will help you to decide how much time you want to devote to each. As I mentioned earlier (and will continue to do throughout this book), I'm a huge proponent of having a personal life. If you're quite content being a workaholic and not having a personal life, *no problema*. But you probably wouldn't have picked up this book if you were happy with that.

- What's on your bucket list?
- What is your definition of a great life?
- Based on your definition, do you have a great life? If your answer is "Yes," kick up your heels and give yourself a high five! If your answer is "Not yet," how close are you to it?

Getting specific about the kind of life you want to have and the personal accomplishments you want to attain will help you to carefully guard your time. When you protect your time, you'll be able to achieve the balance that you seek between work life and personal life.

That wasn't so bad, right? It's just a little exercise to get your brain juices flowing. While we shouldn't dwell on the past, sometimes a little historical recon, combined with thoughts about the present path we're on and future paths we might like to take, helps us to figure out what our next steps in life are.

Get ready to do some mind shifting. You're about to embark upon a glorious mission: your Time Management Revolution. Godspeed!

PART 1

CREATE CLARITY

*Mind Management Is the Key
to Time Management*

1

It's All in Your Head:
End the Overwhelm
by Adjusting Your Mind-Set

The fear of clients not returning for more business, the worry of running out of time for anything and everything, the urgency to burn the midnight oil in order to finish the next task on your never-ending to-do list...these things don't work. That's why you're reading this.

As businesspeople who want to succeed, we can so easily get sucked into the mentality of "I must do this task or project for my job or business, or else I'll lose out!" What if we turned the tables around and thought that way about our personal priorities? "I should spend time supporting my health or family or marriage, or else I'll lose out!" Will saying yes to that "one more thing" for work support your priorities in life?

If you read nothing else in this book, but you understand this strategy, this concept — "I should spend time supporting my health or family or marriage, or else I'll lose out!" — *and live by it*, know this:

You will be productive *and* have a life outside of your business or your job.

Time management.

Productivity.

Happiness.

Success.

Peace.

It's all about mind-set and mind management.

It truly is...all in your head.

A MONSTER LESSON

Have you seen the movie *Aliens* lately? It's the second movie in the franchise. Sigourney Weaver stars as Ellen Ripley and kicks some serious space-monster booty! Ripley wakes up after hurtling through space back toward her home planet, spending 57 years in a deep sleep after escaping from a nasty, slimy alien beast on a colony planet. After her recovery, the powers that be ask her to return to the planet with a crew of Marines because the current settlers on the planet have stopped responding. Hmmm...I wonder what happened to them.

Fast-forward to aliens with razor-sharp teeth, covered in slime, chomping down on one Marine at a time, until they're down to just six people in command central. Bill Paxton's character, Private Hudson, has been whining the entire time about everything that's going wrong. "We're gonna die!" "What are we gonna do?" "There's no way out!"

Ripley takes a deep breath, looks around at everyone, and calmly says to Hudson, "Now I want you to get on a terminal and call up some kind of floor-plan file. Do you understand? Construction blueprints. Anything that shows the layout of this place. Are you listening? I need to see air ducts. I need to see electrical access tunnels. Sub-basements. Every possible way into this complex. We don't have much time. Hudson, just relax."

In the midst of meltdowns by other crew members who were overwhelmed by the mayhem surrounding them, Ellen Ripley was able to remain calm and keep things in perspective.

The situation was critical, but she knew: You have to take your time to save time.

She understood how to **C**reate Clarity.

YOUR SECRET WEAPON IS...

I meet folks from all professions and walks of life when I speak as The Inefficiency Assassin. I also have wonderful phone coaching clients all over the world. The number one question I get asked is, "What is the best _____ to use?" You can fill in the blank with such words as *calendar, file folder, file cabinet, task app, cord manager* — you name it. I'm always asked about a *product*. Or if a company wants to hire me to present at their conference or training, they want me to include a "Top 10 Tools" list as one of my deliverables. Everyone wants to know the secret quick fix.

Depending on how much time I have at that moment, I try to briefly explain that tools are just tools and won't work unless something else, something bigger — an extreme strategy — is learned.

Since you and I have the time right now, let's talk about what that mind-bending concept is.

What is the key to organization and productivity?

I can tell you that there are no shopping lists involved. There's not an inventory of tools or supplies to purchase. No containers. No apps.

Do you want the answer to the question they always ask? Do you want to know what your Time Management Revolution needs in order to work?

Here's a hint: you already possess the most critical tool a person needs in order to be successful with time management.

It's your brain!

That's right, my comrades-in-arms. Your brain is your secret weapon! There's nothing special to buy! Managing your time comes down to how you train your brain *to think*.

Now, don't get me wrong; calendars and apps are tools you can utilize. But the key tool is your brain — because it's your brain that decides what goes on those calendars and what tasks get added to those apps or lists, whichever you choose to use to track what you need to do.

Your brain is what will make you, and it is also what can break you.

Every decision you make, from the time you roll out of bed in the morning until the time your head hits the pillow in the evening, will affect your personal life and work life.

Your brain makes your decisions.

Therefore, that gob of gray matter that resides in your skull is your key to failure...or success.

Your brain is in total control of everything you do. It decides how much time you waste and how much time you utilize. It decides whether you'll procrastinate or jump in and get things done. Your brain determines your reaction and response to every person who communicates with you and every situation in which you're placed. And if you've got too much spinning around up there, you can end up with brain constipation.

It's important to understand that you can't be on autopilot. You must be conscious, aware, intentional, present, cognizant — whichever term you prefer to use — regarding your decisions about how you use your time. Your brain will help you to implement your Time Management Revolution.

CREATING AND CARING FOR
YOUR SECRET WEAPON

In this first part of the book, we'll be discussing the **C** in CIA — **C**reate Clarity. You'll learn how you can care for and utilize your secret weapon — your brain.

In order to **C**reate Clarity, we must do the following:

- Capture our priorities
- Identify our targets
- Administer self-care
- Reflect with power
- Be open to change

When you achieve this part of the mission, completing the rest of the productivity operation — parts 2 and 3 — is that much easier.

Ready? It's time to do some capturing!

2 Capture Your Priorities

What would you do if flames were spreading quickly in your home, and you had just a few minutes to evacuate? My client Carol was once, unfortunately, in that situation. She lived in the Midwest on a quiet street, in a two-story house with a wraparound front porch and white picket fence. The fire in her house started in the middle of the night from an electrical short in the basement, so she and her family had to scramble down the stairs from their bedrooms and get out of the house as soon as possible. When I asked her what she grabbed as she ran out of the house, she replied, "I realized in that moment that my physical possessions were pretty unimportant. I made sure my family was out, our pets were accounted for, and we had our medications to stay in good health."

Those frightening moments brought Carol's priorities into focus. She was reminded that the most important thing in her life was the well-being of her loved ones. That fire devastated the house, and they were forced to rebuild. But this experience changed her perspective on how she spent her days. Having that clarity about her life's priorities helped her to make better decisions in the future about how she wanted to use her time. She realized that work would always be there, but her family might not.

GOAL

Make any and all decisions in work and life based on your priorities. Post your priorities in a place where you can view them daily.

TACTICS

Capture Your Personal Priorities

1. Brainstorm: Write down (on paper or digitally) everyone and every goal that's important to your life.
2. From this list, write down your top three or four personal priorities.
3. View your personal priorities list every day.
4. Make decisions in your personal life and in your work life based on these priorities.

Capture Your Work Priorities

1. Brainstorm: Write down (on paper or digitally) every belief, objective, and concept that's important to your work.
2. From this list, write down your top three or four work priorities.
3. View your work priorities list every day.
4. Make decisions in your personal life and in your business life based on these priorities.

STRATEGY

In order to stay focused on what you're trying to accomplish in your career, you need to understand what your priorities in life are. We often think we know what they are because we've casually thought about them from time to time, but until we set our priorities down on paper (or in the computer) in a place where we can view them on a daily basis, they do not become ingrained in our thoughts. And when they're not ingrained, we tend to lose sight of the big picture and wind up lost — off our path, in the opposite direction of our mission.

While we all have daily priorities like ensuring that we have enough gas in our vehicle to get to the next meeting, or making sure that we have dinner at some point in the evening, we need to examine the bigger picture.

I have multiple clients who, when their careers first started taking off, would work all day long, take a break to have dinner with the family, and then go right back to working on their computers. The time they used to spend in togetherness with their families in the evenings had been replaced by quality time with the computer. And that put a bit of strain on their relationships. They had lost sight of two of their priorities: their spouse and children. The decisions they were making at the time were not supporting their relationships with their families. That needed to change.

Many of my clients struggle with guilt. They'd wanted to attend all their kids' games, but they began missing many of them because their schedules became so hectic. In the back of their minds, they knew they wanted to be on the sidelines to root for their children, but they did not have this priority listed in a place where they could view it when it came time to plan their calendars. "Attending my kids' games" was one of the first items they listed when we put together their priorities list.

By the way, who should be at the very top of your priorities list? That's right — you! What's this, you ask? Why you? Well, when it comes down to it, it really is all about you.

Let's use an analogy. It's one I'm sure you've heard used many times, but I'm going to use it again here because it's so accurate. If you've ever flown in an airplane, then you know the drill that the flight attendants go through during their preflight safety checklist. Frequent fliers are still talking on their phones or flipping through magazines and usually ignore the verbal safety instructions. During the presentation, this line is uttered:

> It's a helluva start, being able to recognize what makes you happy.
> — *Attributed to Lucille Ball*

"In the event that cabin pressure changes and oxygen masks are needed, please adjust yours first before helping others around you."

Mmm. So true. How can we help others if we can't breathe ourselves?

So, it's time to put on our own oxygen masks.

Knowing what our top three or four priorities are in our lives gives us the clarity to make better decisions about how we use our time each day. No need to wait for a fire or near-death experience to force you to reevaluate your life!

When we move from having thoughts float around between the conscious and subconscious parts of our brains, to having those thoughts reside fully in the conscious part, we become more aware and focused. That's what happens when we write down our goals and view them daily. They're no longer random thoughts that pop in and out of our minds. The wiring in our brains that helped us to capture these ideas helps us to turn those random thoughts into focused goals.

As you mull over the questions I'll ask in the following paragraphs, don't focus yet on when these things will happen. Instead, focus on what it is that needs to happen.

People

Whom do you want to keep happy in your life? Your significant other? Your kids? Who is important to you? They will be your people priorities. Whatever future decisions you'll need to make will be based on whether the action you take will support the relationship you want to have with your people priorities.

Activities

What activities will support the relationships you want to have with your people priorities? Is participating in a religious organization a priority? Is travel a priority? What activities will bring you peace? What activities will support your own personal health and well-being? Whatever future decisions you'll need to make will be based on whether the action you take will support your activity priorities.

Work

Is your career a priority? What is your company's mission? What business goals are you trying to accomplish? What activities will bring you income or revenue? If you work for a company, which tasks get you the highest rankings on your annual evaluations? Whatever future decisions you'll need to make will be based on whether the action you take will support your work priorities.

Ah, clarity. You now have a clear idea of your mission in life. This will allow you to make better decisions about how you use your time. The next time your brain tries to drag you away from the present and you have to decide whether to follow that tangent, or the next time someone asks you to do something, make a decision based on the priorities that you've just written down.

Will doing xyz task help you to achieve a priority on your list?

If the answer is yes, get it done. If the answer is no, don't do it. If you have a boss who disagrees, be sure to read part 3, in which we discuss how to communicate with others. If you are your own boss, you have the power to make these decisions.

Hang on to your brainstorm exercises. We'll be using these, along with your priorities lists, a little later. We'll learn how to use these lists to schedule your days, and I'll go into more detail on how to make better decisions about how to use your time.

ⅢⅢ➡ PLOT YOUR NEXT STEPS

- Where will you post your personal priorities list?
- Where will you post your work priorities list?
- When, each day (or evening), will you view these lists?
- Viewing your priorities lists on a daily basis has most likely not been a tactic you've applied regularly. How will you remind yourself to do this every day?
- Where can you store these lists so that you can readily view them when you need to make a decision?
- How will implementing the strategies and tactics in this chapter benefit you?

3 Identify Your Targets

Richard had grown tired of the corporate world. He wound up resigning and purchasing a franchise. He figured that if he was going to work long hours, he may as well be the owner and get paid better.

Boy, was he overwhelmed in no time. There was so much that went into running a business, even if it already came with its own operations manual and training courses. He spent less and less time at home. And when he was home, he was still working, oblivious to everyone around him.

When an employee or manager called and asked him for something, he'd jump and do it, no matter what time it was. Yet somehow he was rarely available to tuck his kids into bed. He promised his wife that he'd spend more time with her. He promised his kids that he'd spend more time with them.

When he got to bed, he'd look at his watch, then look at the photos of his family on his nightstand, and realize that once again he hadn't spent "more time" with his family. Richard knew in the back of his mind and in his heart that he wanted and needed to spend more time with his family. He knew that his family was a priority, so why couldn't he make this happen?

He knew this, but those thoughts had not been moved to the conscious part of his brain. *He had no visual reminders of his priorities and targets that would focus his thinking.*

GOAL

Make any and all decisions in work and life based on your targets. Post your targets in a place where you can view them daily.

TACTICS

Capture Your Personal *Targets*

1. Take out the personal priorities list that you created in the previous chapter.
2. From this list, write down your top three personal (and measurable) targets.
3. View your personal targets list every day.
4. Make decisions in your personal life and in your work life based on these personal targets.

Capture Your Work *Targets*

1. Take out the work priorities list that you created in the previous chapter.
2. From this list, write down your top three work targets. (These also should be measurable.)
3. View your work targets list every day.
4. Make decisions in your personal life and in your business life based on these work targets.

STRATEGY

According to multiple studies, we are more successful when our goals are challenging yet realistic — *and* they can be measured. When your goal cannot be measured, it's easy to bow out and, therefore, never obtain the success you want.

> If you don't know where you are going, you will probably end up somewhere else.
>
> — *Laurence J. Peter*

The research says it all. Be specific.

Because most people never sit down to define specifically what it is they want, they feel as if they're constantly chasing what they can't reach. But if you don't know what you're aiming for, how do you know that you're not there already?

How do we know if we've hit the bull's-eye if we don't know what the target is?

So many times, we feel like we need to keep burning the midnight oil because we haven't made it yet. In actuality, many of us have accomplished far more than the average bear, but we haven't given ourselves credit because we didn't know what our specific target was in the first place.

If your health is one of your priorities, you can choose a target related to it, like walking 30 minutes each day. If spending time with your spouse is a priority, you can choose a target related to that, like spending two solid hours with him/her this weekend. Creating a specific target from your priorities list will help you to focus on creating a life outside of work. Having this target will help your brain to make better decisions about how you use your time.

A major snag in the goals lists I've seen people create is that they contain intangible or unmeasurable goals. When I ask clients what their goals are, here are typical examples they give:

I want to...

- be successful in my career
- make enough money to support my family
- spend time with my family
- be healthy
- be happy

All that is wonderful, but how do you measure it? Does the airline website on which you book your plane ticket post a notice stating, "You'll earn a wad of miles for this flight"? Or does it clearly state, "You'll earn 5,321 frequent flier miles"?

When you say, "I want to get better" or "I want to make more money" or "I want to spend more time with my kids," those aren't specific targets. Words like *more* and *better* are relative. It's crucial to choose measurable targets — numbers.

It's time to be specific so that you know what you're trying to achieve. Let's take apart the sample goals listed above and transfer them from general, unmeasurable terms to specific, measurable terms.

Be successful in my career = I will...

- work X hours per week
- make $X per year
- get X new clients
- earn the X title

- earn X percent on customer service ratings
- earn X on my employee evaluation, etc.

Make enough money to support my family = Our monthly budget is $X, so I want to make $Y in order to live comfortably.

Spend time with my family = I want to...

- spend X hours per weekday with my kids
- spend X hours per weekday with my significant other
- spend X hours per weekday with my _____ (insert other family member)
- spend X hours per weekend with my kids
- spend X hours per weekend with my significant other
- spend X hours per weekend with my _____ (insert other family member)

Be healthy = I will...

- use no more than X sick days this year for actually being sick
- have a cholesterol level of X
- have a blood pressure level of X
- get X hours of sleep each night
- drink X ounces of water each day
- walk for X minutes daily
- eat out no more than X times per week, etc.

Be happy = Is this a separate definition, or is it what you defined above?

When you write down your goals, you're more likely to accomplish them. So in addition to being specific, it's important that they be written down. If you write down your targets, you'll be more likely to reach them, since you're bringing them out of the mists of your subconscious and into the forefront of your brain, as Richard (whom you met in the beginning of the chapter) eventually did.

> People who have goals succeed because they know where they're going.
> It's as simple as that.
> – Earl Nightingale

How do you know which targets to start with? Perhaps you'll want to choose the ones you can attain the most quickly so that you feel success sooner. Or decide which are more critical for you to reach now.

Writing down specific targets from your priorities lists will help you to focus better on your work and also will help you to focus on creating a life outside of work. Having and viewing these targets will help your brain to make better decisions about how you use your time.

NEXT STEPS

Richard put these strategies and tactics into play. He set specific targets for the various parts of his work life and personal life. He concentrated on spending a specific amount of time with his wife and kids each week. He also made it a goal to not work on business-related tasks at all during designated family time. Within a month, he was working the hours that he chose and spending the promised amount of time with his family.

IIII➡ PLOT YOUR NEXT STEPS

- Where will you post your personal targets list?
- Where will you post your work targets list?
- When, each day (or evening), will you view these lists?
- Viewing your target lists on a daily basis has most likely not been a tactic you've applied regularly. How will you remind yourself to do this every day?
- Where can you store these lists so that they're available for you to view when you need to make a decision?
- How will implementing the strategies and tactics in this chapter benefit you? .

4 Administer Self-Care

Nancy was a typical client. Before we started our sessions, she worked constantly and never took time for herself. She always had her computer on and was doing *something* on it. Morning...afternoon...evening...often well into the wee hours of the night. Six days a week, sometimes seven. She stayed hyped up on caffeine, drinking more cups of coffee than she could count on one hand. All her food came out of boxes or cans or restaurants. Her brain was always going a mile a minute.

One day, she had a huge proposal presentation to deliver to the C-suite of a major player in town. If she could land it, this account would be her cash cow for the next two years. She already had a lot on her plate and always seemed to address those other items first...until the day before that big presentation, she realized, "Holy cow! I need to get this together!"

She'd been up late every night that week as usual, trying to catch up on everything. This night, she stayed up until 2 AM to finish that proposal and was up at 6 AM to get ready. She was confident that she'd just developed the most awesome presentation slides ever created on this earth, and with her people-friendly personality, she knew she'd nail it.

Unfortunately, she did not nail it. Her brain was so exhausted from the lack of sleep and so blown out by caffeine that she didn't rock the presentation. She was all over the place and didn't exactly make sense at times. She lost the account — and her credibility with that company.

• • •

My friend Cary Corbin runs her own PR business, Corbin & Associates. In July 2014, for the first time in 10 years, she decided to get her family together for a two-week vacation in Florida.

She notified all her clients about what she was doing and tied off all loose ends before leaving. She knew she could check email on her phone in case of emergency, so she felt confident as she and her family headed off on their family vacation.

On the first Monday into the trip, she thought she'd sneak a peek at her email just to make sure that everything was still fine. She couldn't get her email to come up on her phone! She panicked. She took the phone to her sons so that they could figure out what was wrong. They couldn't. She could not check email! She walked around, took a deep breath, and decided, "I'm on vacation. I let everyone know ahead of time. I'm going to enjoy myself." And she did exactly that.

When we met up after her return, she told me, "I went away for two weeks. I never checked email, never checked voicemail — and my business is still running. You know what I realized? I don't need to work 24/7. It's okay to slow down. My business will still be there. Not only that, but this is the most rejuvenated I've felt since I don't know when!"

Vacation time is your chance to experience special moments in your life. Plus, allowing your brain to rest from work revitalizes you and allows you to make better decisions about how to use your time.

GOAL

Make your health and well-being a priority by implementing all the following tactics. Add on one at a time, at your own pace.

TACTICS

Breathe Deeply

1. Whenever you are asked to take on a new project or task, pause for a few deep breaths while looking at your calendar before making a decision about that action.

2. Whenever you are feeling stressed, pause for a few deep breaths before making a decision about that action.
3. When you get out of bed in the morning, pause for a few deep breaths, and tell yourself that today is going to be great.
4. When you slide into bed in the evening, pause for a few deep breaths, and reflect on at least one thing that happened during the day for which you're grateful.
5. When in doubt, breathe deeply!

Sleep

1. Turn off all electronics *at least* 30 minutes before going to bed. Even mindless internet searches and texting activate subconscious brain sensors and keep us awake.
2. Use a real alarm clock instead of your phone.
3. Go to bed at least seven to eight hours before you need to be awake. Eventually, you'll figure out your sweet spot — the number of hours you need to function *well*.
4. Eat or drink nothing but water within two hours before going to bed. This helps with both weight loss and deeper sleep throughout the night.

Eat Nutritiously

1. Yo mama was right. Eat fruits and veggies daily.
2. Increase the percentage of your from-home meals.

Hydrate

1. Drink water.
2. Eat foods like fruits and vegetables that contain water.

Walk Daily

1. Go on a walk whenever you catch yourself procrastinating.
2. Schedule a daily walk, during which time you can decompress from the day.
3. Whenever you feel stressed, go on a walk instead of reaching for food or drinks or social media.
4. When you need to make a big decision, take a deep breath, and go for a walk.

Take Breaks

1. Take a break to celebrate whenever you complete a task. Do a happy dance around the room.
2. Whenever you feel like procrastinating, take a break by getting up to refill your water glass.
3. When your derriere starts feeling numb from sitting too long or your wrists start aching from too much typing, take a break by going on a five-minute walk.

Go on Vacation

The next time you are faced with deciding whether to keep working and possibly catch a new opportunity that might come your way, or taking a break from work and focusing on one of your personal priorities or targets, try out the latter — even just a half-day staycation next weekend. Make plans for some kind of getaway within the next year. Minimum: two days. Maximum: your choice!

STRATEGY

> Eat food. Not too much. Mostly plants.
> — *Michael Pollan*

Karoshi. It's a Japanese term that means "death from overwork." For decades, Americans have poked fun at the Japanese work ethic, but when you look at our rising numbers of heart attacks and strokes due to work-related stress, you'll soon realize that overwork and lack of self-care are a serious matter.

Research tells us the following:

- We need to breathe deeply to clear our minds.
- We need six to eight hours of sleep.
- Our bodies and brains need a balance of nutrients in order to function.
- Our brains operate better when our bodies are hydrated.
- Walking clears the mind and leads to creativity.
- Both our brains and bodies need to take breaks.
- We live happier lives if we go on vacation.

You know what studies haven't found? That working the longest hours and not having a life mean more money and happiness. Nope, not a bit.

No, you haven't picked up the wrong book. You're still reading a time management / productivity book. So why the heck are we talking about self-care in a bloody business book?

When we know that we're good at what we do, it's easy to feel invincible. After all, we need to have confidence, right? But there's a difference between confidence and overstepping what we're physically and mentally capable of completing when our brains aren't getting the rest, nutrition, and care that they need.

Your vitality depends on your mental, emotional, and physical well-being. For most of my clients, this fact is often cast aside in their race to make everyone else in their lives happy — their kids, their spouse, their friends, the parents of their kids' friends, their boss, their coworkers — you name it. Everyone else around them, everyone else in the world, but *not them*.

Let's be frank and earnest. (Who are those guys, anyway?) If you don't take care of *your* health first and foremost, then productivity will not happen.

I repeat:

If you don't take care of *your* health first and foremost, then productivity will not happen.

Why is that? Because productivity and time management are all about *mind* management — a healthy brain that makes good choices. So if you're not in good health, your brain won't have clarity. If your brain doesn't have clarity, it won't make good decisions. And if your brain doesn't make good decisions, you may as well flush all your calendars and apps down the toilet because they won't dig you out of any holes that your brain creates. So it's absolutely vital that you take care of yourself — and your brain!

> What's the point in working yourself to death?
> — *Cesar Chelala, MD, PhD*

Overall, the strategy is to increase your time management skills by creating brain clarity, which will happen when you care for your body and mind. There are so many modern advances that are supposed to help us to do this, but they actually often cause us more problems. Examples:

Fast food is easy to grab on the go, but we end up with more health problems because of the lack of nutrients and the abundance of calories and nonnatural substances. We might save time in the short term because we're getting our food in 10 minutes instead of spending 30 minutes cooking, but in the long run, we'll need to spend more time working out to lose the weight and more time at the doctor to deal with health issues.

Smartphones are awesome tools that allow us to operate a mobile office, but they can become a tool of procrastination and distraction. When we don't want to do what's in front of us, it becomes an easy habit to grab our phone and "play," thereby putting us further behind in what we're supposed to do. Smartphones also interrupt sleep patterns and contribute to sleep issues when we leave them dinging, buzzing, and vibrating next to our bed — waking us up throughout the night and never letting our brains and bodies reach deep sleep. As you continue reading, you'll discover better ways to use your smartphone as a tool instead of an avoidance crutch.

It's cool to be able to have a mobile office in hip coffee shops, but using caffeinated drinks to hydrate can actually slow us down.

Gyms are tremendous tools, but just plain old walking will still provide plenty of health benefits.

Wanting to be "liked" by all beings in the physical and virtual worlds is a hindrance that affects daily life. So many times we instantly say yes to someone's request for our time — in fear of not being liked — before taking the time to assess if completing that action is going to benefit us, or if the time frame given to complete the action fits our availability. We tend to drag in past worries and emotions and maybe even guilt and respond with a quick "Yes!" instead of focusing on current conditions and determining if this is a good move for us. In our haste to rush and squeeze in as much as possible, and in our fear that someone might not like us, we end up saying yes to way too many things, overtaxing our brains, and backing off from mental and physical time-outs. Getting as much information as possible and pausing for some deep-breathing time will help you to make better decisions and will allow you to better harness your time.

> Try to find one more minute,
> Squeeze one more thing in it.
> On track for a heart attack
> if I don't do some kicking back.
> Don't you think it's high time
> to make a little more time for that?
>
> — Clint Black, "Time for That"

Hurry up. Do more. "Gotta do more, gotta be more!" (Remember that line from the movie *Dead Poets Society*?) We might think we're functioning just fine until we discover how much better we can be when we take our time, breathe deeply, get sleep, eat well, hydrate, go on walks, take breaks, and get away. Our brains and bodies need recharge time. You let your phone charge overnight, and that's just a little machine. Your brain and body are vastly more complex and need at least that, if not more.

And to top it all off, fewer and fewer Americans go on vacation. No wonder we're so stressed!

You have to take your time to save time.

We lose time when we run ragged and get sick. We think we don't have time to cook healthy meals or exercise, yet we're forced to create time to go to doctor appointments and miss work to sleep off whatever illness struck us down. Why not stay healthy instead, and use the "illness time" saved to have fun?

Let's take time for self-care.

NEXT STEPS

Nancy focused on implementing the tactics in this chapter for a solid month. Every time she felt like returning to her old ways, she reminded herself that those old ways were exactly why she was a frazzled wreck. After this focused, intentional month of concentrating on her self-care, these tactics slowly became habits and no longer seemed like a chore. With her brain running on all cylinders, she made much better decisions about how she used her time.

> **▬▶ PLOT YOUR NEXT STEPS**
>
> - What elements of self-care are you already practicing?
> - Which element of self-care would you like to add to what you already do?
> - How will you make sure that it gets implemented?
> - How will implementing the strategies and tactics in this chapter benefit you?

5

Reflect with Power

My sister-in-law's family is from Hawaii, so every other summer she and my brother (who's a genius with elevator repairs) go there for vacation. The last time my brother came home from Hawaii, he called me and said, "I want to move there." From the tone in his voice, I could tell that he was pretty serious. And when he said, "We looked at some places to live," I knew he was completely serious.

I said, "You must have had a fantastic vacation!"

He told me, "They have such a laid-back life there. The beach is five minutes away. The food is fresh. It's so much better than L.A."

"Awesome!" I exclaimed. "If you guys move there, we'll have a place to stay for free!"

After giving him some support, I started asking him a few questions about the future move.

"How were the houses you saw?"

"They're really expensive. We'd have a bigger mortgage over there."

"How far would your commute be to work?"

"There aren't any tall buildings nearby."

"How far is your house right now from the beach?"

"About five minutes."

"When I come visit you next time, will you take me to the farmers' market down the street from your house?"

"Sure."

About a week after this conversation took place, my brother called me to say that they had decided not to move. You see, after reflecting and writing down everything they liked about Hawaii, they realized that they have almost all of that where they currently live. They just took it for granted. This past summer, they went to the beach three days a week after work. And they're enjoying all the delicious food in their area. They began to look first at what's good in their life and what they already have before examining any perceived deficits. They examined each situation's pros and cons objectively. They planned before diving in. That's reflecting with power.

GOAL

At the end of each day, celebrate all your wins — both minuscule and grand — as well as what you have in your life, before trying to improve upon what didn't work. Never start with, "I didn't get *xyz* done."

TACTICS

Take a few moments each day (or at least each week) to reflect on what you've been doing to work toward your personal priorities and targets and your work priorities and targets.

Ask yourself:

- What tasks (small, medium, large, and extra-*grande*) did I finish and need to celebrate?
- Have I stopped and made any decisions based on my priorities and targets? (Celebrate!)
- Have I said no to something that wasn't going to fully benefit me? (Celebrate!)
- What worked? (Celebrate! And keep doing this.)
- What are the lessons I learned from all this good stuff I did?

Reflecting on at least one positive step forward will give you the encouragement you need to stay focused on your personal and work priorities and targets, which will help you to make better decisions about how you use your time. This is reflecting with power.

Next, ask yourself:

- What glitches occurred?
- Why did they happen?
- What did I learn from what transpired?
- What can be done to prevent them from happening again?
- What do I need to make more time for?
- What do I need to take off my plate to make more time for that?

When most folks reflect, they skip the prior "round one" positive questions and celebrations. They instead start and stop with only the first question in this "round two" section. And then they stay frustrated. Raise your hands in the air and let out a big "Yahoo!" for taking the time to reflect with power on *all* these questions, as doing so will increase your positivity and brainpower, which will in turn improve the decisions you make about how to use your time.

If you have a team to whom you delegate or with whom you work, reflect at the end of each week:

- What did each team member do well?

Let them know! Communicate this as they complete a job well or at the end of each week. If all they ever hear is what they did wrong, that'll be a bummer for them and will not motivate them to do their best for you.

Next, ask yourself and your team:

- What glitches occurred?
- Why did they happen?
- What did we learn from what transpired?
- What can be done to prevent them from happening again?

Don't let miscommunication or noncommunication evolve into shoddy work and animosity. Nip it in the bud by addressing this during your weekly team meeting (which we'll discuss in part 3, "Assemble Your Team") or setting aside separate time.

STRATEGY

My husband and I have many goals and targets, but this one is particularly important to us: go on vacation at least once per year. It's our marriage retreat/

relaxation/rejuvenation/carpe diem getaway. It never fails, however, that while we're abroad, we develop wild fantasies about how sweet life would be if we lived elsewhere.

I realize that we're not alone in these musings when we talk to other folks who dream big dreams when they're on vacation.

"Life would be better here."

"If I lived here, I wouldn't have *xyz* problems."

"This is the good life."

Whenever we step off a train on vacation, I'm nearly swept away by the romance of train stations — the large open areas full of bustling people, the huge skylights, the architectural wonders...it's just like the movies! I want to live in this town!

But watch commuters wherever you visit. They look and feel the same way that commuters do where you live. Why? Because they're not on vacation.

The grass is always greener on the other side of the hill, so the saying goes. Instead of trying to get over to that grass, why not cultivate and nurture the grass under your feet and make that as green as possible?

What does this have to do with productivity? Reflection is an important part of any improvement process. But if we focus on chasing unrealistic dreams, and we never acknowledge what we have in front of us, we pretty much just end up frustrated from chasing our tail in circles. Too many times we try to hunt down something that won't necessarily benefit us or that we might already have in our lives. This causes us to spend time and resources on something we don't actually need. We will also stay frustrated and beaten down if we keep focusing on everything we haven't done.

Of course, examining what needs to be improved and dissecting what things didn't work and why is absolutely critical to growth and improvement, but it shouldn't be done first. When it is, we forget about all the great stuff we've done, and all that goodness just gets pushed aside and forgotten. So many times we get wrapped up in work that we forget to examine what we've experienced. We lose out on celebrating victories and accomplishments. We also miss out on learning from what we've experienced and creating new and better ways to get things done. Our accomplishments are swept under the rug until some random person points out what we did

> If you think you are sh*t, you are drawn to sh*t.
>
> — André (played by Jamel Debbouze), in the movie Angel-A

right, and we mutter, "Oh yeah." We spend so much time beating ourselves up for what we didn't do yet, or for what we did wrong, that we forget to congratulate ourselves for everything that we have accomplished. That's not a good way to stay motivated.

When we don't take the time to reflect with power, we often just focus on what's left on our never-ending to-do list. That's definitely not motivating. We also tend to focus on what went wrong. This is also not motivating. For example, if you say something like this at the end of each day, it's going to get depressing: "All I got done today was..."

Egad! Start with what you *did* get done. You might learn that you've accomplished more than you ever thought you would. You just haven't given yourself credit for it yet. When you start with what you accomplish, you'll begin to refrain from using negative language like "all I got done" because you'll realize how inaccurate the "all I got done" phrase is.

For those of you who journal, you know the therapeutic feeling this exercise can bring. For those of you who hate writing things down, I ask you to humor me and jot down at least a few thoughts. The transformation that can take place when you read your own thoughts on paper (or a screen) is amazing. You look at your words, and they "sound" quite different from the words that are inside your head. Suddenly, you can find solutions to your problems as you talk and write things out.

It's extremely important to review your life at least once per week, if not daily. Using a personal example, based on my schedule, Friday is the best day for me. At the end of the week, I take a deep breath and think back to the events that took place during the week. I do a happy dance for everything I finished, no matter how big or small — or important or unimportant — in the grand scheme of things. If I finished something, let's high-five it! Here's an example from last week:

Got the laundry washed and folded
Remembered to bring my reusable bags into the store with me
Enjoyed my Saturday afternoon cooking date with my hubby
Finished step 2 of 10 on one of my long-term projects
Rocked the house with my killer keynote at a conference in Dallas

After acknowledging my wins, then it's time to take a look at what needs improving. I make any necessary adjustments to tasks that didn't go quite right, let the idea of change set in over the weekend, and then hit the ground running on Monday morning. It's also during this reflection time that I tweak my schedule for the following week and create my action plan for Monday.

Perhaps you'd rather do this on a Saturday or Wednesday. The point is, choose a day and get your reflection on. Take stock of:

- Wins
- Lessons learned
- Glitches
- Adjustments

In that order.

In the past year, I've begun capturing my wins in a digital document as they occur. I use this document each month when I meet with my accountability group. Capturing wins is so much more encouraging than focusing on deficits!

We are pros at picking ourselves apart. That's why I'm repeating yet again that we must empower ourselves through reflecting first on our victories, large and small.

▌▌▌▌➡ PLOT YOUR NEXT STEPS

- On what day(s) each week will you have your power reflection?
- Where will this reflection take place?
- What reminder will you set for yourself to make sure that it happens?
- How will implementing the strategies and tactics in this chapter benefit you?

6 Rendezvous: Your Date with Change…and Discomfort

When my client Julie (the one who had kept working right through her son's first home run, completely missing that special moment) tried implementing some of these steps you and I've been talking about, she confessed that she felt, well, a little uncomfortable. She said, "I feel strange talking about all this clarity stuff. That's a little woo-woo for me. And pausing to breathe? Who does that stuff?"

She also commented that it felt "different" to pause to look at her lists of priorities and targets before she made a decision about how she would use her time. She'd tried doing that for two days, but she wasn't used to it. It felt odd. So she stopped.

> Discontent is the first necessity of progress.
>
> — *Thomas Edison*

I asked her how she had felt when she missed Ben's home run. "Terrible," she muttered.

"Do you want to keep doing what you're doing and miss more special moments?"

"No!"

"So if you don't want to keep doing what you're doing, what needs to happen?"
She paused, took a deep breath, and said, "I need to…*change*."

GOAL

Acknowledge the discomfort you'll feel, and try at least one change that I recommend in this book for at least three weeks.

TACTICS

1. Recognize when you feel uncomfortable about trying something new.
2. Rejoice in the fact that you feel discomfort. It means you're taking forward steps in making a change!
3. Include reflecting on this change — trying out this new strategy or tactic — during your weekly reflect-with-power session.
4. Try out the new strategy or tool for at least three weeks before you consider throwing in the towel.

STRATEGY

Change.

People try it and give up when the first steps toward it don't go smoothly.

People fear it because they're not sure about what they're doing, or they're not sure if they'll do it right.

People avoid it because they feel discomfort in doing something different from the norm.

Discomfort is an abstract feeling, so Julie and other clients have found it hard to describe not only what it felt like, but also what was causing this odd feeling. They just knew that they felt different when implementing new strategies and tactics, so they stopped these new procedures after only a couple of days. Purely because it felt different. And — in the beginning — they went right back to their old ways.

> All progress takes place outside the comfort zone.
>
> — *Attributed to Michael John Bobak*

Change seldom happens overnight. Rather, it's something you struggle with initially because it feels different; it feels unnatural because you can't be on autopilot, and you have to remind yourself to do it. You have to push through because if you don't keep up the discipline to do it, you'll go back to your old but comfortable routines — and unsuccessful ways. Change can be a tedious process because it takes effort to form a new habit. This may take weeks. And for some habits, even longer.

I'd like to tell you a little secret:

Change can be scary, but when you march through a transformation you've determined to begin, and then you succeed, it feels remarkably empowering. It's an accomplishment. You looked fear of the unknown in the face and kicked its bootay!

Instead of being comfortable with shying away from change, try craving the feeling of accomplishment. Instead of allowing the fear of change to dominate your outlook, focus on the desire to feel the success of following through with this change.

It's all in your head.

It's human nature to stay in a groove — even a bad one — because we've become comfortable in those ways. The minute we try something different, our brains go into a bit of a panic mode because we've left that comfort zone. So if you feel a little discomfort from walking off your problems, taking deep breaths, and making decisions based on your priorities, I congratulate you! That's awesome! It means that change is happening.

As you implement the productivity strategies and tactics in this handbook, recognize the discomfort you might feel from trying something new — and celebrate it!

The discomfort you might feel means you're taking a step forward. Do a little happy dance because implementing these strategies and tactics we're discussing during our sessions together will help your brain to maintain clarity and make better decisions about how to use your time.

NEXT STEPS

Julie faced her discomfort and celebrated each day that she implemented her positive changes. She realized that she was more successful when she implemented only one or two changes at a time, so she stuck to that method.

ⅢⅢ➡ PLOT YOUR NEXT STEPS

- Do you feel any discomfort from trying to change?
- If so, how will you work through it?
- What will your reward be for getting through the change?

PART 2

IMPLEMENT STRUCTURE
and FLOW

Support Your
Time Management Revolution
by Controlling These Five
Key Elements of Your Workday

7

It's All in Your Head: Prevent Drowning through Structure *and* Flow

I'd like to share with you a journey involving a client of mine. Nancy, whom we met in chapter 4, always has a smile and wants to know what's new with you. She's just delightful. She's a super-hard worker, but she felt like she wasn't getting anything done — despite her long hours at work and multitasking. In addition to her self-care challenges that I shared with you in that chapter, she had ADD, she procrastinated, she felt constantly interrupted, and she never finished what she started because of the interruptions.

One day, we made arrangements for me to shadow her in her office for a two-hour session. I was a fly on the wall that day. Well, not a fly, more like a mannequin on a chair shoved into the corner. Nancy often attempted to multitask: She read email while talking on the phone; filed while printing checks; listened to voicemail while composing emails. She had a huge project deadline coming up and still had more than half of the project to complete, yet she read an email about a conference that she *might* attend in two months, and the article had hyperlinks about people involved with the event, so she went down that rabbit hole for a good 20 minutes. A few times she just sat staring at her desk with her hands cupped around her coffee mug. She told me later that in those staring minutes, she was in a state of panic because she knew that she had millions of things to do and plenty of piles on her desk to attack, but she had no idea of what she needed to do next.

Strategically, when you take over how you run your day, you also take over time. You harness it. Once you're able to tell your time what to do (as we'll explore throughout part 2), you'll have the mental bandwidth to apply the necessary tactics to cut inefficiency from your day.

Nancy learned that rushing and diving into action without a plan were not helpful tactics. She needed to map out her plan of attack. She had to take her time in order to save time.

She learned that she must understand both scheduling and modification... routines and flexibility, structure and flow.

She learned the **I** in CIA: **I**mplement Structure *and* Flow.

Say what? Aren't those opposites?

Yes, it sounds crazy, but we need to **I**mplement Structure *and* Flow. We need to have processes for how we handle documents and communication. We need to set up our go-bags, mobile offices, and work spaces based on what we need to accomplish. We need to have structured routines and time blocks for completing work; yet we need to be able to adjust those routines and time blocks, and morph — move them around as needed — and still get everything done that we need to.

On the one hand, if we have *only* structure in our day, any little variance or hiccup might throw us into a tornado of overwhelm. Take for example a detective named Monk, played by Tony Shalhoub in the television series *Monk*. Monk had such a precise routine for every part of his work and life that if there was any deviation from it, that sent him into a panic attack. I'm a big proponent of having routines and a foundational structure, but we also need to be able to go with the flow when "stuff happens."

Martial arts legend Bruce Lee espoused a philosophy that we need to "be water." We need to adapt, depending on the situation. He said, "Be formless, shapeless, like water. You put water in a cup, and it becomes the cup. You put water in a bottle, and it becomes the bottle. In a teapot, it becomes the teapot. Water can flow or drip or creep or crash. Be water."

In order to be an agent of change in your Time Management Revolution, you must have a form, a structure, yet be willing to modify, adapt, and flow whenever necessary.

Implement Structure *and* Flow.

In a January 20, 2013, article by Michael Ordoña in the *San Francisco Chronicle*, actor Jeremy Renner, who has starred in such films as *The Bourne Legacy* and *Avengers*, revealed that he works on a multitude of projects throughout the year:

Acting in films
Producing movies
Writing music
Renovating houses

Those aren't little 10-minute tasks. They are big-time, long-term projects that require many steps and components to complete.

When Ordoña asked how all this was possible, Renner replied, "Fluidity."

At first I was worried that he would say something like, "I just wake up and go with the flow. There's no plan. I just do whatever."

I was pleasantly surprised by the answer he gave when he described what "fluid" meant to him: "Being prepared as you can be, but willing to let it all go because it's not working. To be fluid and to allow change, move around the obstacles."

Today, Nancy still procrastinates, but only a few minutes a day instead of hours each day. She does her blah tasks first thing in the morning to help avoid most of the procrastination. To help with her ADD, she sets a timer for 15 minutes of concentration. She plans her action list at the end of each day for the following day, and this list keeps her focused on what she needs to do. She's become her own agent of change. She recognizes when one of the AGENT components — the five areas of the workday to control, explained below and throughout part 2 — is getting out of whack and stops to make adjustments.

To reiterate (hint: I'm brainwashing you at this moment), we need to have structured systems, routines, and time blocks for completing work; yet we need to be able to adjust those systems, routines, and time blocks, and morph — move them around as needed — and still get everything done that we need to.

In order to be an agent of change in our Time Management Revolution, we must **I**mplement Structure *and* Flow. We must be able to control, yet also modify, these five key components of our workday:

Assignment and Task Completion
Go-Bag and Work-Space Layout
Electronic Communication
Notes, Document, and File Management
Time Protection

By understanding that everything you must do during a workday corresponds to one of these five components, your brain is able to zero in on the areas that are not currently under your control. By implementing the strategies and tactics in part 2, you'll be able to build the infrastructure you need each day to manage these five different components. By being in control of these areas and understanding how they need to operate, you'll also be able to apply flexibility when technology or your fellow humans throw a wrench into your plans.

We're not robots, but we do need enough structure and systems so that there is time for spontaneity, putting out fires, and...fun!

When you achieve the first part of the mission, Create Clarity (part 1), it makes completing this portion of your Time Management Revolution that much easier.

Ready? It's time to head out on Operation: Implement Structure *and* Flow!

8 Manage Long-Term Projects with Mega-efficiency

Susan is a top-notch consultant in her field. She is sought after by companies and agencies all over the world to bring in her expertise. She is always calm and collected, and her feathers never appear to be ruffled. Her advice is spot-on, whether she delivers it through individual consulting or trainings or workshops.

Behind the scenes, however, she is a hot mess. She struggles to balance work tasks with personal time. She is constantly working. She says yes to every project and every proposed date that is put in front of her. She'll book anywhere from one week to one year out, yet she'll work until 2 AM the night before a presentation or client meeting to prepare.

She says there's not enough time to do everything she needs to get done.

GOAL

Schedule time for every step of a project into your calendar as soon as you know this project has become yours to complete.

TACTICS

1. Get out a piece of paper and pencil or open up a fresh digital document.
2. At the bottom of the page, list the due date and the finished task for an upcoming project you have. Example:

June 25   Presentation

3. Working your way backward, list out the steps it will take to complete the request.
4. Next to each step, note how much time each step will take.
5. Pad in extra hours or days for each step to allow for people who don't hit their deadlines, as well as Murphy's Law hitting you with mishaps.
6. Starting at the bottom and working your way backward, assign due dates to each of these steps, based on the time you need.
7. Use this timeline to schedule time for these tasks in your calendar. Now.
8. Communicate this timeline to everyone involved.

STRATEGY

Do you know when Christmas is?

Even if you don't celebrate the holiday, you know that Christmas is on December 25. Every year. Since about the fourth century. So why do people exclaim the week before Christmas, "Holy cow! Christmas is next week! I've got so much left to do!"?

It's because they know in the back of their minds that Christmas is rolling around, but they haven't taken the time to map out what all needs to get done and by when. So their holiday cheer turns into mad, mad steamrolling, and they end up in disillusionment and nonjoy to the world.

A lot of folks just dive into a big project in the same manner — without giving it much thought — so they soon find themselves a bit lost. After they've spun a little while longer and felt like they weren't getting anywhere, overwhelm sets in. Once good ol' overwhelm starts infiltrating, the brain begins to shut down, decisions can't be made, and soon the towel is thrown in.

Instead of just diving in blindly, it's important to take the time to plan what you're doing.

- What are your goals for the project?
- What steps will you need to take to get there?
- What materials and resources will you need for each step?
- Who all will need to be involved with each step?
- How much time will each of these steps take?

When a big project is broken down into smaller pieces, it becomes much more manageable. For example, let's look at what the San Antonio Sports Foundation did with their "ING Kids Rock" program back in 2012. A marathon is

26.2 miles. That's a heck of a long distance to run. If you're only five years old, it will seem like forrrrrrrrever, and you may not want to do it. Instead of having little kids — kindergartners through second-graders — attempt to run a marathon in one day, they broke down the task into manageable chunks. The kiddos ran a little each day at school until they hit 25.2 miles. The grand hurrah of their last mile took place during the San Antonio Rock 'n' Roll Marathon weekend events.

The children were able to say they'd run 26.2 miles. It wasn't all at once, but they still got the job done. And that's what mattered.

You might be saying to yourself, "That's all fine and dandy for little kids, but what about for adults like me?" Okey-dokey. Let's use an adult project, a presentation, as an example:

Your presentation will be given June 25. You'll write that at the bottom of your page.

Will you have to submit your presentation slides or handouts ahead of time for distribution? If so, when are those due?

Whether or not you have to submit early, make your due date the day before the work is due to allow for technical difficulties.

In order for you to submit your presentation and/or handouts, you will have needed to rehearse to make sure that this is what you want to present.

Before that, you need to finish the PowerPoint (or Prezi or Keynote or whatever software you use) slides.

Before you can finish the slides, you need to have graphics and a format/layout/design chosen.

Before you can pretty things up, you need to have content.

Before you have content, you need to decide what you want to teach or what point you want to get across.

Before you can decide that, you need to know the objective.

Before you can pinpoint the objective, you need to communicate with a representative from the group you're presenting to in order to determine what your purpose is.

Phew! That's a lot of planning! Yes, it sure is. It takes this much planning to make a project happen. We haven't even included figuring out how long each one of those steps will take, or what materials, resources, or people we'll need to be involved.

So, when you do think about everything that's involved with your project and invest the time in planning, and assuming that you'll have other tasks to work on or clients to meet with during the same time period, your task list for your project might look like this:

> May 24: Confirm scheduled presentation, plan timeline, and inform parties involved what your timeline is, as well as due dates for which they have responsibilities — 30 minutes.
>
> May 25–27: Discuss objectives with group, and finalize desired outcome — 3 hours.
>
> May 28–June 3: Plan content for the slides — 1 hour per day.
>
> June 4–11: Put together the slides — 1 hour per day.
>
> June 12–14: Acquire and drop in graphics, finalize format — 1 hour per day.
>
> June 14–15: Rehearse one-hour presentation, at least three times — 3 hours.
>
> June 16: Make final changes on handouts and slides — 2 hours.
>
> June 17: Finish handouts and slides — 1 hour.
>
> June 18: Handouts and slides due; send electronically — 30 minutes (it should take only five minutes, but allow for technical glitches — file doesn't load, server is down, internet is out, etc.).
>
> June 18–24: Rehearse one-hour presentation, at least seven times — 7 hours.
>
> June 24: Travel — 4 hours.
>
> June 25: Presentation (network before and after) — all day.
>
> June 25: Travel — arrive home late.
>
> June 26: Debrief; any to-do's from presentation? Plus catch up on phone calls, emails, mail — 3 hours.

W.O.W. That's a full month of prep time, if you're not working on it all at once. (FYI, you might now understand why consultants and speakers charge "so much" for "just" a one-hour presentation.) If you don't want to work seven days per week, you'll need to take that into account for your timeline.

This is why just putting "Work on XYZ project" on your calendar doesn't cut it. That's too broad. You look at it and think, "Yeah, I'll do that later," because your brain doesn't know what part of that project it needs to work on. Suddenly, the day before it's due, you think, "Oh, crud! I need to finish XYZ project!" Then you stress, drop everything else for this "emergency," and probably end up burning the midnight oil and becoming sleep-deprived — and maybe gaining weight from stress eating or grabbing fast food because there's no time to cook. And getting into a tiff with a loved one because you snap, since you're in a foul mood. Mmmm. That's not a joyful way to live.

If you don't create presentations as a part of your work, no worries. You can apply this same thinking to developing the company budget, writing a book, rolling out your company's marketing plan, gearing up for the holidays if you're in retail...It doesn't matter what industry you're in; developing a timeline will save you. And if you have similar projects throughout the year, you can reuse your timeline template.

You're reading this book because you're tired of operating in hurry-up frenzied mode. So, if you want to lower your stress levels, you'll need to change how you operate. This means investing time in your health and mental well-being by planning out your projects. Taking 15 to 30 minutes of your time to map out the steps for a project will save you hours of wheel-spinning and gosh-awful stress down the road.

It's crucial for you to schedule time blocks for every step of a project into your calendar as soon as you know that this project has become yours to complete. By operating in time blocks, you'll be able to shift work times around as necessary, but you'll still allow yourself enough time to complete each stage of the project without working yourself into a frenzy.

NEXT STEPS

Susan implemented a great deal of change. It wasn't all at once, but it was a concerted effort over a six-week period.

She applied the strategies and tactics from the **C** in CIA — **C**reate Clarity.

Next, she worked on the **I** in CIA — **I**mplement Structure *and* Flow.

In particular, she focused on the A and T in AGENT. She began to create timelines for what was being asked of her, so that she could either accept or decline offers. For the offers she did accept, she scheduled the steps from the timeline into her calendar. If other requests arrived or opportunities arose, she'd check her calendar before adding to it.

> Generating revenue should not come at a cost to your well-being.
>
> — *Helene Segura*

She realized that her fear of losing out on income was driving her to say yes to an unrealistic schedule and an impossible list of tasks. This crush of to-do's was actually costing her income because of the physical, mental, and marriage side effects that forced her to seek — and pay for and lose time to — medical assistance.

It soon became clear that she could obtain the same or better *profit* level by slowing down.

You have to take your time to save time.

Implement Structure *and* Flow.

> **⫸ PLOT YOUR NEXT STEPS**
>
> - How has not using a detailed timeline affected you?
> - How will creating a timeline for your long-term projects help you?
> - You probably already have deadlines set for various projects. Have you already completed task timelines for each one and scheduled time blocks into your calendar? If not, which project will you start with in creating a timeline?

9

Get It All Done in 24 Hours: Turn To-Do Lists into *Done* Lists

Tim is a financial planner who works for a large national firm. There are rules and regulations he must follow, and deadlines and quotas he must meet, but he has the freedom to decide his schedule each day.

He knows what he needs to do. He has to make cold calls to total strangers. He has to make warm calls to people he's been referred to or folks he met at networking events. He needs to go to those networking events to meet contacts. He needs to prepare quotes and examples for those with whom he can schedule appointments. He has to follow up with his current clients to make sure that their needs are being met. He wants to do more than a yearly review with his clients; he wants to get to know them.

That's a whole lot that he needs to do. His to-do list usually has 20-plus items.

Yet, on a morning when I spied on him, he spent a total of two hours answering fellow planners' questions or just shooting the breeze with them while being sociable and playing pool in the employee break room, as well as piddling around in his email inbox while filling out various forms.

In the back of Tim's mind, he knew exactly what he needed to get done. Yet he didn't do it. He said he didn't have enough time in the day.

GOAL

Accept the fact that as long as you have a full life and thriving career, at the end of the day, you will always have something still left to do.

Accept the fact that you can get done what you absolutely need to do because you are in total control of how you handle your day. Total.

TACTICS

At the end of each workday, choose the top three tasks you need to complete the following day. You'll also want to choose the next three most important tasks you can work on. These are your 3+3.

1. On your paper or digital calendar, schedule in your personal priorities for the next day.
2. Have within your view your calendar for the upcoming week.
3. While reviewing the project timelines you created in the previous chapter and looking at your next five to seven days of activities on your calendar, add in any tasks you must complete into open time blocks.
4. Choose your 3+3 for the next day. Number them on your calendar 1, 2, 3, 4, 5, 6, in order of priority.
5. Block off two half-day CHOP sessions per month to clear the annoying crumbs from your plate. See page 65.

STRATEGY

There is time in the day to do what truly needs to get done.

The Philosophy behind My 3+3

It's time to take a step back and take a deep breath. In and out. In and out.

Our lists of everything we need to do will always be long. If we have a full life and successful career, there will *always* be something else to do. That is a fact of life we must accept. The day we have nothing on a to-do list means our job has become obsolete. So rejoice that you have a lot to do!

If the long list of tasks to do is overwhelming, are you willing to go to a 3+3 for each day? You see, when we try to work from one long list of everything we need to get done, it's not motivating to see the list never shrink. And it doesn't, because as we cross off things we finish, we also add tasks that have cropped up. There's nothing wrong with having one master task list to capture all the things you need to do over time. But having a *short* list to complete on a *daily* basis is psychologically more soothing, plus it's motivating to see more items crossed off than not.

Another challenge with trying to work daily from a long list of to-do's is that they're just items on a list. They are not tied to times. If you were to look at the list of 25 things you have there and assign time blocks to them (example: It'll take me 30 minutes to do X and two hours to do Y), you'd discover that it's not humanly possible to get all those things done in the day, in addition to the regular daily tasks you complete and the personal life you'd like to live.

> If a man does not know to what port he is steering, no wind is favorable to him.
>
> — *Seneca the Younger*

By choosing only three absolutely critical tasks we must complete the next day, we are setting ourselves up for success. A list of only three tasks is doable, so we'll get those crossed off and be able to celebrate. "Yes! I finished my list!" A list of only three tasks is easy to focus on. When shiny objects appear or interruptions happen, it's simple to get back on track and refocused on those three tasks that need to get done that day.

Now you might be saying, "Hey, crazy lady! I do a helluva lot more than three things each day!" Yes, absolutely you do. There's checking email, returning phone calls, completing daily tasks related to your job, and so on. But all these tasks are usually not the ones that are of the greatest responsibility or highest value for your job, yet you spend waaaaay too much time on them. Sometimes, all day. By choosing three high-priority, high-value tasks to work on, you won't fall down the rabbit hole of low-value work.

So, once you choose your top 3, then you choose your +3. This is the bonus round. If all the stars align in your day — everything goes absolutely perfectly — and you end up finishing with time to spare, you can celebrate, and then start working on your +3 to get ahead. Or, if the opposite happens — everything goes haywire, nothing is going your way, the internet is down, you can't get the answers you need, people flaked out — and you can't move forward on your top 3, then you can move into your +3. Usually, when bad things happen, we pitch a fit, and then a mental roadblock goes up because we don't know what to do next since things didn't go as we wanted or expected. With the +3, you'll be able to get back into focus and still move ahead, even if it's not in the order that you originally planned.

Another reason why you want to choose your 3+3 is so that you can procrastinate productively. Let's say that you don't really want to work on task 1 or task 2. Instead of popping into email or piddling around on something else that's nowhere near a high value for your job, you can procrastinate — temporarily avoid the task — by working on something else from your 3+3 that will keep you on track or put you ahead.

Schedule Only What Truly Needs to Get Done

How do you know which tasks to put on your 3+3 list? Start with your current list (or scraps of paper) of your to-do's. (Eventually, this is the part where you'll take out the project timelines that you completed in the previous chapter. It's okay if you're not there yet. You will be.) Work through the following three questions:

What types of tasks or projects are "Urgent Priority"?

These tasks must be completed or else you'll lose your home, your health will suffer, the health of your household members will suffer, you'll get fired, you'll go out of business, your relationship with a household member will suffer, or something terrible will happen to you or a member of your household or work team. If you don't get this done, you'll be in a world of hurt.

What types of tasks or projects are "Priority"?

If these tasks are completed, your personal health will remain at least status quo, the health of a household member will remain at least status quo, you'll earn income, you'll keep your job, your business will remain afloat, your home's condition will remain at least status quo, or your office's condition will remain at least status quo. If you get this done, you'll stay afloat.

What types of tasks or projects are "Proactive Priority"?

If these tasks are completed, your personal health will improve, the health of a household member will improve, you'll increase income, your home's condition will improve, your office's condition will improve, the status of your job or business will improve. If you get this done, you'll be ahead of the curve.

Let's reflect for a moment. What types of tasks or projects fall into none of the previously mentioned categories, but you often spend a lot of time on them?

Gradually, as you become more efficient, you'll find yourself needing to complete fewer and fewer last-minute "Urgent Priorities," so that you'll have more time for focusing on "Priorities" and, eventually, "Proactive Priorities." Before long, you will be scheduling your tasks several days ahead, then a few weeks ahead — instead of just the next day.

Schedule Using Time Blocks

Whatever tasks you want to complete should be assigned to time blocks throughout the day. Block off 30 minutes at the end of your workday for reflecting on what you finished, processing what needs to be ready for the next day, and scheduling your 3+3.

Assign time blocks for each task in your 3+3. Pad in at least an extra 25 to 30 percent of time over and above the amount of time you think it'll take. This will help you if you struggle with underestimating how much time you need. For me personally, since I still battle with perfectionism, plus I want to have time in my day for putting out fires or taking advantage of an unexpected opportunity, I pad an extra 50 percent. If I think something will take me 60 minutes, I block off 90.

By working in time blocks, you know how much time of your day should be spent on which kinds of tasks — both low value and high value. Should you need to change things around, no problem. Implement Structure *and* Flow by flip-flopping time blocks around to different places. You're moving them, but you're still allowing time for them.

Build in a Fail-Safe

When we second-guess ourselves or worry about what we might forget, we lose time. Building your 3+3 at the end of each day will help remove the worries and give you that time back. It's even more confidence building to have a backup plan, so build in two half-day CHOP sessions per month for this. What do you work on during your CHOP day? I'm glad you asked!

Crap
Highly hay
Odds and ends
Piddly stuff

These are tasks that are

> boring *or*
> difficult *or*
> annoying *or*
> delayed because you won't make a decision *or*
> avoided because they require untangling a mess

and have been carried over on to-do lists each day because they're not at the top of your priority list, but they still eventually need to get done. The blocked-off focus time allows you to chop through stuff you still don't want to do, or perhaps even chop tasks from the list for good because you realize that you don't really need to do them. More important, this time allows you to chop the weight from your subconscious that these un-done tasks add. Eventually, you might be able to cut it down to one CHOP hour per week instead of two half days per month.

> Whatever keeps you from reaching your goals today had better be important — it's costing you a day of your life!
> — *Nido R. Qubein*

You don't have to remember each individual letter of CHOP (like "highly hay," which is my term for scuttlebutt that has the potential to turn into a rumble — a.k.a. you have a situation in which the proverbial crap is about to hit the fan). Just remember to CHOP these clingers-on from your plate because they're subconsciously weighing you down.

Choosing your 3+3s and seeing what tasks from your list you don't have time to complete will help you to decide on what tasks you should consider asking for help with or delegating to others. In part 3, "Assemble Your Team," we'll discuss how to do this.

If you're thinking to yourself, "Good golly! Who in heckfire wants to be this structured?" I understand. It can be a little scary at first.

But once you realize that the more structure you have in your life, the more time you'll have for fun...

The more structure you have, the more you'll have room to flow...

The more structure you have, the more a crisis will be just an inconvenience...

The more structure you have, the more peace you will have...

Then it will no longer feel scary or constrictive.

It will feel... p o w e r f u l !

NEXT STEPS

Tim started blocking off the last 30 minutes of each day to plan his 3+3 for the next day. It's not as though he could just wipe his calendar clean and start over, so at first, some of his days were full of client meetings he'd already set up. He realized that his clients were the 3+3. Eventually, he learned to leave breaks in his day to have time for non–client meeting 3+3s.

Initially, Tim had to squeeze in time to work on the various steps from his project timeline lists, but with future projects he eventually scheduled those steps on his calendar immediately after creating the timelines, so the time crunch lessened.

He learned to schedule East Coast calls first in the day because their business day ends first. Then he'd work his way west toward the West Coast and Hawaii. (If you deal with Europe, Africa, Australia / the Pacific Rim, or Asia, figure out the best phone-conference times around your time-zone differences.)

Instead of operating from a tremendously long list of tasks that were not attached to time blocks, Tim used a digital calendar that included his 3+3 and kept him focused and on task. Plus his calendar sent him reminders. He was still sociable, but he now had a time block for playing pool and hangin' with his fellow agents, so he knew how much time he could spend on that and still have time to get everything else done. He no longer dilly-dallied in his email inbox because he knew what his time block was for dealing with email. His fail-safe plan was to schedule a CHOP hour every Friday afternoon so that he could empty out his worries and mind, and fully enjoy his weekends.

Tim did find time to get everything done.

IIII➤ PLOT YOUR NEXT STEPS

- When will you determine your 3+3 for the next day?
- Do you currently use only one long task list, or do you pull a few tasks out from there to work on each day?
- What aspects of your current system are working or not working for you?
- Based on what you read in this chapter, what changes will you make, and why?

10 Set Reminders, and Never Forget Again

Rhonda is a social worker for a nonprofit agency. Her days are spent running group sessions, as well as conducting individual sessions. She also must document every contact she makes with her clients and complete the necessary paperwork for the county and state. Her clients are a bit transient in that some drop out of the program, only to return a few months later, so those individuals need to be exited, tracked, and reentered.

Rhonda's greatest fear is forgetting to do something and then getting fired as a result. She is so fearful that this will occur that she spends up to 10 minutes at a time at various points in the day having a panic attack about possibly forgetting something.

GOAL

Utilize checklists and create a reminder system so that you never forget anything or lose time second-guessing yourself.

TACTICS

Create a checklist for each regular project or task you complete.

Weekly

- Reflect with power on all the tasks you completed correctly.
- On the off chance that you left something off your checklist, capture those steps at this time.

Daily

- Use your checklists.
- Have a colleague double-check any tougher tasks or projects, or those that contain a new twist you haven't before seen.
- Do your 3+3 at the end of each day.
- As a fail-safe, implement a Mind Liberation and utilize a backup reminder system.

STRATEGY

Worrying and panicking can be such a terrible hindrance. If you have these tendencies, you may have experienced some of these success-blocking behaviors:

- You can't look at your work only once or twice. You need to keep checking and checking to assure yourself that you haven't forgotten anything.
- Even after you finish a task, you review it to see if you might have forgotten to do something.
- There are times when you realize that you don't want to take the next step because you might forget to do part of the step.

> Worry is a meditation on sh*t.
> — Mike (played by Tim Robbins), in the movie Thanks for Sharing

- You sometimes pause and think back to yesterday or the day before or the week before, wondering if there's anything you forgot to do.
- You occasionally lose all sense of time and presence because your mind is so obsessed with living out all the possibilities that could occur based on whatever you are worrying about. You play every variation of scenarios and write and rewrite scripts in your head.

These behaviors end up costing you more time.

Much of this worry and anxiety occurs when you don't have a reliable workflow system in place and/or you have other thoughts weighing on your mind. It also occurs because you don't give yourself enough credit for everything you do right.

Create a checklist for each regular project or task you complete.

Creating a checklist for each regular project or task you complete will help you to keep your work flow organized. The checklist should contain all steps — no matter how insignificant they may seem — so that even if you get amnesia, this list will allow you to complete every piece that must get done. So-called no-brainer items like "sign it" and "date it" — *all* steps — should be captured on these checklists. Even if you complete this same process 10 times per week and should have it memorized, use the checklist. When you have a lot going on around you, your checklist will keep your brain focused.

This checklist is your new wingman — your new partner who will stick with you through thick and thin and make sure that you complete your mission. Utilizing a checklist will remove the worry that you might have forgotten something. If you want an additional wingman, consider having an assistant or colleague double-check your work on projects that are especially tricky or don't fit the "normal" pattern.

As a fail-safe, implement a Mind Liberation.

Go-getters have heads that are full of ideas — the ideal conversation to solve a customer's dilemma, the next great business venture, the next awesome marketing plan, an amazing blog idea, the most incredible new product, the perfect power-team partnership, the…thoughts are endless. It's because we cram so much up there that we fear forgetting one of those things. So this leads to worries getting added to the mix. When you have too much floating around in your brain, all those great ideas and plans get imprisoned, and often the worries get pushed to the forefront.

How do you relieve this cramped holding cell and set your great ideas and thoughts free? I recommend to my clients that they complete a Mind Liberation a minimum of once a week. For my clients with sleep issues, I recommend that they do this every evening. Get all the ideas out of your head and onto paper or into your phone or computer. Purge your mind to make room for the creativity that needs to happen in order for you to take action and implement the thoughts and ideas that have been swirling around up there. Capture all your thoughts to relieve your worry about the possibility of forgetting something.

Get it all out of your head:

What you're excited about
What you're worried about
Things you need to do tomorrow
Things you need to do someday
Anything that's swirling in your brain

You can capture all these thoughts in one continuous list, or you can create a new document each time. The key is, do this any day you're feeling like your head has too much internal action, or if you constantly worry about forgetting something. You can use your Mind Liberations in helping you to plan your 3+3.

As a fail-safe, utilize a backup reminder system.

I should really call this a *Fifth Element Backup System*. (Nod to the movie *The Fifth Element*, starring Bruce Willis.) After all, you already have a checklist that you've created for the project or task. You'll reflect with power at the end of each day. You'll ask colleagues for an extra set of eyes on tougher projects. You'll manage your tasks during 3+3 time. That's four different ways to prevent things from falling through the cracks and four ways to catch the very few that might. The fifth way is to use a reminder system through an app or software. (Or maybe we can call this your "sixth sense." Ha! Bruce Willis fans will get that one!) What reminder systems are out there?

Calendar: If you use a digital calendar, it most likely also has a reminder system.

App: Examples of task list systems are Remember the Milk, Evernote, and Toodledo.

CRM: Your customer relationship management software may include a task-management or reminder system. You can tie these reminders to your digital project files and documents. Multiple people working on a project can see who has done what and when, as well as what's up next.

Assistant: Before computers, secretaries would remind their bosses of everything they needed to do. If you have an admin assistant, you can make this a part of his/her job if it makes sense.

Digital reminder systems allow you to set email or text alerts to remind you to do something. I'd like to caution you to set your reminder for *before* something is due or *before* you're supposed to be at a meeting, and not when something is actually due. When your reminder goes off at 2:00 PM to tell you that your project is due at 2:00 PM, that's not helpful. Use chapter 8, "Manage Long-Term Projects with Mega-efficiency," to help you break down tasks and set reminders for benchmarks along the way. If you don't have long-term projects, here's an example of how to block off time on your calendar and set reminders for a single appointment:

Appointment:
    Wed, April 18, noon–1:30 PM — lunch review with financial planner
Appointment + Reminder:
    Wed, April 18, 1:30–1:45 PM — debrief lunch meeting notes
Appointment + Reminder:
    Wed, April 18, 11:30 AM–noon — leave for and travel to lunch
Appointment + Reminder:
    Tues, April 17, 3:00–3:30 PM — materials needed for 4/18 lunch? Prep!
Appointment + Reminder:
    Mon, April 16, 8:00–8:05 AM — email to reconfirm 4/18 lunch

Not only have you set reminders, but also you've blocked off time on your calendar for these things to happen.

Stop the fantasy world in your head!

If your worry comes from imagining hypothetical situations, your course of action should be to focus on what you can control. If you've completed your 3+3, you'll have a list of objectives to stick to and help get your mind back on track when you wander off into what-if land. If you implement all reminder systems in this chapter, you have five (count 'em, five!) backup systems in place. There's no need to worry. But if your brain slips into its old ways and goes into worry mode, ask yourself: How is this worrying serving me?

Asking your brain this will lead to an answer of "It's not," which will allow you to tell your brain that it's time to get back to your objective at hand.

And be sure to celebrate all your wins. When you acknowledge all the great things you do correctly, you'll build up your confidence, which will help crush all that second-guessing.

NEXT STEPS

When Rhonda completed the weeklong time journal that I had assigned to her, she discovered that she lost up to 30 minutes panicking each day. Because of that high anxiety level, I asked her to complete a Mind Liberation each day, which helped her to build up her confidence as she implemented the tactics in this chapter and solidified her new habits.

In five years as a social worker, Rhonda had never forgotten anything so important that she was threatened with getting fired. But lately, because her workload had increased and she had begun to doubt herself, she caught herself leaving off a few steps in her casework, and twice she was corrected by her supervisor when she forgot to initial a page. The mistakes drove her anxiety levels even higher.

We created task lists for each project. We created checks-and-balances systems, so that there was no way for anything to fall by the wayside. We had her implement a Mind Liberation and create her 3+3 each day before she left work. She also set up a reminder system through her digital calendar.

Did entering information into these systems take a few minutes each day? Yes, it did. But these few minutes saved her 30-plus minutes per day. With foolproof systems in place, there was no need to panic about forgetting anything. She was able to gain back time — not to mention lower her stress levels and stress eating — by cutting out panic attacks from her day.

ⅢⅢ➤ PLOT YOUR NEXT STEPS

- What effect do you think implementing a Mind Liberation will have on you?
- When each day will you complete this Mind Liberation?
- What capture mechanism will you use for your daily/nightly Mind Liberation?

Spiral notebook

Paper

Task app

Task function within your CRM or project management system

Document on your computer

Other:

- Would you prefer that this be a free-for-all capture without structure, or do you want your ideas placed into categories (work/home, this week / next week / next month, etc.)?
- How will you remind yourself to do this?
- Speaking of reminders, what reminder system(s) are you already using?
- Are they working? Why or why not?
- If they're not working as well as you'd like, what checks-and-balances systems can you put in place, making it darn near impossible to forget anything?
- If you fear forgetting to do something, what can you do to push past that thought and move forward?
- How will you remind yourself to not let second-guessing get in your way?
- How will implementing the strategies and tactics in this chapter benefit you?

11 Set Up and Maintain a Productive Work Space

My first office as an adult was actually a classroom. I set up my classroom the same way I remembered my favorite English teacher had hers set up, with my desk in the corner of the room opposite the door and all the students' desks lined up in rows facing the front chalkboard and door. That didn't quite work for me. It took me too long to reach my desk. I wound up changing my furniture layout several more times during the school year.

Throughout the year, I added bookshelves so that I could store books and supplies that my students needed to use. I preferred taller bookshelves to shorter ones because I was able to utilize vertical space instead of taking up precious floor space. By the time I had acquired all my furniture, the room looked like a consignment store — an old oak teacher's desk from the sixties, three different styles of student desks, a beat-up brown metal file cabinet, a dark metal four-shelf bookcase commandeered from my future mother-in-law's plant patio, a rosewood-colored bookcase that my future husband brought home with him after college, and an unfinished pine bookcase that a student's parent made for his daughter's favorite teacher. It was an interior designer's nightmare, but it functioned for me.

The lessons I learned from setting up my classroom are the same ones I applied when I set up my own office and those that I teach to my clients when they struggle with creating functional work spaces.

GOAL

Invest the time to set up your office according to *your needs* — not a picture in a magazine.

TACTICS

1. Divide your space into zones.
2. Decide what you need in your primary work space in order to function.
3. Place your supplies by frequency of use.
4. Set up your desk/workstation.
5. Contain your supplies and projects.
6. Put everything back in its place before you depart.

STRATEGY

I get asked nearly every day what the perfect office setup is. In a society that wants instant fixes, many people bristle at my answer: "It depends."

Unfortunately, there is no one perfect office layout, no one diagram, no one set of directions for furniture positioning, no one shopping list of the supplies that are needed. The perfect office is the one that meets all *your* needs. So how do you set it up so that it does exactly that?

Divide your space into zones.

What tasks do you need to perform? Bill paying, filing, making phone calls, researching, designing…list everything you do in your office. On your computer or a separate sheet of paper, sketch out your office. Using sticky notes, assign the tasks you just listed to specific areas of your office. The key is to keep tasks that use the same supplies bundled by zone so that you don't have to walk back and forth constantly while working on an assignment or task.

Decide what you need in your primary work space in order to function.

Take another look at your list of tasks and the zones you created. What kind of furniture would be best for your workday? Do you need a large table for spreading out your work? Do you need a desk for a computer? Do you print out documents all day long and need a printing station? Reconfigure your current furniture or purchase/request new pieces if necessary. It's better to spend some money on a piece of furniture that will make your workday function, rather than struggling every day with furniture that does not. If your employer thinks otherwise, you'll need to retrofit the company pieces as much as possible, or ask permission to purchase your own.

Place your supplies by frequency of use.

Your most-often-used items should be within easy reach so that you do not have to walk or roll anywhere to get them. Less-often-used items can be kept a little farther away. Rarely used items can be stored on the opposite side of the office or cubicle. The easier it is for you to get to your supplies, the easier it will be to *return them*. (Aha! That's the key to maintaining your office!)

Set up your desk/workstation.

Your layout will depend on which tasks you need to complete at your workstation and, therefore, which supplies need to be kept nearby. Not everyone needs a desk. Some folks don't have one because they never sit down. Instead, they use a table as their workstation when they need to complete various tasks.

Where should you put everything? Here are a few possibilities:

- A container with a fairly small diameter (think soda can instead of coffee can) can be used to store your most-often-used writing implements. You don't want something so large that it becomes cluttered and you can't easily grab what you need.
- Your top desk drawers should house items that you utilize daily or almost daily. Use drawer dividers to hold items in place so that they don't slide all over your drawer, making items difficult to find when you need them.
- Your lower desk drawers should store lesser-used items.
- If you'll need to refer frequently to books, workbooks, or binders, keep them stored vertically on a shelf near your desk. If you don't have the luxury of a shelf, line these up vertically on the edge of your desk, and use bookends to keep them in place.
- Most desks come with a file drawer. Use hanging files to keep papers easily accessible — and to make it easy to drop them in.
- When you are working at your desk, you should not have to get up multiple

times each day to retrieve supplies from elsewhere. When you are sitting at your desk, what do you need to have access to within arm's reach?

• Sit in your chair and go through your daily routine in your head. Make sure those supplies are within reach. Set up what you think you'll need. You can always make adjustments at the end of the week if you've forgotten about a certain supply or if you need to switch locations of items. You won't know what works for you until you get in the driver's seat and test-drive what you've created.

Examples of zones in an office and supplies placed by frequency of use:

Primary work space — desk

Daily files — desk drawer

Daily office supplies — desk drawer

Lesser-used files — file cabinet in back of office

Printer/scanner/fax, used multiple times per week (but not daily) — corner, near desk, within one roll of the chair

Project files, materials, and daily reference books — shelves near desk, within arm's reach

Project work space — open table for spreading out work, along wall between project materials and file cabinet

Lesser-used books and reference materials — bookshelves, back of office, across from file cabinet

Extra office supplies and paper — bookshelves, back of office, across from file cabinet

At this point, you might be saying to yourself, "That sure is a whole lot of time and energy spent on deciding what goes where!" Here's a little secret: If you don't invest the time now to decide where you'll store your items, you'll spend far more time looking for supplies when you need them.

Contain your supplies.

Once you've determined how often you'll use your supplies and where everything will be stored, it's time to get your supplies into containers and placed where they need to be.

Clear containers are the best to use because you'll be able to see what's inside.

The best size container to use is determined by the sizes of the objects that need to be stored. If you buy a container that is too large, not only will you waste space on a shelf, but you will end up dumping in items that don't belong or putting too many other objects in there. Why is that a big deal? If you mix categories, it will be harder to find what you need. And if they're mixed, you'll have to empty the container onto a table or pick through it in order to get what you need. That's not very efficient and will cost you time.

Clearly label each container so that everyone who comes into contact with that container will understand what is stored in it and what should be put back in it.

Containers that store daily items do not need lids. Lids get in the way, especially when it's time to put objects away. If you need to be able to grab supplies and put them back, consider keeping those particular containers lid-free. Containers that hold lesser-used items, on the other hand, can have lids.

If you're short on shelf space and need to stack containers, make sure that your lesser-used containers are on the bottom of the stack, as you'll need to access them less often. Or you can stack similar objects — such as reams of paper — in any order, since you can just grab from the top. It's not optimal to stack bins or place containers on their sides, but if you're in an office with minimal space, you need to make every square inch of storage count and utilize vertical space. Just make sure that their placement is based on place of use and frequency of use.

An alternative to stacking is using helper shelves so that each individual item is simple to slide out. By dividing up your vertical space with a shelf, you create two levels of easy-to-reach storage. Or consider using a plastic drawer system where each drawer can slide out when needed.

Contain your projects.

Many people have a specific set of supplies or papers that they use. Keep those supplies in a container that's simple to tote around the office, or keep the papers in an easy-to-reach file. Some of my clients have a shelf of baskets — one basket per client — because their projects involve 3-D objects. Other clients have a file sorter on their desk to store ongoing project files. By having a designated place for your clients' project materials, you'll know exactly where to put those loose notes from meetings and phone conversations. There will be no more frantic searches for the nugget of inspiration you scribbled on a napkin.

Put everything back in its place before you depart.

There is no better way to start your day than walking into an orderly office. You feel in control from the get-go, which empowers you to plow through the day.

> A productive environment is an intentional setting in which everything around you supports who you are and who you want to be.
>
> – Barbara Hemphill

Walking into an office in which you have piles of unfinished projects or stacks of who-knows-what is a deflating way to start your day. These piles wreak havoc on your subconscious. They silently sucker punch you throughout the day, bringing down your energy. They envelop your brain and grind your thinking down to a halt. They sabotage everything you attempt to do throughout the day. That's why you need them cleared out. (See the next chapter for help on digging out.)

Visual learners most especially get distracted by objects and clutter. Piles of items can also negatively affect your subconscious because your brain is reminded of how much you have going on around you — or how much you haven't yet done.

By returning everything to its home at the end of the day — even if you will need it again the next day — not only will you keep your office in order; you'll also keep your mind in order.

As a fail-safe method to make sure that your office stays orderly, include among the things you do during your CHOP days (see chapter 9, "Get It All Done in 24 Hours: Turn To-Do Lists into *Done* Lists," for details) addressing those pesky renegade papers and objects that have snuck into your office under the radar. Not only will these check-ups help you to keep your office in shape, but also they will help you to prevent any projects and tasks from falling through the cracks. Having this built-in backup system will give your brain the confidence that you won't flake out or forget, so you don't have to leave everything out on your desk in order to remember to do it.

Invest the time to set up your office in a way that will work for you. You have to take your time to save time. It will pay dividends in the long run for your Time Management Revolution.

ⅢⅢ➡ PLOT YOUR NEXT STEPS

- What about your current office is working for you? Why?
- What about your current office is not working for you? Why?
- Based on what you've just read, what types of adjustments will you need to make?
- What zones will you need to create in your office?
- Will you be able to make these changes in one full day of rearranging or in a weekend, or will you need to work 30 minutes a day on different sections until the project is completed?

12 Dig Out from a Buried Office

My client Julie had a beautifully decorated office. The walls matched the curtains matched the shelves matched the chairs matched the area rug. The problem was, you couldn't actually see the chairs or shelves or rug because papers, bags, and whatsits were strewn everywhere. The *bigger* problem was that Julie lost time every single day looking for something she needed.

She said she didn't have time to devote to getting her office in order; yet each day she lost at least 30 minutes in total looking for items. After journaling where her time was going, she realized that she could save almost three hours per week by making sure that everything in her office had a home.

GOAL

Block off time on your calendar to eliminate the piles in your office.

TACTICS

Use my *Cinco* P method to defeat the stacks in your office:

1. Plan
2. Pace
3. Purge
4. Partition
5. Place

STRATEGY

I've always loved the sound of the word *syncope* (pronounced SIN-co-pee). According to the Merriam-Webster dictionary, *syncope* means: "1. loss of consciousness resulting from insufficient blood flow to the brain : faint. 2. the loss of one or more sounds or letters in the interior of a word (as in *fo'c'sle* for *forecastle*)."

Whether we're talking about the human body or words, either way, it means a loss. And a loss of time is exactly what happens when piles of papers and objects weigh down your subconscious, resulting in insufficient energy flow to your brain, which prevents your brain from operating at optimal capacity. A loss of time is what happens when you can't find what you need.

I thought it would be ironic to take a word that expresses loss and turn it into a method that eliminates loss. So, drumroll, please...

To prevent this loss of time in an office that's crowded with too much stuff, apply my *Cinco* P method to dig out.

1. Plan

You've got it! Everything in this book — every theory behind a successful Time Management Revolution — is related to mind management and planning, so it should come as no surprise that planning is involved here too, when it comes to physical space. What's normally happened with my clients before they started working with me is that they decided to clear out their space by coming in one Saturday afternoon or staying late one evening. They didn't think about what their goals were, what steps they needed to complete, or what resources they would need. They were completely unprepared when they dove in, so they didn't accomplish what they had set out to do. The lack of project completion in a single session brought them crashing down, and the pileups just continued because they gave up on their project.

To prevent that from happening to you (or to move past it), let's create a plan for your office decluttering project.

- Will you need to sort in your office space, or can you pull things out a little at a time to a separate area? (You'll be making a big mess. It'll get worse before it gets better!)
- What boxes or containers can you use to set up the various categories you'll divide items into?

- Where can you set up all the above boxes, so that you create a mini "store" for your categories of items? (Picture Walmart or Target or your grocery store. There are aisles of items, and each aisle has specific items…unless you shop at my local Ross, where it's hard to find things because items are strewn all over the place!)
- Where can you take the shredding?
- Where can you take the recycling?
- Where can you take the trash?
- Where can you take the donations?
- Is there anyone who can help you with this process?

2. Pace

For some reason, we think we need to finish projects in one short sitting. Perhaps it's because we live in a microwave society and expect to have things nuked — or fixed — instantly. Unfortunately, it doesn't quite work that way, unless you're willing to just throw away everything in your office without even looking at it.

Therefore, you'll need to decide at what pace to work. Are you physically, emotionally, and attention span–ly capable of working for several hours at a time? If so, schedule blocks of time on your calendar to work at this pace.

If you work better for 15 or 30 minutes at a time, schedule your blocks of time accordingly.

When I'm working with clients and forcing them to stay focused and on task, it takes about one hour to get through a Bankers Box amount of small objects or papers. I don't give them the time to read every single word on a document. They take five seconds to scan with their eyes, and then *boom!* decide where the paper goes.

I share this estimated time passage with you so that you can realistically estimate how much time the project will take. That's half the battle — creating a timeline you can live up to.

If you have the equivalent of 25 boxes of papers and stuff hanging out in your office, you should plan for *at least* 25 hours to work on and finish your project. This is why pacing yourself and scheduling are so important. Choose a pace that works for your brain, body, and calendar. If you spend 30 minutes per week on this project, you'll finish in a year. If you spend an hour per week on this project, you'll finish in six months. If you spend 30 minutes per weekday working on this project, you'll finish in just under three months.

Be realistic about your time.

To help yourself to work around the room and see progress, divide your desk and the room up into squares, like a checkerboard. You can do this figuratively in your mind, or (if your boss doesn't mind, you never host clients, and this won't cause a safety issue) you can physically lay out string or tape on the floor. Work on one square at a time.

Once you dig in, start at the top of the pile in a single square, and work your way down that stack. Psychologically, we feel like there's more space in a room when we can see the floor. So if you work on one column at a time from top to bottom, you'll see more visible progress compared with randomly grabbing from the tops of various piles. The more progress we see, the more motivated we are to continue and finish.

3. Purge

Set up boxes for donations, shredding, recycling, trash, and objects/papers that belong to other people. Your first round should be spent on simply clearing out a little space. Don't dig too much at this time. Just start in checkerboard square 1 and scan with your eyes. What jumps out at you? What can go immediately?

At the end of each week (or sooner if the boxes fill up), take the contents of the boxes to the appropriate destinations.

As you move to step 4, "Partition," you'll revisit this process as you dig through your columns.

4. Partition

We'll be doing this on two levels: macro and micro. You'll need some boxes or containers (and, eventually, hanging files) for this.

First, gather all the papers and objects you've been working with in the past two to three weeks. You'll most likely still need them as you progress through this project. Set them in a safe spot, such as a container on your desk, so that you don't lose them during this project.

Partition — Macro Sort

Set up boxes for the various papers and objects you'll find. Typical categories to start with:

Office supplies
Client files
To do
This year's papers
Prior year's papers
Cables
Gadgets
To read
Reference material
Paper (printer, card stock, etc.)
Memories (certificates, photos, awards)

And, of course, you still have your boxes from step 3, "Purge": donations, shredding, recycling, and objects/papers that belong to other people.

Feel free to set up more as you go along. This is why you need an area to work on this project.

Starting in square 1, you'll quickly work your way down through the column, glancing at each paper or object for about five seconds — just long enough to decide in which category it should be placed. Don't think too deeply at this point. You're doing this macro sort so that you can know what's in your office and make easier decisions when you get to...

Partition — Micro Sort

This is where your hanging files will come in. You don't need fancy totes or empty file drawers yet. (If you have them, great. If not, no worries!) You can use Bankers Boxes to hang your files.

Label your file folders with sticky notes. No need to make permanent labels until you're sure you need that file.

Once you're done with the macro sort, it'll be time to address what's in all your boxes. By having like things together, you'll be able to more quickly weed out duplicates and gather papers that belong in the same file.

It's also at this point in the project that you think to yourself, "Why the heck did I save all this?" and "Why the heck did I not deal with this stuff sooner?"

Use these thoughts as motivation to purge even more. And use these thoughts as motivation to sit down and process your papers at the end of each day so that you'll never have to go through a monstrous months-long project like this again.

Work on one box/category at a time. Depending on how you best address your projects, you can start with what you deem to be the easiest box so that you can finish it faster and feel more successful sooner. Or you can start with what you deem to be the toughest box so that you can get the worst over with first.

Purge what you can. Whether you want to scan the papers eventually or keep them in paper format, create file folders for your major categories so that you have a place in which to drop the papers as you work.

See chapter 18, "Set Up a Simple Filing System That Works," if you need more structure for this part.

With the boxes of objects you have, you'll go through the same process. Purge what you can, via donating, giving to others, or tossing in the trash. With what's left, move to the next step.

5. Place

This should be the fun part because it's the step during which you complete the project. But this is where a lot of people get overwhelmed because after all the purging and partitioning, there's still crap all over the place! Actually, there shouldn't be any crap because that should've been purged. So, if you refer to anything at this point as crap, perhaps it missed its calling during the "Purge" step!

Seriously, though, when people see that there are *still* boxes of papers or objects after *all* the time they've spent purging and partitioning, they feel a little frustrated at this point. They want to just shove the boxes into a corner and move on to something else. As the band Pink Martini sings, "Hang on, Little Tomato!" The light is at the end of the tunnel!

> The very cave you are afraid to enter turns out to be the source of what you are looking for.
> — Joseph Campbell

Round 1: Taking a box at a time, place your daily-use items first, closest to where you'll need them.

Round 2: Taking a box at a time, place your weekly-use items either behind or underneath the daily-use items.

Round 3: Taking a box at a time, place your monthly-use items either behind or underneath the daily- and weekly-use items.

What you're doing here is consciously placing your most vital information and resources in places that will be easy for you to reach — and easy for you to put things away.

As you run out of space, you need to ask yourself, "If I don't need this daily or weekly or monthly, do I truly need it?"

Do I want to install floor-to-ceiling, wall-to-wall shelves to hold everything I own, or am I willing to let go in order to create space in my office, in order to create a work space that's conducive to efficiency and productivity…and peace?

If you don't want to wash-rinse-repeat and reexperience huge decluttering projects like this, be sure to have a maintenance plan of returning items to their homes at the end of each day — and deciding on homes for new objects when they enter your work space.

NEXT STEPS

Julie's office had roughly 10 boxes of papers/items that needed to be dealt with. Her ADD limited her attention span to about 15 minutes, so she set her timer for that amount of time and chipped away for two to three sessions per day. It took her a total of approximately eight hours to purge and partition and about two hours to place. She now has zones and can find whatever she needs in less than a minute. She processes all papers and objects at the end of each day instead of waiting six months (or in some cases a full year) before addressing what's mysteriously crept into her work space.

⇒ PLOT YOUR NEXT STEPS

- When will you set aside time to plan?
- Based on what you read in this chapter, what kind of pace and timeline do you want to schedule for yourself?
- What motivation and/or accountability partner will you use to make sure that you finish this project?

13 Create a Go-Bag and Mobile Office for Road Warriors

Jack, a pharmaceutical rep, spends most of his week working out of his home office and car, driving to appointments. On multiple occasions he did not have enough documents or the right samples to leave behind because he'd forgotten to check what his clients had needed and reload. His shoulder bag contained all his supplies, but not in an orderly structure, so he could never find anything when he needed it. His apologies for making prospective clients wait while he fished something out of his bag became almost second nature. His trunk hadn't been organized since day one, and, being completely full, it caused him to migrate his newest piles to the backseat.

GOAL

Make time to create a mini-me office that contains your must-have daily supplies in your go-bag and/or trunk.

TACTICS

1. Use triplicates.
2. Have a go-bag with compartments.
3. Set up your trunk office.
4. Go digital whenever possible.

STRATEGY

Thanks to laptops, smartphones, and tablets, professionals around the world are no longer tethered to their desks. But with this ease of portability comes the need to adjust to a mobile office in order to stay efficient and productive while out on the road.

My clients who spend little time in an office tend to have these two major challenges:

- How to keep track of supplies and files in up to three different locations — home, work, and car (that's the focus of this chapter)
- How to squeeze in as many client appointments as possible without being late and without having to do paperwork until midnight (see chapter 25, "Scheduling for Road Warriors")

It takes a little bit of a mind shift, but here's how you can begin to manage those challenges and increase your productivity. In addition to reading chapter 11, "Set Up and Maintain a Productive Work Space," implement these strategies and tactics.

Use triplicates.

It sounds funny for someone who talks folks into getting rid of things to say that you should have duplicates or triplicates, but if you work in multiple spaces, there's no need to keep transferring the same supplies around. Utilizing multiples will prevent "I forgot that" incidents and will annihilate lost time because you'll never have to look for that item that you wound up leaving back in your other office. Have one set of supplies in your home office. Have a separate set of supplies in your work office. Have a third set of supplies in your go-bag or trunk office.

Have a go-bag with compartments.

Often, my clients will have purchased a shoulder bag or case on wheels based on looks or price, and they end up with a great deal on a nice-looking bag that has just one compartment. They inevitably dump all their supplies and files into one black hole and lose time looking for what they need. Instead, figure out what items you need to carry with you on the go, and purchase a bag that contains different compartments to hold what you need. Or retrofit your black-hole bag with containers that will hold items from your various categories, such as a laptop or tablet, files, gadgets, cords, brochures, notepad, writing utensils, and so on.

Set up your trunk office.

My sales consultant clients have to be ready for each client appointment with brochures, cards, product information, and samples. If they're seeing multiple clients in one day, they can't fit all this in one go-bag. So we set up a trunk office. Crates hold hanging files with the different forms and brochures. Separate containers hold the various samples. For my clients who commute via train or subway, their trunk office is a roll-aboard suitcase with these same categories. Their go-bag rests on top of the roll-aboard and contains whatever they need for the client in front of them. (Note: To prevent thieves casing a parking lot from knowing what you've got stashed in your trunk and then breaking in when you leave your vehicle, load up for your next appointment in the parking lot of the client you're just leaving.)

Go digital whenever possible.

Having access to all your client information and files from any location is extremely helpful. If you're digitally inclined, consider using a cloud-based file cabinet such as Evernote — or Dropbox, which (if you've installed the desktop version) allows you to access files on a laptop even when you're not connected to the internet. For security reasons, you never want to log in to the internet through public Wi-Fi, so using a program such as Dropbox that allows you to see your files without an internet connection is a bonus. If you can log in via nonpublic Wi-Fi while on the road (such as a secure tethering option on your phone), consider using a CRM system to house everything related to your clients. If you don't feel comfortable with digital, please do not fret. If you're more comfortable with paper, stay with paper. Use whatever works best for you.

Increasing your efficiency and lowering your stress levels will happen as you gradually implement these strategies and tactics. It may seem counterintuitive to slow things down, take your time, set up storage in multiple places, and have triplicates of supplies, but doing so will give your brain clarity and allow you to better focus on what you need to get done. When your brain is focused, you'll produce higher-quality work and make better decisions about how you use your time.

NEXT STEPS

Jack eventually sensed that his prospective clients didn't have faith in him because they witnessed him fumbling to retrieve items. He noticed a complete about-face once he showed up with structure — in his roller bag and in his go-bag. He was even proud to open his trunk in front of doctors if they happened to cruise by his car in the parking lot. They were impressed with his "deals on wheels" office. A guy who had it that together would surely have it together enough to take care of their orders properly.

> Our greatest glory is not in never falling, but in rising every time we fall.
>
> – Oliver Goldsmith

ⅢⅢ➡ PLOT YOUR NEXT STEPS

- What about your current mobile office is working for you? Why?
- What about your current mobile office is not working for you? Why?
- Based on what you've just read, what types of adjustments will you need to make?
- What compartments will you need to create in your go-bag and/or mobile office?
- Will you be able to make these changes in one full day of rearranging or a weekend, or will you need to work 30 minutes a day on different sections?

14 Set Boundaries in the Digital Age

When was the last time you saw two people sit across the table from each other and just talk, making eye contact the entire time? Instead, it usually goes a little something like this:

Jan sits down to wait for Ricardo. While waiting, she pulls out her tablet so that she can report her geographic location via social media. She's so engrossed that she doesn't see Ricardo walk up, and he startles her.

Ricardo sits down, setting his smartphone on the table. As their conversation starts, his phone rings. He picks it up, looks at who's calling, and then apologizes for leaving the ringer on. He turns off the ringer and returns his attention to Jan.

Another minute into the conversation, Jan sees out of the corner of her eye something change on her tablet screen. She glances at her screen, swipes something on it, and then looks back up at Ricardo.

Ricardo's phone vibrates on the table. He looks at the number on the screen, apologizes, and says he must take this call. "Hi, Nathan. I'm in a meeting and can't talk. Can I call you back later?"

And this is how their meeting goes. Thirty minutes of constant interruptions. There is never any truly focused time when the person across the table is the only thing in the world that matters and, therefore, has the utter and complete attention of the other. This is a case of not being intentional.

The art of *focus* is a dying one. And that's why so many people are spinning their wheels. They're in such a hurry to get everything done that they stumble, make mistakes, forget things, or get sidetracked, and, ultimately, get *nothing* done — or at least, very little.

GOAL

Do you control your phone, or does your phone control you? Turn off your notifications, and set a schedule for checking communication on your devices.

TACTICS

1. Turn off the message indicators on your phone, tablet, and computer.
   Messages = text, email, social media, voicemail.
   Indicators = sounds, vibrations, numbers popping up on the screen.
2. Move your "temptation" apps off your home screen and onto a back screen (or completely off your device).
3. Decide at what intervals during the workday you'll check your messages (every 10 minutes, one hour, three hours, etc.).
4. Decide at what intervals during your personal time you'll check your messages (every five minutes, 30 minutes, three hours, etc.).
5. Decide which form of communication will be the primary mode used for work.

STRATEGY

I always meet with my clients in their place of business. I sit with them at their desks and interview them. I listen intently, but I also watch their body language; figure out their personalities, brain types, and work styles; and pick up on their habits. During nearly every initial meeting that I've had with business clients, there is one top time-waster that I've observed and that I recommend they quit. Those who don't follow that particular recommendation miss out on the easiest way to cut disruptions and eliminate lost time. Those who do follow my recommendation tell me that just by doing that one little thing, they gain an incredible amount of time back and increase their productivity exponentially.

What is this simple fix that people hear about but usually don't implement?

Turn off your message indicator.

I've worked with executives, solopreneurs, office managers, authors, media consultants, physicians — you name it. Those with the indicator turned on took longer to get through our interview because their attention was constantly drawn to the little blip on the screen that kept popping up, or the little beep that let them know that a new email or text message had arrived, or the number displayed on their email tab that crept higher.

At the end of our interview, after giving them other recommendations based on my findings, I pointed out how many times they checked their email or texts and shared with them the total number of minutes eaten away by a lack of focus and their need to regroup their thoughts or be reminded of where we were in the conversation.

Everyone is a bit taken aback by this. They start apologizing for being rude. I explain to them that my observation has nothing to do with social etiquette. It has to do with time and reaching a higher state of brain function. If you just lost 20 percent of your time with someone you were paying to sit in your office to coach you, how much do you lose when there's no one here? In one hour, we've lost 12 minutes. Over an eight-hour day, you'd lose about 90 minutes. In one week, you'd lose over seven hours. In one month, you'd lose nearly 30 hours. In...

"Okay, okay! But I can't turn it off. I need to know what's going on."

"Unless you're an emergency dispatcher who needs to send paramedics to sites or you were hired to answer customer questions within 30 seconds of receiving an email, it can wait until you're ready."

"But...I *like* it. I think I might be addicted to it."

"Try this. After I leave, turn off your email indicator for one hour. Work on something for 10 minutes, and then check your email. Work on something for 10 minutes, and then check your email."

"Fine. But I know I won't like it."

"I know, but please humor me."

Another common pushback comment is, "But what if it's the school calling to let me know my child is hurt, or the hospital calling to say my spouse is there?"

My answer: "If you spend each moment waiting for a horrific phone call to come, then it will. What if instead you focused on having a great day and great life?"

Turn off your notifications.

To be clear, I'm not suggesting you stop checking altogether. What I am recommending is that you check when your brain is ready to focus on communication,

> We think we are so much more connected because we carry these devices around with us so we can press buttons and talk to someone immediately. But...we are actually coming further and further away from true connection.
>
> *— Zachary Quinto*

instead of letting yourself get interrupted constantly throughout the day. It takes the brain an average of 60 seconds to restart when switching tasks, so that's what you lose each time you go Pavlovian and check when the indicator goes off. You can check every 10 minutes if you'd like. Set a timer. Focus on your work for 10 minutes. Allow your brain to work efficiently, at full steam.

Every single client who accepted my challenge reported back that they had the most amazing hour in their professional lives. They had never realized how unfocused they were because it had been so long since they had focused. They got stuff done. Even more important, they created a clarity in their brains that they hadn't experienced in many moons. Not only did they complete more tasks; they produced better-quality work.

It was scary to quit their addiction cold turkey, but it was the most productive they'd been in ages. One reporter called me back two days after our interview and said, "That changed my life! My mind was electrified. Who knew?"

Is this a sexy topic? No.

Is this earth-shattering advice? As with all the other strategies and tactics in this book, to those who start *doing* it, yes.

A nonclient once said to me that I needed to give more exciting and original advice. "If *Forbes* interviewed you, would you talk about turning off your email or text indicator?"

If it gave someone back nearly *four full business days per month* and the mind clarity that leads to greatness, hell yeah.

Remove temptation and deliver us from evil.

Tablets and smartphones allow us to pick and choose which apps to house on our home screens. These should be the ones we use the most, and the lesser-used apps should be stored on the rear screens. But what if some of the apps you use more often are tempting time sucks, and one of the ways your time is smuggled away each day? Seeing the icons for your favorite social media or gaming apps right there in front of your face makes it very tempting — and super-easy — to slip into another world. The more time you spend in that other world, the more inefficient you are in this one. Move the app(s) off your home screen so that it takes a little effort to waste time. If you want to take extreme measures, remove the app from your phone completely. You can still use social media or play games through your computer or laptop, but it will take a little more effort to reach those screens, which will help prevent you from going down that rabbit hole.

Decide which form of communication to use for work.

Some companies allow their employees total freedom in how they communicate with customers, clients, and coworkers: internal messaging, email, text, Facebook messages, Twitter direct messages, LinkedIn mail, and so on. I once watched a client spend 15 minutes searching for information she knew she'd received because she didn't remember which platform was used to convey it. And that wasn't the first time she needed to search for information. She was losing quite a bit of time doing these searches.

Let your customers, clients, and coworkers know which two methods you prefer. If they forget and use one of the other formats, simply transfer the conversation back to one of your preferred methods. That way, you have to search for conversation threads or information in only two platforms instead of a plethora.

NEXT STEPS

It's really important that we focus on the present, that we be intentional with everything we do. When we rush around from here to there, when we allow ourselves to be interrupted by our gadgets, when we allow our apps to become procrastination crutches, our brains get jumbled up with mind clutter and more thoughts of other things we're supposed to do, which breaks our concentration from the present.

The more connected we are to our devices, the more disconnected we are from the people who are in front of us and the tasks for which we're responsible. We don't pay attention. We don't stay in the moment. We're constantly flit-flitting to whatever catches our eye. Our minds are swirling with overwhelm. Additionally, in our zeal to "stay connected," we let our gadgets interrupt us constantly throughout the day.

Implement Structure *and* Flow. Set structured boundaries with your devices to allow more time for flow.

> ➤ **PLOT YOUR NEXT STEPS**
>
> - Are you going to be the boss of your time, or are you going to let some computer or phone own you?
> - When will you turn off your notifications?
> - What schedule will you set for emailing, texting, and checking/posting on social media?
> - On the home screens of your devices, are there any apps that tempt you?
> - If so, when will you move them to the rear or remove them from your device?
> - How will implementing the strategies and tactics in this chapter benefit you?

15 Manage Your Incoming Email

My client Robert had email anxiety. He dreaded email because he had so much of it, and he spent all day working out of his inbox. He would begin his day without his 3+3 list. The first thing he'd do was open up his inbox. He would open one email at a time. He'd read it. He'd type up a quick reply. Then he'd hit send.

He wound up opening a lot of emails that were junk or didn't apply to him.

He also discovered as he kept opening emails that some of the responses he'd sent earlier didn't quite fit the situation because he hadn't read through all the emails in the chain.

As he kept working in his inbox, he'd revert to the latest email that popped up on his notification. He wanted his supervisors and coworkers to know that he was on top of things. To him, that meant answering every email as soon as it arrived. He'd quickly read it, type up a hurried response, and hit send.

Then he'd forget where he was and what he was doing in his inbox.

He would end up falling behind on projects and not completing anything he'd hoped to because he'd answered emails all day.

At other times, he would quit email cold turkey and not look for two days because he was just so overwhelmed.

It was a love-hate relationship. No matter which way he approached his email inbox, neither was doing him any good. And neither way proved to his supervisors and coworkers that he was on top of things. At times, he had 5,000 unread emails. He just wanted to bury his head in the sand.

GOAL

Your email should not control your day; *you* should.

TACTICS

Checking/Reading Emails

1. Set your timer for 15 minutes.
2. Scan your inbox for emails you don't want or need, and delete without opening:
   a.   Obvious spam
   b.   Sales announcements
   c.   Events you know you can't attend
   d.   Other?
3. Scan your inbox for emails that don't apply to you, and delete without opening:
   a.   Information that doesn't affect you or your department
   b.   Reminders for events you've already RSVP'd to
   c.   Reminders from others about projects/tasks you've already completed and submitted
   d.   Other?
4. Look at your to-do list and 3+3 for the day. Read emails related to those tasks and situations, and draft responses.
5. Read emails that are related to other important tasks or situations — but weren't on your 3+3 list for the day — and draft responses.
6. If there's time remaining in your email session, read the less important emails, and draft responses.
7. Send any drafts that truly require your response before your next email check.
8. See the "Writing Emails" section for best practices on responses.

Writing Emails

Originator emails

1. Decide on the purpose of your email. Know the one-sentence message that you're trying to convey and what actions you're requesting of the recipient.
2. Will it take less time to cover this in a phone call? If so, make that call. If not...
3. Draft a thoughtful email, including all the possible scenarios and questions that might arise.
4. Utilize a template for repeated communications.
5. Leave the draft until your next email check.
6. During the next check, add any other thoughts or ideas that have cropped up.
7. Include when you're available for email or phone responses.
8. Read your email out loud to verify accuracy.
9. Type in a subject line with your requested action and due date.
10. Hit send.

Replies

1. If you're not sure of the answer, acknowledge receipt of the email and let the recipients know when you'll have an answer for them.
2. Do all of the above in the "Originator emails" section, plus:
3. Reread the email to which you're responding to verify that you've covered all questions and topics.

Out of Office

If you'll be unable to reply to emails within your normal time frame, set your out-of-office autoresponder. This message will automatically be sent to everyone who emails you and should state when you'll be back in touch, as well as who else can help them in the meantime.

STRATEGY

Email should not run your day. *You* should run your day.
"Giveth and you shall receiveth."
Send less. Receive less.
You have to take your time to save time.

It's as simple as that. The more email you send, the more you will receive. Too many times, what should be a five-minute conversation on the phone turns into 10 or 20 emails going back and forth because little thought went into the responses. And too many times, we rush in our responses, so we end up losing time when we backpedal — clearing up misunderstandings, correcting typos, or repairing the damage from a communication that shouldn't have been sent.

If you run a technology help desk, customer service center, or emergency response team, your job obviously is to check email in order to respond to communications immediately. But unless you have a job like that, your responsibility is not to be at someone else's beck and call. Your job is to achieve your business targets. And you won't be able to achieve your targets if you're living in and operating out of your inbox all day long.

Message Indicators Kill Productivity

First and foremost, turn off all your indicators and notifications — on your phone, tablet, and computer. Each time you allow your device to interrupt you with a notification that a new email, text, or social media post has arrived, you're losing an average of one minute in brain restart time. According to some studies, the average person receives 11 electronic communications per hour, so 11 notifications would cause you to lose 11 minutes per hour. In an eight-hour day, you've caused yourself to lose 88 minutes! Just turning off your indicator alone will save you 1.5 hours per day!

Before you have a heart attack and think that I'm asking you to never check email, let's calm down and set the record straight — that's not the case. I'm not asking you to ignore email. Instead, I'm asking you to forbid your phone and tablet and laptop from controlling you. I want *you* to control *them*. They are your tools, not your bosses.

Set designated times to check your email. For many jobs, an acceptable response time is the same day. So you could check email in the morning and again in the late afternoon. For some industries, response time may be expected within a few hours. If so, check email once every two hours. Heck, even if you check email once every 10 minutes, you'll still be more productive than allowing yourself to get interrupted 11 times per hour. If you run your own business, you as the business owner decide what an acceptable response time is.

Once you determine your email check-in schedule, share this time frame with any contacts or clients with whom you communicate. For example, my clients know that I check email first thing in the morning, at midday if I have a chance, and when I return to my office at the end of the day. Because I've set that expectation and shared it with others, I feel no pressure to check email more often. In fact, I saw a post from one of my clients the other day on Facebook, referring me to one of her friends. She let her friend know my phone and email schedule! Awesome!

Checking Email

When you do dig in to check email, set your timer for 15 minutes so that you don't get sucked into a time vacuum. It's easy to intend to check email for just a few minutes, and then get sucked into links and links of links... and end up losing half an hour... or two. Set a timer to keep you focused on answering the most pertinent emails.

You'll actually do multiple rounds of scanning your inbox. Round 1 will be for scanning for emails that are advertisements, unwanted newsletters, spam, and any other emails that don't apply to you. It'll take you about 60 seconds to scan your inbox for these and place check marks next to them, and then click or press the delete button. That's right! You'll delete them without even opening them. Booyah! You just saved time!

During round 1, you'll get an idea of who's written to you.

During round 2, you'll go back to the emails that apply to your 3+3 list, which covers all important items you need to complete that day. Therefore, you should first look at communications related to them.

During round 3, you'll read any other emails related to important clients and projects on which you're working.

During round 4, you'll read what's left.

Writing Emails

One of the reasons email strings can go on forever is because they're typed and sent without much thought. We just hurriedly punch out a quick response off the top of our head, and then we hit send. Because we don't take the time to closely read the email from the recipient, we sometimes misunderstand what he is requesting or saying, or we miss some of the questions he is asking. Because we don't take the time to give a well-thought-out answer, we can be unclear or leave out important details. All of this leads to mistakes, miscommunication, and more questions — all of which will cause us to lose time from our day.

Instead, take your time. That's right. You have to take your time to save time. Carefully read the email to which you're responding, and make sure that you understand the content.

What kind of response will you need to give?

Is this a complex situation?

Will it take less time to have a phone conversation about this and then follow up with an email confirmation of the conversation?

Sometimes picking up the phone will take only 10 minutes, versus 30 minutes or more of back-and-forth emails.

If you do need to reply via email, thoughtfully craft a response that covers all possible questions and angles. End with the questions you need answers for or actions you need the recipient to complete. Summing up the actions and giving a deadline will let the recipient know that you're competent and mean business. The first time you do this, she might be a little shocked by someone being so straightforward. But when you deliver quality work on time, she'll know why. You should also state when you'll be available by email or phone to answer questions or continue the discussion. Will stating your availability take an extra 30 seconds to type? Yes. But this will prevent lost time through phone tag or unrealistic expectations about when you'll respond via email.

Example of a formal request:

Next steps: To ensure that we move forward, please send me your responses to the following three questions by Thursday, November 18, 5 PM PST:

1.
2.
3.

If you have any questions, I'll be available by email from 8 AM to 5 PM PST, Monday through Friday. I'll answer by the end of the business day.

Or, if you prefer to discuss this by phone, I'll be available at 1-800-IM-GOOD:

Tues, 8:00–8:30 AM PST

Wed, 4:00–5:00 PM PST

With your help, I look forward to hitting this project out of the ballpark for you!

Sincerely,

Then let the email rest in the draft email folder.

What?! Yes, that's right. Let your email rest — especially if it's about a touchy situation. Sometimes our first reactions are very emotional, and sending that first draft can lead to a world of trouble — and lost time — down the road. Let your email bake for as long as possible in the draft oven. If you can wait until your next email check to review it and send it — great! If you can't wait until the next go-round, and you truly need to send it right away, at least wait until the end of this round to reread it one more time before sending.

Most email systems offer spelling check. If yours offers the option of marking misspelled words as you type, definitely use the option. If not, run the spelling checker. Also take the time to read your email out loud. This will help you to catch omitted words, incorrect words (it happens when we have a lot in our head!), and emotionally loaded words. Taking an extra minute or two to edit can save you from problems in the long run.

What if you'd like to do all this, but you don't know the answer you need to give? Respond to the individual to acknowledge your receipt of the message, and let the person know when you'll be back in touch with the answer. Will it take you a day to find out? Tell the individual two days. Give yourself some time. If you don't deliver by the set time, the individual might be displeased with your tardiness. If you find out earlier, the person will be pleasantly surprised. The latter is always better!

Subject Lines

"Hello!" is the most worthless subject line on this earth, next to a blank one. It does not tell you what the subject is or what action is required of you. Set the example for everyone you communicate with (and make your life easier at the same time). Use subject lines that state the call to action and the due date. If someone has sent you an email with an uninformative subject line, change the subject line to something more informative. Here are some examples:

Bad:

Hello!
What's up?
Did you know that...
Need your help

Good:

> Status of xyz project needed by June 25, 12 PM EST
>
> FYI — Ryder engineering stats may be of interest to you
>
> Need your Feb newsletter edits by Jan 15, 5 PM CST
>
> 911 — Mr. Client found dead; issue press release ASAP!

You can be softer and less blunt if you wish — but still get to the point. The rest of the details that the recipient needs will be in the body of your email, but the subject line will help him to sort his email. How thoughtful and efficient of you!

If your response is only one line, your subject line can be the entire email, ending with "EOM" ("end of message"):

Original email subject line:

> question about rates on McNally project

Subject line of your response:

> Received, will have answer by June 25 (EOM) — Re: question about rates on McNally project

Using this technique will save your recipients time because they won't even need to open your email to know your response. They'll love you for this efficiency!

Use Templates

If you find yourself stating the same responses or instructions in emails, create a template in your word-processing software so that you can use it as needed. There's no need to reinvent the wheel each time. Copy and paste from your template into your email system, and make any modifications as needed.

What If You Can't Respond Right Away?

If I'm working out of town or presenting all-day trainings in town, I set my autoresponder to take that pressure off of having to respond the same day. Whatever task is in front of us — whether it's working on a proposal or meeting with a customer or readying display shelves — deserves our absolute full attention.

Checking email should not be a priority if you want a productive day and better-served clients.

You might be saying, "If I've told my clients or contacts that I'll email them by the end of the day, how will they know when my schedule changes?"

Good question. But that's not your worry. Seriously. Your worry is your personal priorities and targets and your business priorities and targets. But it can be hard initially to let go of that fear of not being so readily available. So here's what you can do.

When you're having an email conversation with someone, let her know when you'll be available for phone or email responses. It will take you an extra 30 seconds to add this information at the end of your email, but it will save you possibly hours of time because you won't be fixated on your worry about not responding right away to that person. If you're working on a project, let participants know in advance of your out-of-town or unavailable dates.

> The first rule of any technology used in a business is that automation applied to an efficient operation will magnify the efficiency. The second is that automation applied to an inefficient operation will magnify the inefficiency.
>
> *— Attributed to Bill Gates*

What if you're not in a conversation with them? What if they initiate an email from out of the blue? If you've set expectations with them about how you give your focus to projects and clients in order to provide better service, they will understand when they receive the autoresponder you've set. And if you haven't yet had "the expectations conversation" with them, you can do so when you return their email.

Be sure your autoresponder lets your emailing fans know whom they can reach while you're gone. Here's an example:

> Thank you for your email! I'm currently working out of town and will respond to your email on Tuesday, February 12. If you need assistance before then, please contact:
>
> > Individual consulting/coaching and media interviews:
> > Maribeth — 210-892-4990 x73 or saoffice@livingordersa.com
> > Keynotes, workshops, trainings, and bulk video or book orders:
> > Wilene — 210-892-4990 x79 or speaking@livingordersa.com

If you're in the middle of a project, include contacts specific to that project.

If you're a solopreneur wishing you could have "peeps" to list in an autoresponder, you'll pick up some pointers in part 3, "Assemble Your Team."

NEXT STEPS

By following these strategies, Robert was able to gain the upper hand on his email challenge. He handled incoming email efficiently and began working on other tasks — instead of just email.

He set a structure by deciding on an email-checking schedule. He stopped checking email on his phone at all hours of the day and night. He discovered that he got a better night's sleep because he no longer felt nagged by his phone and all those darn emails.

By not peeking into every email in the order in which it appeared in his inbox, he instantly shaved time from the email process. Just getting rid of 10 unnecessary emails at once in round 1 instantly relieved his email anxiety and gave him the motivation he needed to push through the other rounds.

Robert now plows through his email on a mission to rid the world of what's in his inbox. And it works.

ⅢⅢ➤ PLOT YOUR NEXT STEPS

- Do you control your email, or does your email control you?
- What is one email tactic discussed in this chapter that you already use and will continue to do so because it saves you time?
- What is one new email tactic that you will begin implementing today in order to save more time?
- What types of templates might save you time?
- What will those templates need to say?
- How will implementing the strategies and tactics in this chapter benefit you?

16 Dig Out from a Flooded Inbox

In the previous chapter, you met my client Robert, who had email anxiety. He dreaded email because he had so much of it — sometimes 5,000 unread emails.

Each time he saw a three-digit number next to his inbox, indicating the number of emails waiting for him, he'd just cringe. When that number hit quadruple digits, he began to suffer increased anxiety. The day he showed me his inbox, I could see his body stiffen up and his facial expression change from the smile he had greeted me with to one of hopelessness.

He'd previously never had time to keep up with the incoming emails, so how the heck could he comb through all those old ones and get rid of them?

GOAL

Set aside blocks of time to eliminate the clutter in your inbox.

TACTICS

Planning

1. Decide if you have small chunks of time or large chunks of time to declutter your inbox.
2. Schedule these time periods on your calendar.

Decluttering Sessions

1. Set your timer for the chunk of time you want to work.
2. Scroll to your emails from the prior month.
3. Focus on one month at a time or one reading pane's worth at a time.
4. Scan this section for emails you don't want or need, and delete without opening:
   a. Obvious spam
   b. Advertisements
   c. Invitations to events you know you can't attend
   d. Invitations to events, offers, and due dates that have already passed
   e. Other?
5. Scan this section for emails that don't apply to you, and delete without opening:
   a. Information that doesn't affect you or your department
   b. Reminders from others about projects/tasks you've already completed and submitted
   c. Conversations that have already expired
   d. Other?
6. Read emails related to any current important tasks or situations, and draft responses.
7. If there's time remaining on your timer, move to the previous month or the next viewing pane.
8. Send any drafts that truly require your response before your next email check.
9. See the "Writing Emails" section in the previous chapter for best practices on responses.

What to Do with Emails after You've Read and Responded

1. If you might need to refer back to the information in the email, and it's not readily available online, save the email.
   a. In Gmail, Outlook.com (formerly Hotmail), and other web-based email services, you can archive an email without placing it in a folder.
   b. In Microsoft Outlook, set up folders, and file the emails there.

c.　If you don't need to save the correspondence, or you can find the information elsewhere, delete the email.

What to Do with Emails That Remind You to Do Something

1.　Keep the email in your inbox if you'll do that task this week.
2.　If it's a longer-term project, use your reminder system, and then file your email.

Prevention

1.　Unsubscribe from newsletters and announcements that no longer interest or serve you, from senders you know.
2.　Set filters or rules for disposing of newsletters and announcements from unknown senders.
3.　Use a generic email address on business cards and when submitting web forms; save your "real" address for your clients, your colleagues, and vetted contacts.
4.　Teach your friends and colleagues to use the BCC line.

STRATEGY

Keep your inbox as cleared out as possible. Your email inbox is not a receptacle for delayed decisions and actions.

Decide on Your Work Time

If your neck, back, eyes, and attention span can handle it, block off an hour or two to declutter your inbox. If you have only small increments of time to work, don't be afraid of setting aside as little as 15 minutes at a time to devote to this project. That's still 15 minutes of progress.

However much time you decide to spend on this, be sure to schedule it on your calendar. If you leave the intention in your head, you most likely will forget about it, or something else will take precedence. If you have

> I attribute my success to this: I never gave or took any excuse.
>
> — *Attributed to Florence Nightingale*

the time blocked on your calendar, you'll be far likelier to stick to the plan. If you're in the process of improving your time management / mind management, but you want to be done with clearing your inbox sooner rather than later, you might need to do this project after hours.

Reading (Browsing) Email

Set a timer to keep you focused on this task.

You'll do multiple rounds of browsing your inbox. Round 1 will be for scanning for emails that are ads, spam, and any other emails that don't apply to you. Scan your inbox for these, place check marks next to them, and then click or press the delete button. You'll delete them without even opening them. Woohoo! Be free of these old emails!

During round 1, you'll get an idea of who's written to you. During round 2, you'll go back to the emails that still require a response. The further back in time you go, the less you should need to respond. See the previous chapter if you need more detailed instructions for processing your inbox efficiently.

What to Do with Emails after You've Responded

If your email program allows you to archive your emails, this is a great option. Your subject lines will have keywords in them, so if you ever need to search for an email on a particular subject or from a particular person, you can search the archived emails. Archiving also saves you from having to choose a folder into which to drop an email.

If your system doesn't offer a searchable archive, you can set up an electronic file cabinet for the emails you do need to save. These would be the folders you can create in the navigation bar on the left side of your screen.

What are the major categories of your incoming email? Here are some examples:

Department
Management Memos
Schedules
Projects
Procedures
Warm Fuzzies
Clients

What else comes in that you need to save?

Set up a few folders to get started, and then as you process your email, create new ones as you recognize larger categories.

You'll want to limit your categories to 10 or 15 at the most. You need to be able to easily drop into a folder any emails that you should save. If you have 100 folders, you'd waste time scrolling through all of them and deciding on the best place to store your emails. Keep it simple — just a few folders.

By the way, you can apply this same process to the electronic documents on your hard drive. If you have a good search function on your computer, the folder names aren't as important because the computer will search for keywords in the document.

If you do not need to save a record of the correspondence or if you can obtain the information in the email from another source, consider deleting the email instead of saving it.

What to Do with Emails That Remind You to Do Something

A number of my clients have so much going on in their head that they often become forgetful. This fear of forgetting something drives them to leave to-do emails in their inbox as a reminder, even if the to-do is months away. This is part of the reason why their inbox is so crowded.

If it's something that needs to be done this week, and the number of inbox to-do's won't raise your blood pressure, keep the email in your inbox. In two or three days — after you complete the task — you can file away or toss the email.

If it's a longer-term project, or if the number of to-do emails will clog up your inbox, use your reminder system, and then follow the previous instructions for filing your email.

Prevention

Guard your email address carefully. If you own your own company, consider setting up a generic address (like sales@ or office@) to put on business cards that you hand out when strangers approach you or that web forms will use to send to you when people find you online. You can check this address when your brain is ready for that mode. You can also eventually allow a contractor or employee to be in charge of this separate address when you expand your team. Use this email address if you decide to sign up for a newsletter or enter a contest. If you end up trusting the vendor, you can always modify the email address and have the email sent directly to your main inbox. If you're an employee, you'll need to check the company policy on having dual email addresses.

Have a separate email address — your main one — that you'll check on a regular basis. This is the email address that you'll give to your contacts and clients.

Keep your personal conversations out of work email. Most people have their own personal email address (@hotmail.com, @gmail.com, @yahoo.com, @me .com, etc.). Use your personal email address for your personal conversations. Our brains work better when they're focused on one subject at a time. If you have to switch back and forth between various topics at work, plus various topics in your personal life, that's too much brain scatter — which will lead to lost time from brain sluggishness. Be sure that your personal contacts know to send personal items to your personal email address.

If you work for a company, the company owns the company email address and has the right to monitor your email and delete at will. That's another reason to restrict your personal emails to your personal account.

If you shop online often, consider having a separate email address just for shopping. Many online stores sell their email lists to other entities in order to generate more revenue. That means you'll get on a slew of other email lists. Since you know when you order something and you don't need to check this account except when you're confirming order status, you'll be able to delete everything in this account whenever you do stop by to check.

Request that your friends and colleagues use the BCC (blind carbon copy) line instead of loading up everyone's email address in the TO or CC lines. This will prevent one more way that you get on spam lists, plus you'll never lose time from a chain of reply-all emails that don't apply to you. Now, there may be some times when you do have to list everyone — for example, if you serve on a board and you need to vote by email between meetings, or a few of you working on a project can't talk via phone but need to share some input with each other. But in most cases, such as when a response is not needed — it's just general information being announced — the BCC line is the way to go.

Unsubscribe

If you know the company that sent the email, it should be safe to use the unsubscribe link at the bottom of the email. If you're not familiar with the company and don't know how you got on their list, or if you're absolutely sure the email is spam, using the unsubscribe feature might actually confirm that your email address is "good" and is therefore worth more money when selling a list of emails. I know — that stinks!

Hopefully, your email account has a good spam blocker so that most of those unwanted emails will automatically go into your spam folder. It's easier to scan your spam folder for any "real" emails and delete the rest. If you find that unwanted emails land in your inbox, go to the help section of your email provider and read the tutorial on how to filter your email. You can ban email addresses and domain names from your inbox in this way.

Get Tech Help

If you're struggling with some of the techie steps I mention here — such as setting up separate email addresses or filtering emails or setting up an email file cabinet — it will be worth it to ask your company's IT genius to assist you, or hire a consultant who specializes in this, or take your techie friend out to dinner in exchange for helping you do these things. Your time is worth it!

NEXT STEPS

By following these strategies, Robert was able to gain the upper hand on his email challenge.

During his next business trip, he set aside the time he spent waiting at the airport terminal for his old-email-processing time. He started with the most recent unread emails and scanned the senders and subject lines. He was able to get through the previous six months while waiting for his plane to take off.

On his return trip, he did the same thing at the airport. But this time he realized that everything was more than six months old and either had been dealt with or no longer applied. So he deleted items in bulk even faster. Five thousand emails. Done. Total project time: 3.5 hours.

Robert no longer has thousands of unread emails in his inbox. Or even hundreds. Or dozens. He uses the tactics in the previous chapter to deal with his daily incoming email, so that he no longer gets these terrifying backlogs.

➤ **PLOT YOUR NEXT STEPS**

- How many emails do you have in your inbox?
- What maximum number of emails in your inbox would you be comfortable with?
- What timeline will you use to complete this project?

17 Utilize the Telephone More Efficiently

Nancy absolutely loved to talk on the phone. She answered her phone every time by the middle of the second ring. She'd listen to everything you had to say. She also could talk your ear off. You could easily spend an hour swapping stories with Nancy.

Nancy, as it turns out, is a nurturer. She feels like it's her duty to take care of everyone, so everyone is her friend when they call. She doesn't want someone to hang up and feel unhappy or feel that they don't like her.

Nancy, as it turns out, also procrastinates severely. Talking on the phone is one of her subconscious task-avoidance techniques. She uses the technique well. That's why she's so far behind on her work all the time.

GOAL

No one else but you should dictate how much time you spend on the phone.

TACTICS

Receiving

1. Record a voicemail message that states when you'll call people back.
2. Don't answer your phone during laser-focus work time.
3. When you do answer the phone, state how much time you have to talk.
4. Upon ending the call, verify who's doing what by which date.

Calling

1. Set aside a specific amount of time for phone calls.
2. If you get someone's voicemail, leave not only your name and phone number, but also what information you were seeking from the call, as well as your best call-back times.
3. When you begin the conversation, state how much time you have to talk.
4. Upon ending the call, verify who's doing what by which date.

STRATEGY

Receiving Calls

Record a voicemail message that states when you'll call people back.

To help relieve the tension and pressure you might place on yourself — worrying about what the caller thinks about your response time — record a voicemail that states when you'll call the person back.

In some industries, this might be 15 minutes. In other industries, calling someone back within three hours is acceptable. In others, you might have two days. Determine what is acceptable in your industry and fits your schedule. A sample message greeting might sound something like this: "Howdy! This is Helene. Please leave your name and the best way and time to contact you, as well as your question. I'll return your call by the next business day."

By setting the expectation of when you'll return the call, you instantly relieve any pressure or guilt you might feel about not immediately responding.

Don't answer your phone during laser-focus work time.

As you'll learn in chapter 31, "I Multitask, but I Still Can't Finish Everything," we disrupt ourselves when we multitask. We also disrupt ourselves when we answer the phone.

For some strange reason, we feel like we are at everyone's beck and call, and therefore we must answer the phone immediately each time it rings. You are capable of just letting the phone ring without answering it. After all, do you answer your phone if the CEO of your company is staring right into your face? Do you answer the phone while you're having sex? Unless you're some kind of emergency responder or you're on call for emergencies during your shift or you work the customer service desk for your company, you don't need to answer the phone right then and there.

And please don't pick up the phone to say you can't talk. Some genius invented voicemail many moons ago. Let's use it. Hold 21st-century technology to your head, but not utilize the 1980s technology of allowing people to leave a phone message? Oh, the irony.

If you're a decision maker for your company, you need focused time to work on projects and make those important decisions. However, if you work in a field that requires — not wants, but *requires* — immediate contact and answers, then someone else should be answering your phone for you in order to filter the noise and provide as much information as possible before you're able to return any important phone calls.

When you do answer the phone, state how much time you have to talk.

Procrastination is a productivity killer, and talking on the phone is one way to increase procrastination. As you greet the person on the other end of the line, let him or her know how much time you have to devote to this call. Your greeting might sound something like this: "Hi, Julie! It's great to hear your voice, but I only have 10 minutes before my next appointment. How can I help you?"

If it's not great to hear from the person, think of something else positive to say before setting the expectation. If you don't feel like you'll be assertive enough to end the call when the 10 minutes are up, set a timer that will emit a sound loud enough for the caller to hear it.

And you're not lying when you say "my next appointment." You have appointments with yourself all day long to complete tasks. But you don't have to go into this technical detail with the caller...unless you just want to blow an hour. But I don't think you do — otherwise, you wouldn't be reading this book.

Upon ending the call, verify who's doing what by which date.

If it isn't a social call, then there should be some kind of purpose to it. Summarize the decisions on the call to make sure that everything is understood. If next steps are required, identify the following:

- what the next actions are
- who will do them
- what the deadline is
- in what format the deliverable should be

By reviewing all this information, you'll cut back on confusion and save time in the long run.

Outbound Calls

Set aside a specific amount of time for phone calls.

Many times we want to grab the phone if we have a quick question. In making these impromptu phone calls, we don't mentally grasp the entire situation, which means that we ask about only one minor detail that's popped into our mind, and we end up needing to make multiple phone calls before everything gets put in place. We often feel like we can't move forward if we have to wait for that person's answer. But sometimes our questions can be answered if we think through the situation a little more or finish browsing the emails or plowing through a few more tasks from the day.

If you still need to call someone even after thought time and/or scrolling through all the information that's landed on your desk, then you might want to consider:

- Who is the best person to call?
- What specific information do you need to get from the call in order to make it worthwhile?
- When will be the best time for you to make this call? When will this call not be interrupting what you're working on, and when will it have your full attention?
- When will be the best time to reach the person in order to prevent phone tag?

When you do make the call, as mentioned in the "Receiving Calls" section, above:

- When you begin the conversation, state how much time you have to talk.
- Upon ending the call, verify who's doing what by which date.

If you get someone's voicemail, leave not only your contact information, but also what information you were seeking from the call, as well as your best call-back times.

Imagine getting a message like this: "Hi, this is Allison. I have a question. Can you call me, please?"

Who is Allison? What is the question? How much of a priority does this become for me? What information must I be knowledgeable about in order to answer this question? Will I need access to certain materials when we talk? What type of decision might need to be made? Do I really want to talk to this person? I bet she's trying to get me to buy something. Maybe I shouldn't pick up the phone when she calls again.

Leaving an ambiguous message is not efficient. You may as well not have called. Instead, do yourself and the other person a favor by stating what it is you need. That way, when he calls back, he will have the best answer ready for you.

Additionally, consider letting the person know when you'll be near your phone so that you won't lose time playing phone tag. Even if you've left him a detailed message about what you need, and he should be able to leave that information on your voicemail, a discussion might be required, so you don't want that delayed by phone tag.

Wait-Time Calls

There are times in life when you have to make a call that requires waiting on hold for what seems like an eternity to speak with a human. Or what if you're stuck in a meaningless conference call during which you will have zero participation, and you'll never be required to regurgitate the information shared? When you know that you need to make this call, have something to work on that requires relatively low brain output but still allows you to knock something off your to-do list. Perhaps you can clean out emails from the prior year, or open up the mail on your desk and toss the envelopes. Technically, this is not multitasking if you're not listening closely or talking.

NEXT STEPS

Now, we didn't want to go about making Nancy unfriendly and uncaring. What we needed to do was get her to see how spending so much time on the phone was detrimental to her productivity. She tracked her phone time, and when she saw it on paper, she couldn't believe where so much of her time went. She also came to understand that the more stressed she was about having to make a decision or finish a project, the more likely she was to grab the phone when it rang or make a bunch of unnecessary calls. Once Nancy implemented the tactics outlined in this chapter, she saved a couple of hours each week. She was still nice and caring — just in smaller doses.

> Don't water your weeds.
>
> *— Attributed to Peter Lynch and Harvey MacKay*

ⅢⅢ➡ **PLOT YOUR NEXT STEPS**

- Do you unnecessarily spend time on the phone?
- If so, what do you think is causing this?
- Which of the tactics are you already implementing?
- Which of the tactics will you start implementing?
- How long can you go without answering your phone?
- What will your voicemail greeting state?

18 Set Up a Simple Filing System That Works

Back in the first part of my adult life when I began my career as a teacher, I had a really fancy filing system with file folders for each and every administrator, counselor, and department at the school. I eventually realized that I seldom looked back at the memos, so why was I wasting all that time on a fancy system? And why have a file folder for only a few papers? Those folders took up a lot of space in the cabinet.

I began to ask myself that question at home, as well. I had a file for every single vendor I'd ever paid, in addition to the companies we paid monthly bills to, plus a file for every single account we had with a company. My papers would pile up throughout the month, and I would avoid filing like the plague. What was wrong with me? I had a totally organized file cabinet! So why was it so hard to file and keep up with my paperwork?

GOAL

Create a file system that is based on how often you *retrieve* papers, is easy to drop papers into, and has only a few categories from which to choose.

TACTICS

1. Determine what papers you need to retrieve on a daily, weekly, monthly, or yearly basis.

2. Determine the categories of papers you receive and retrieve.
3. Determine the best locations for your papers.
4. Determine what kinds of paper folders or containers would be easiest for you to use.

STRATEGY

Let's set up a simple, realistic processing and storage system for your papers. Our goal is to have the smallest number of steps, take the least amount of time, and touch the papers the fewest times possible. If you already do parts of this well, don't fix what isn't broken. Keep doing what is successful for you, and make adjustments only to the tasks that aren't currently running as smoothly as you'd like.

Determine what papers you need to retrieve on a daily, weekly, monthly, or yearly basis.

We're about to go through how to manage and store the various categories of papers. But before we do that, I'd like you to consider how you want to spend your filing time.

> I find it hilarious that you'll run into a gunfight with nothing but your sword, but paperwork makes you panic.
>
> — *Curran in* Magic Rises, *by Ilona Andrews*

Studies show that we refer back to fewer than 20 percent of the papers we file away. If we hardly ever look at those papers, why spend a lot of time on the front end, dividing papers into dozens of categories and having to file those papers into dozens of file folders? That's way too tedious and takes up entirely too much time, which is why filing becomes such a big turn-off and why we let papers pile up...because we don't want to face the filing.

One question I want you to ask yourself is: How often do you truly go back and refer to your files? Once a day? Once a week? Once a quarter? Once a year?

Instead of taking 30 minutes per day (150 minutes per week) to file things away in a complex system of multiple folders, you could take 10 minutes per day (50 minutes per week) to drop papers into just a few files. When you do need to pull something up, you could invest your time *then* (some of that 100 minutes per week — or 87 hours per year — that you're saving!) to look for the paper.

Determine the categories of papers you receive and retrieve.

We don't want a bazillion categories because that will just complicate things. Instead, let's narrow it down to as few as possible. If the paper is in only one of 5 or 10 files (instead of 30 or 50), it will be easier to find.

All employees will have a different set of categories depending on what their job responsibilities are. Here's an example from a client who worked in her company's accounting department:

TYPE OF PAPER	RECEIVE	RETRIEVE
Expenses		
Vendor bills	Monthly	Rarely to never
Credit card statements	Monthly	Rarely to never
Insurance statements	Yearly	Never
Receipts by department	Daily	Rarely to never
Income		
Bank statements	Monthly	Rarely to never
Client payments	Daily	Rarely
Operations		
Company announcements	Monthly	Before event
P/L reports	Monthly	Monthly
HR policies	Monthly	Rarely

What are the categories for your particular position?

Here's an example for a typical entrepreneur who operates out of a home office:

PERSONAL		
TYPE OF PAPER	RECEIVE	RETRIEVE
Expenses		
Bills	Monthly	Rarely to never
Credit card statements	Monthly	Rarely to never
Insurance statements	Biyearly	Never
Receipts	Daily	For returns
Income		
Investment statements	Quarterly	Never
Bank statements	Monthly	Rarely to never
Operations		
Kids' schoolwork	Daily	Semiweekly
Invitations	Weekly	Before event
Coupons	Daily	Weekly

BUSINESS		
TYPE OF PAPER	RECEIVE	RETRIEVE
Expenses		
Bills	Monthly	Rarely to never
Credit card statements	Monthly	Rarely to never
Insurance statements	Biyearly	Never
Receipts	Daily	For returns
Income		
IRA statements	Quarterly	Never
Bank statements	Monthly	Rarely to never
Client payments	Daily	Rarely
Operations		
Invitations	Weekly	Before event
Client documentation	Daily	Weekly

Can you think of any other categories for your situation? Noodle on this one while you read through the rest of this chapter.

Determine the best locations for your papers.

Many of us don't actually need to retrieve most of our papers. We just keep them because of company retention guidelines, or for tax or documentation purposes. If you never have to refer to a paper, but you must keep it for one of these reasons, there's no need to spend a great deal of time filing those papers into multiple file folders by vendor or company. Check with your company's HR and/ or tax department to find out how papers need to be presented in the case of an audit, and use those parameters as a guide for helping to narrow down your categories. If you're an entrepreneur, you can drop your papers into monthly January–December files for personal and monthly January–December income and expense files for business. *Bam!* They're all ready to go for tax season. (Thank you to good friend, colleague, genius, and Clutter Diet founder Lorie Marrero for teaching me about monthly files back in 2006.)

Papers that you need daily can be divided up into specific categories or client files, and placed as close to your desk as possible, such as in the desk's file drawer or in a file cabinet under or right next to your desk.

Papers that you need less often can be in broader-category files in a file cabinet that doesn't necessarily have to be right next to your desk.

For my personal setup, I have two narrow slots on my desk — one for incoming expense and income papers for my business, and one for expense and income papers for our household. These get recorded at bookkeeping time and then filed away.

I keep my business January–December expense files and January–December income files in the left drawer of my desk. As receipts come in and invoices get paid, or as check stubs come in from various clients, they get dropped into the appropriate month slot after they're processed at bookkeeping time. No need to get up, walk across the room, and find 20 different files to place papers into; simply open the drawer and drop the papers into the month slot. If you receive a great deal more paper, you might consider getting a separate file cabinet or scanning.

My personal January–December files are kept in the personal drawer of a file cabinet in the back of my office because these papers don't come in daily since I'm set up on paperless for most of my accounts.

Each of my current clients has a file, and these are kept in the right drawer of my desk since these papers come in almost daily, and I need to access them at least weekly. Archived client files are kept in a separate file cabinet until it's time to shred them.

Other business papers I need on at least a weekly basis are stored in project files in a file sorter in the left side of my work area. (I'm right-handed, so I don't want objects taking up space in my right-hand work area.)

All other papers are divided into general category files that reside in the personal drawer or business drawer of the file cabinet in the back of my office.

Whether you work for a company or for yourself, take the time to determine where the best locations for your files will be, according to how often you need access to them.

Determine what kinds of paper holders or containers would be easiest for you to use.

If the paper-capturing devices that you use are not über-easy to manipulate, then you won't have an easy time storing those papers. If this step isn't as simple as possible, then you won't do it. So, what works, and what doesn't?

Binders: These are great for holding reference materials that you need occasionally. They're terrible for holding papers that you need to file or handle every day. I used to be a binder girl. I had binders for everything. But then I realized that it took far too much effort to use them. I had to punch holes, then pull out the binder, then open it up, then open up the rings, then load the paper, then close the rings, then close the binder, then put the binder back where it belonged. Egad! That's a lot of work to do every day! Now, if I had nothing else to do, I'd have time to load binders all the livelong day. But if you're like me and have a ton of other tasks that need completing, don't use binders to store incoming daily papers.

Cubbies or stacking trays: These are terrific if you deal with a lot of hand-outs and brochures or printer paper. It's hard to see what all the different papers are in one slot, but if they're all the same, it doesn't matter, since you just need to grab from the top of each stack.

Accordion or pocket folders that have flaps that fasten with a band: These are terrific if you are mobile and need to keep your papers organized as you get in and out of your car. They're terrible if you're planning to use them for filing daily incoming papers for the same reason as the binder above — they're too much work to open, load, and close. Find flapless accordions for daily incoming papers.

File sorters: Taller ones are a convenient way to store manila file folders that you're currently working with — say, for client files or project files. Shorter sorters can store your *Do something* papers (see chapter 19, "Deal with Incoming Daily Paper").

Magazine holders: These are great for holding thicker materials such as magazines and bound material, or for holding a large amount of papers related to the same subject. They're not so great if you have only a few papers at a time in that particular category, because the papers will just flop over.

Hanging files: These are awesome! Open the drawer, open the file (per Lorie Marrero, the tab should be on the front of the folder so that it easily opens), drop the paper in, and close the drawer. Sooo much easier! These can be utilized in a file tote or crate on top of your desk for daily papers, in your desk drawer for weekly papers, and in a file cabinet for all others.

If you're going to ask what order the folders should be in, I'll have to give you my standard answer: whatever order works for you. Examples:

Alphabetical

Chronological

By subject

By frequency of use

There's no law on how the folders in your file cabinet or container should be placed. What will function best for you?

I have a "Favorite Products" list at www.HeleneSegura.com/30tactics if you'd like to see some examples of containers for your office. There's also a brief video on how to contain papers on your desk.

At this point, it's perfectly fine if you don't yet know which containers you want to use. But your brain should be pondering this as you sort through your papers and set up your system.

What about going digital?

My husband, who teaches high school English, will be annoyed with me for sharing this with the world, but it will help make my point. He is the least digital person I know. He has a "dumb" phone (a non-smartphone that predates the BlackBerry, Androids, and iPhones). He learned how to attach documents to emails only a couple of years ago. He doesn't tweet or post on Facebook or text, so he doesn't understand a lot of lingo and acronyms that people use, like LOL, IMO, DH, and so on. Yet this most undigital man keeps his file cabinet on a key ring. That's right. The guy learned how to use a flash drive! He has his lesson plans, assignments, and handouts on that little piece of digital heaven. If he can do it, I think there's hope for everyone else out there! (He's working his way toward eventually storing documents in the cloud, but one step at a time.)

If you do scan papers and store everything electronically, you'll still need to have some type of electronic filing structure, similar to how we set up the physical papers in this chapter. Be sure to use a backup! Do you keep your documents on both your hard drive and in the cloud? Do you use a backup service like Mozy, Carbonite, or CrashPlan? Can you get to your documents if you don't have access to the internet? If you go paperless, make sure that you have a backup in place.

NEXT STEPS

Are you asking yourself, "Really? Do I need to think about my papers? Do I need to dissect what I have? Do I need all this structure?" If you want to be even a little bit organized and know where your papers are, then the answer is, "Mmm-hmm, that's right."

Half the battle of getting organized is figuring out your own brain. Once you discover how your mind works when it comes to your thinking patterns and work preferences, you'll understand how to structure your systems. When you have systems in place that fit who you are and how you work, you will get *and stay* organized. Right down to all the papers in your office.

Take a deep breath, and get ready to dive in. This will be like scuba diving. It's not exactly fun to go through the pre-dive checks and tasks, and it's a little scary the first time you jump into the water, but when you realize that serenity awaits you, you're ready and willing to do what it takes to get to that place.

If you are antsy to get started on setting up your notes, documents, and file management system, then get goin'! Block off some time on your calendar this week and next for when you will work on it. You may have to come in to work early or stay late a few days to work through some of these steps. Or you can use your break time each day over a week or two. Regardless of how you choose to work on this project, the time that you invest will be worth it.

On the other hand, if you're feeling overwhelmed and the thought of starting in on structuring a file system is making your head spin, then begin by deciding where your *Do something* papers will go. Start with something small, so that you can feel success sooner.

Take one step forward at a time, at a pace that's comfortable for you.

Remember that it will take some time to develop a structured system that works smoothly for you. The important thing is to set up something. Use it for two weeks. Then step back and reflect. What worked? What didn't? Adjust your system based on your reflections.

ⅢⅢ➡ PLOT YOUR NEXT STEPS

- What is working with your current system that you should continue implementing?
- If you're reading this chapter, there is something bothering you about your current filing structure. What do you think that is?
- What types of papers do you need to retrieve on a daily, weekly, monthly, quarterly, or yearly basis?
- Determine the categories of papers you receive and retrieve. ˙
- What types of storage containers will work best for your situation?
- What are the best locations for these storage containers?
- How will implementing the strategies and tactics in this chapter benefit you?

19 Deal with Incoming Daily Paper

Julie is like most of my clients. Unless it's a check from one of her customers, she finds paper to be annoying and overwhelming, so she tosses papers into the four-inch-deep basket sitting on her desk. And that's where they stay until she has to dig through the stack to find a paper she needs for something she forgot to do. She's grown weary of this panicked paper pushing and wants to stop worrying about what's lurking in that pile.

GOAL

Process all incoming papers each and every day.

TACTICS

1. Schedule time each day to **DID** your papers.
2. First third of the **DID** paper session:
   Divide your papers into three categories:
   a. **D**o something
   b. **I**mportant info to keep
   c. **D**iscard
3. Second third of the **DID** paper session:
   File papers that landed in your *Important info to keep* pile.

4. Last third of your **DID** paper session:
   a. Place *Do something* papers in your action area.
   b. Recycle or shred your *Discard* papers.

STRATEGY

When I was in college in the early 1990s, we used floppy disks to save our information on the computer, and email was just emerging in mainstream America. We were told that the world would soon be paperless.

Ha! What a load of hooey!

Granted, nowadays we can digitize and use the cloud all day long, but there's more paper floating around today than there was 20 years ago.

Paper continues to be a big challenge for many of my clients. I personally detest paperwork and filing. Knowing that about me, you might think this next statement is counterintuitive, but please bear with me:

If you hate paper, it is vital that you process it every single day.

Whu-huh? If you despise paper, why would you want to look at it and deal with it every day? Well, it goes a little something like this...

If you loathe paper and keep tossing it off to the side to manage later, that pile just continues to grow. You tell yourself, "I'll deal with it at the end of the week." But the end of the week rolls around, and you take one look at the pile and say, "Man, forget it! I don't feel like dealing with that now. I'll deal with it next week." So the pile grows until the papers start sliding around, because there are now so many that they can no longer stay neatly stacked. Instead of processing that mountain of papers, you decide, "I'll just put them in this box and deal with them later." The papers get scooped up, the box gets shoved under the desk or back in a corner, and you forget about that box until you get in trouble for a missed deadline or run across the box while you were hunting for something else.

Sound familiar?

If so, we need to do two things:

1. Get you into the habit of processing your papers multiple times per week, if not daily. (This chapter.)
2. Set up a paper system that's easy-peasy to use, so that filing is no longer a tedious chore. (The previous chapter.)

If I'm going to have to drag you kickin' and screamin' to get you to do #1, I ask you to consider a mind shift in how you view paper. Please indulge me for a moment...

Do you take a shower every day? (Hell, at least every other day, right?) Or do you wait until the end of the month and just shower for a couple of hours? I'm serious. Answer the question. Why do you bathe every day? Maybe because if you don't, you'll stink. This will lead to problems at work because, let's face it, who wants to work around someone who reeks? And this will lead to problems in your personal life for, well, pretty much the same reason. You also probably bathe for hygienic reasons. If you didn't remove the dirt, grime, and bacteria, you'd eventually develop all sorts of disgusting diseases that have multisyllabic names. So showering might not be the most exciting thing to do, but you do it on a daily basis because if you don't, bad things will happen.

Why don't we apply that same concept to processing papers?

> Happiness doesn't depend on any external conditions; it is governed by our mental attitude.
>
> — Dale Carnegie

We might not get stinky just by pushing papers off to the side, but if you replace "stink" with the word "stress," that will build in the same way. Whatever we put off doing today will double our workload for tomorrow. So why should we put it off?

We shouldn't.

Whether you like it or not, documents, notes, information, and objects will continue to enter our lives. It's just a fact that we need to accept. So it's important to have a system in place to handle it. Without a daily routine, you might miss something important or, even worse, feel overwhelmed everyday by backlogs.

Shower daily. Process papers daily. It's as simple as that.

So how should you process your daily incoming papers? Use my **DID** system to get your papers *done*!

Schedule time each day to DID your papers.

In order to prevent pileups and things slipping through the cracks, it's important to set aside processing time each day to review every new piece of paper or object or piece of information that has entered your life. A great time to do this is at the end of each day, right before you choose your 3+3. The first time you **DID** your incoming papers for the day, allow 30 minutes. You'll be able to cut the time as you get faster with the sorting and decision making. Try setting a timer. Have it right next to you to remind you of what your focus is supposed to be. Increase or decrease the amount of focus time as you feel comfortable.

(If you have a heap of older papers to go through, see chapter 12, "Dig Out from a Buried Office," for help with attacking that project.)

What should you process?

Papers
Business cards
Receipts
Notes from meetings, conversations, ideas capture, Mind Liberations, etc.
Any papers or objects that have crossed the threshold into your office (physically or digitally)

Divide your papers into three categories.

You'll do this during the first third of your **DID** session. There are only three things that you can do with a sheet of paper. (Or with an email, for that matter.) That's it. So you'll divide your papers into these three categories, **DID**:

1. **D**o something
2. **I**mportant info to keep
3. **D**iscard

What do those mean?

Do something.

The paper requires you to take an action such as calling someone, emailing someone, responding with a letter, or going somewhere.

Important info to keep.

What the heck should you keep? A common stumbling block in purging papers is not knowing what to keep and what to toss. It's always best to check with your employer and/or legal and tax representatives for the precise answers for your situation, but the following are a few general tips.

Overall categories of papers that should be kept:

Proof of identity and status

Proof of ownership

Proof of correct tax return numbers/calculations

Proof of legal, tax, government, investment, and real estate transactions that still affect you today

Proof of insurance coverage

Client files

Human resources documentation, contracts, and records

Keep forever (timeless):

Proof of identity and status — birth certificates, social security cards, passports, marriage certificates, divorce decrees, death certificates, business setup documents, etc.

Keep for seven years for tax/IRS purposes (tax archive):

All supporting documents used in filing your tax returns. These support the numbers and calculations you make on your returns. (Technically, you need to save documents for only three years, but if you get audited and the IRS questions anything, they can ask for up to seven years of documents.)

Keep indefinitely (semi-timeless):

Legal documents with original signatures

Real estate transaction documents with original signatures

Proof of ownership — home, auto, high-value items for insurance purposes (personal); shares of company, property, and equipment (business)

Year-end statements that involve cost-basis transactions

Tax returns

Proof of insurance for coverage period

Current client files

Human resources documentation, contracts, and records

(Each company and individual's situation is different, so consult your employer, legal representative, and/or CPA on the length of retention for your documents.)

What you can toss:

Papers that don't fall into one of the above categories

Papers/information that you can access online

Papers that you've already scanned (and have a digital backup of)

Many industries require patient and client records to be kept for up to 10 years. Each company should set its own paper-retention policy so that employees know what to keep, where to keep the documents, and for how long to keep them.

Discard

This is my favorite category! If the paper does not fall into one of the above categories, you'll need to think long and hard for a good reason to hang on to it and let it take up valuable space in your file cabinet or, if scanned, in your digital file storage. *Discard* as many papers as you can into the recycling bin, or shred them on the spot.

File papers in your Important info to keep *pile.*

You'll use the second third of your **DID** session for this. At this point, if you just put these papers on top of the ones that are already in your to-file inbox, they'll stay there and collect dust. Put them away now. All of them. It shouldn't take you long to do this, especially after you've set up your file structure based on the previous chapter.

Place your Do something *papers in your action area.*

After you finish processing your papers, the last thing you want to do is have your action papers get mixed in with other papers. You'll waste time looking for them, you might not find the paper in time to complete the action by the deadline, or you might lose that paper completely. So what are some ways to make sure this doesn't happen?

After you process your papers, follow productivity guru David Allen's advice: If you can do it in two minutes or less, then do it right then and there. Once the action is completed, that paper moves from *Do something* to *Important info to keep* (file) or *Discard*.

If the action will take longer than two minutes to complete, and you don't have the time to complete it at that moment, schedule it on your calendar. If it's necessary to hang on to the paper in order to complete the action, place the paper in your action area; otherwise, *Discard* it. The home for your *Do something* papers will be determined by how your brain processes and remembers. Where is the best place to put them that will trigger you to remember?

- Taped to a cabinet or wall or other eye-level spot right by your desk? The pro is that you'll see them. The con is that everyone else will, too. Another con is that if you don't have enough space, you'll end up taping more actions on top of the ones that were never completed.
- Left on your chair? The pro is that if you like to sit down while you work, you'll be reminded to complete those actions when you sit on your papers. The con is that if you like to sit down at other times, you'll end up moving your *Do something* papers to various places, and you'll lose them.
- Placed in hanging pockets on the wall? The pro is that these papers won't get mixed in with others on the desk or in the room. The con is that if you don't place these in an area that you can easily see or reach, you'll forget that the papers are there. Another con is that if you use pockets that are colored instead of clear, you won't immediately be able to see what papers are stored there.
- Placed in a hanging file tote on your desk? The pro is that it's right on top of your desk. The con is that only the file tabs will be visible, so the papers themselves won't serve as a visual reminder.
- Placed in a file sorter on your desk? The pro is that you'll be able to see in one quick glance what actions are required. The con is that this is not the prettiest-looking display for papers, and it will be out in the open right there on your desk.

Once again, the best system is the one that works for you.

For me personally, I use a file sorter on my desk right by my laptop to hold my action papers. The papers in the front need to be dealt with ASAP. The ones toward the back can wait until the end of the week. Turning on my laptop as soon I get into my office is a daily habit, so I use that as a reminder to look at my *Do something* papers. My backup is that I've scheduled a digital reminder, so I'll get an email to remind me to take that action on the appointed day.

What will trigger your memory?

Recycle or shred your Discard *papers.*

These last two steps (schedule and place your *Do something* papers, and get rid of your *Discard* papers) will be completed during the final third of your **DID** paper session.

Does your company need a DID day?

Forward-thinking businesses can set up **DID** days to address paper pileups on desks and/or in overstuffed file cabinets, and let employees do this together. I love spending a full day at a company to facilitate this. We have a productivity workshop in the morning, purging and organizing time during the day, then a wrap-up workshop at the end of the day. A setup like this is efficient because you have only one day of interruptions — people asking questions about what to keep, what to toss, where to store stuff, who needs to handle what — instead of constant interruptions throughout the year, when employees do this on an individual basis. If you begin to process your papers in the way I suggest in this chapter, you won't need to have **DID** days. But to deal with the piles and boxes you currently have, consider a **DID** day or two.

> Any goal…will make little progress unless it is supported by commitment. Without commitment, the goals we set for ourselves are mere dreams — ideas that don't have the footing to be realized.… Commitment provides the power to stick with it over time so that goals can be actualized.
>
> — *Heidi Reeder*

NEXT STEPS

Ooof! That seems like so much structure — thinking, planning, and setting up — right? Compared with what you may be used to, it might be. But will it be worth it? Oh my stars, *yes!*

You might also be thinking, "I gotta do this stuff every day?" You don't have to. Only if you want to work more efficiently, which will save you time. And you can use the time you gain to make more money or be with your family, friends, and loved ones, which is why you started reading this book in the first place.

The **DID** process that I describe in this chapter may seem quite regimented and structured. But this is what our brains crave — little steps they can handle, one at a time. It takes the overwhelm away from a task that can seem so tedious and downright boring. When you trick your brain into thinking it's easy, when you do a bunch of simple steps one right after the other, this task won't seem so bad, and you'll fly right through it — especially because you'll have only one day's worth of papers instead of 3 or 15 or 30 days' worth.

And if you're having a hard time believing that, try this on for size:

You're reading this chapter because what you've been doing hasn't worked. So why not give this a shot for two weeks? Julie did, and she no longer needs that basket for purgatory papers.

ⅲⅲ➡ PLOT YOUR NEXT STEPS

- How often do you currently process your papers?
- In what state are your papers as a result of your current processing schedule?
- How would you like things to be different?
- At what time each day will you **DID** your papers?
- If you've got a large stack of papers waiting for your attention, what time-line will you use to **DID** them?

20 Take Notes Anytime, Anywhere — and Never Lose Them

My client Sheila is a successful physician. She's moved up in the ranks, so she now attends more meetings than she sees patients. She would become extremely frustrated and agitated when she couldn't find the notes she needed for a meeting, or the notes she needed in order to finally put a dent in the tasks she knew she needed to complete.

She'd check her email, notes file on her phone, Dropbox, Evernote, 10 notepads, four go-bags, three spirals, two purses, and a partridge in a pear tree. Just kidding — but only about the partridge part.

She found herself doing this more and more often. At first it was just a few times a month. Then it became a few times a week. And then, alas, daily. She realized that she was losing at least one hour each day just looking for stupid notes.

The lost time and the frustration had to end.

GOAL

Process your notes daily.

TACTICS

1. Choose a note-capturing tool in paper format that you're likely to carry with you.

2. Choose a note-capturing tool in digital format that you're likely to carry with you.
3. At the end of each day, process your notes.
   a. Review the notes you took, and fill in any gaps.
   b. Schedule any required actions or follow-ups onto your calendar.
   c. File away the notes.
4. Review your notes once per month.

STRATEGY

Choose a note-capturing tool in paper format
that you're likely to carry with you.

If you are 100 percent digital, you may not need to complete this step, but you might want to keep reading to see if it applies to you. Some choices for paper note capture:

- **Mini spiral-bound notebook:** You can carry this with you in your purse or pocket at all times.
- **Regular-sized spiral-bound notebook:** If you carry a large shoulder or attaché bag (or some version of a go-bag) with you at all times, this can reside in the bag. If you'd like, you can have one spiral for each type of meeting you attend, but this isn't necessary.
- **Ampad or ARC notebook:** This is a major upgrade on the spiral. You can remove the pages and place them in a different section of the notebook, which can hold dividers. The dividers can separate the different entities you meet with so that the notes are already divided up.
- **Three-ring binder with paper and dividers:** If you carry a go-bag with you at all times, this can reside in the bag. The dividers can separate the different entities you meet with so that the notes are already divided up.

Is there another paper format you'd like to use?

Choose a note-capturing tool in digital format
that you're likely to carry with you.

If you're not paper-inclined or if you're a hybrid, you'll want to choose a program or app that's available to you on the digital device you normally carry with you. It would also be optimal if you can utilize this program or app even when cell service or Wi-Fi is down. If it can't be used in those situations, be prepared to have paper ready. Some choices for digital note capture:

- **Notepad:** Most devices have a digital notepad program that you can use for capturing notes. Be sure you know how to save and retrieve your notes.

- **Evernote:** This software syncs on your computer and phone, so you can have your notes anywhere.

- **Task apps such as Toodledo, Remember the Milk, or Things:** These are more for tasks, but at least you can capture information here until you can transfer it to a more appropriate location.

- **CRM:** If you already utilize a customer relationship management program, you can record meeting notes directly into the CRM file for this particular client or organization.

- **A document (Microsoft Word, Pages for Mac, etc.) on your device:** You can capture every piece of information possible, and then organize it later.

- **Email:** You can capture information in the body of the email, and then send it to yourself.

- **Moleskine:** Yes, this is a traditional notepad, but Moleskine has partnered up with Evernote on a hybrid that allows you to take notes on the paper, and then send it to Evernote.

For updates on these types of resources, visit www.HeleneSegura.com/30 tactics.

At the end of each day, process your notes.

In a perfect world, you would stick to only one of these capturing tools, and you'd neatly organize your notes by the end of the meeting and file them away where they need to go. But since it's not a perfect world, you might find yourself writing notes on whatever scrap of paper or napkin you can grab or in whatever program you happen to have open on your device, and then scooting off to your next meeting or event. That's why you'll process every day.

> Accept responsibility for the things you are responsible for.
> — *Les Brown*

Review the notes you took, and fill in any gaps.

Sometimes we write down just key words or phrases that make sense at the time. But when we go back days or weeks later to look at our notes, we think, "What in tarnation does that mean?!" During your 3+3 processing time, review your note pages (in paper or digital form), and fill in any gaps so that there's no confusion later.

Schedule any required actions or follow-ups into your calendar.

You most likely will have something you need to do based on the outcome of the meeting. Schedule these tasks into your calendar so that you don't forget about completing them. If you use a task reminder system, schedule your reminder as well.

File away the notes.

Choose one location where you will keep *all* notes, no matter what note-capturing tool you use. This might be one of the following:

- **Hanging file folders in a file cabinet:** Assign a folder to each organization or client with whom you meet, and drop the notes into that file. This assumes that you're predominantly paper oriented, and if you happen to take notes digitally during a meeting, you could either print them out and file them here (Plan A because you look in only one location) or set up a digital file cabinet for your notes (Plan B because now you have to look for notes in two places).
- **Digital file cabinet:** If you're primarily digital but wind up with some paper notes, you can scan them via a traditional desktop scanner or a PDF app on your phone, and then file them away in your digital file cabinet.

By filing away the notes at the end of each day, you'll keep the paper stacks and digital clutter away, and you will always know where your notes for particular committees or clients are.

Review your notes once per month.

This is your fail-safe. On the off chance that you forgot to write down a task, you can catch it when you review your notes for the prior month. If you have a number of client or committee files, the monthly review may not be the best for you. It might make more sense to review the file a couple of weeks after the meeting, then again in the week before the next meeting. Another benefit of reviewing notes is that you can purge any that you no longer need and make space in your physical or digital file.

NEXT STEPS

Sheila initially chose one three-ring binder that she would carry to all meetings. Over time, she found that she preferred just grabbing any old spiral from her desk. This was not a problem because she learned to process her notes at the end of each day, so even though she was still using a multitude of spirals, her notes were filed away exactly where she knew she'd look for them. No more note searching for Sheila!

Through the process of paying attention to — being present for, becoming cognizant of — what she was doing, she made an additional discovery: she rarely needed to look back at her notes. Writing down information helped her to retain it. But what she did need to refer back to were the tasks she was responsible for. So in her notes for each meeting, she left the top half of her first page of notes blank (just under the title and date of the meeting) so that she could add her to-do's there, where they were easy to see as she was flipping through pages in a file.

⸺➤ PLOT YOUR NEXT STEPS

- How much time do you spend looking for notes?
- What capture method are you currently using?
- What about it is working or not working for you?
- What processing method are you currently using?
- What about it is working or not working for you?
- What filing method are you currently using?
- What about it is working or not working for you?
- What changes will you make to improve your situation?

21 Know Where Your Time Goes, So That You Can Tell Your Time What to Do

Have you ever looked up at the clock on the wall, or the watch on your wrist, or the time on your phone, and thought, "Where did the time go?"

How is it that *hours* slipped by, and you have little to show for it?

Such was the case with my client Nancy. As you've read about her already, she worked a lot of long hours nearly every day of the week and swore that there were not enough hours in the day to get everything done.

At the end of our first session, I gave her a homework assignment: track how she used her time over the next week.

Initially, Nancy was dead set against tracking her time. The thought of that project practically made her gag. She dreaded the tedious nature of my request and thought it would take an inordinate amount of time, which — in her mind — would be a huge waste. Plus she didn't have any time to spare. She gave me her crooked smile, which meant, "I'm being polite to you, but I think this is bull crud, and I'm not going to do it."

The next week when we met, she sure enough had not completed her homework assignment. She started crying when she described her previous week. It was another stress-filled, work-all-hours-of-the-day-and-night, full-of-screwups week. I asked her if continuing to do the same thing week in and week out would lead to change. She crossed her arms, screwed up her nose and mouth, and snapped, "No!"

I made a deal with her. If she completed her homework assignment, and if what she learned from it did not improve her situation, she could fire me during the next appointment. No questions asked. No contract squabbles. She perked up and agreed.

After Nancy completed her time journal, she began to understand how her approach to her workday was actually causing her to spend more time at work. Filling in her journal took only 15 minutes each day. And that 15 minutes a day for one week wound up saving her hours each day in the long run.

The only firing that happened was Nancy firing her current ways of attempting to complete work.

GOAL

Know where your time goes every day, and then tell your time what to do!

TACTICS

1. For one week, keep a journal of where your time goes in 30-minute increments, 24 hours per day. Create your own chart, or download my chart from my resources page: www.HeleneSegura.com/30tactics.
2. Determine the sources of your time leaks.
3. Plug those leaks.

STRATEGY

Tell Your Time What to Do

I love that line! My friend Michelle Poteet and I were enjoying a meal one evening, and we got to talking about type A personalities, work ethic, and getting things done. We talked about being in control of our time. She blurted out, "Yeah! Tell your time what to do!"

In order to understand how to use your time, you must understand where your time is going. What exactly do you do — all day, every day? How long does it take you to do these things?

Part of the reason we have difficulty determining which tasks should take precedence is because we're not even sure what tasks we have completed or need to complete. We know that we stay busy all day long working on something, but we're not always able to articulate what actions we've just completed.

When you start paying attention to what you're doing, when you start becoming cognizant of what actions you're taking, your brain becomes more focused on the present. When your brain is focused on the present, it makes better decisions about how to use your time.

Examples from Our Personal Lives

Since the line between our personal and work lives can become blurred, the time we lose in one area can directly affect how much time we have in another area.

When I complete client assessments, I find that my clients spend up to four hours per day on social media, television watching, and volunteering. They don't realize that the time adds up to four hours because they're doing it for 15 minutes here and 15 minutes there, occasionally bingeing for a couple of hours at a time. If these activities do not fully support your personal priorities and targets, as well as your work priorities and targets, the question becomes: Do they belong in your life?

Should you spend the same amount of time on social media, or less? Some people lose hours each day while trolling social media sites. Facebook is a wonderful way to keep up with friends and family. Pinterest is a fun place to spot ideas. But how much time on those sites is necessary for you to live a complete and fulfilling life? How much time on them is necessary for you to meet your targets? This is an individual decision. I bring up social media as a time-waster a lot in this book. I'm personally not against it. I have accounts with almost every platform. I keep mentioning it, though, because this is where I see so much time going, and those folks aren't getting any return on their investment. Decide how much time you'd like to live in cyberspace and how much time you'd like to live being present with the life that's occurring right in front of you.

I once came across a Pinterest bio from "Kori" that said it all: "I'm confused and deeply worried. But I have enough time for Pinterest...?" Great question.

Should you spend the same amount of time watching television, or less? Many of my clients watch digital recordings of their favorite shows. This is a good idea because every half hour of television contains only 20 to 22 minutes of actual programming. So watching the recording without commercials will save you time. However, if you're watching three hour-long shows per night, that's still two hours of viewing time. Two hours per day adds up to 14 hours per week and 60 hours per month. Do all 60 hours of television viewing support your priorities and targets?

Should you spend the same amount of time volunteering, or less? I have one client who now writes a check instead of volunteering for 10 different organizations. She'd rather write 10 checks for $100 each (yes, a total of $1,000) than run around ragged all year long trying to keep up with these organizations on top of everything else. She decided that her choices were to donate $1,000 or pay $120 per hour once a week for therapy because she was about to go over the edge. (Disclaimer: Some people truly do need therapy. This example is not anti-therapy!) I have another client who donates four hours per month (one hour per week) to her favorite cause. Another works on one specific event each year and puts in 15 hours in one weekend. How much time would you like to give to volunteering?

Are there activities you are doing now that you could live without — ones that you could cut back on or stop completely, which would save you time? About 10 years ago, when I realized where a lot of my time was going, I stopped watching TV shows. We watch football on the weekends and Spurs playoff games, but we decided that we get more fulfilling things done without TV. Ironing takes up too much time, so I don't do that. I don't blow-dry my hair. My husband shaves every other day instead of every day. There are so many different ways to shave off time from your activities, once you're firmly committed to your priorities and targets.

Know Where Your Time Goes

When my clients begin to realize how they spend their time, it is very surprising and a little infuriating for them at first. They're shocked at how much time they lose to inane behaviors and tangential tasks, and they're a bit upset with themselves for letting that happen. But then hope sets in, because they understand that much of their time was lost because of *their* choices. And when they make better choices, they'll have more time. And since their brain is in charge of their choices, they have total control over how they use their time. *Capiche?*

For you to become an agent of change — Implement Structure *and* Flow, and tell your time what to do — you must be aware of how you currently use your time. And then protect it.

> In the end, we ourselves — far more than any outsider — are the people with the greatest ability to steal our own time, talents, and accomplishments.
>
> — *Denis Waitley*

NEXT STEPS

Nancy thought that if she stayed busy doing something all day long, that would mean she had a successful day. She discovered that her definition of success was inaccurate. Just because she was busy every minute of the day did not mean that she was getting the most important tasks cleared from her plate or that she was progressing on projects that would boost her career.

She also came to the conclusion, based on her time journal, that what she said were her work hours really weren't — because she wasn't always working. And what she said was her personal time really wasn't — because she was spending 10 minutes here, 30 minutes there, trying to catch up on what she hadn't finished during the workday. There was a big disconnect between what time *she said* she spent working versus what she was *truly spending* on valuable work tasks. Misconception time versus real time.

Nancy discovered that by haphazardly choosing the next tasks, she added variety and the thrill of doing something different to her days, but she was not accomplishing what she needed to in order to bring in new customers, keep her current customers happy, and turn around high-quality work without burning the midnight oil.

After we completed an analysis of her time by studying the details of her time journal, she realized where she could patch the holes in her schedule and gain back time in a hurry. She lost several *hours* each day through the following activities:

- Spending her morning in her email inbox (a.k.a. lack of focus)
- Jumping over to the internet or social media when she didn't feel like doing the task at hand (a.k.a. procrastination)
- Peeking at her phone or computer whenever the message indicator sounded (a.k.a. distractions)
- Shuffling papers around her desk when she had so much to do and didn't know what to work on next (a.k.a. overwhelm)

She also learned that she spent quite a bit of time on tasks that did not bring her direct income and/or were not her strong points:

- Cataloging receipts
- Reconciling accounts
- Designing graphics for presentations
- Proofreading press releases

By discovering how she spent her time, she was able to make immediate changes to her schedule and work habits, which would allow her to complete the same amount of work in far less time — even before delegating tasks to save yet more time. She also learned that she was unrealistically trying to squeeze 75 hours' worth of work into a 40-hour workweek. No wonder she felt so overwhelmed!

Just by understanding your own self-interruptions from procrastination, distractions, lack of focus, and overwhelm, you'll be able to slash lost time from your day!

ⅠⅠⅠ➡ PLOT YOUR NEXT STEPS

- What's your biggest aha from tracking your time?
- There are probably some traitorous time leaks sabotaging your days...a little here and a little there. Where are you losing time?
- What can you do differently to prevent that time from being lost?

22 Schedule around Your Personal Priorities and Targets

Just after the turn of the century (gosh, that sounds so forever ago!), I entered my serial-entrepreneur phase and became an absentee wife.

I worked. And worked. And worked. And worked.

I saw my husband at the breakfast table before rushing over to my computer to check email and get any last-minute items done. We carpooled to work, so we did enjoy some quality conversations. We talked about what our plans were for the day and envisioned everything going great. After work, we carpooled home and reflected on our days. We'd celebrate the good stuff that happened, and then decompress about anything that went wrong.

Once we got home, I went straight to my computer to continue working. Fortunately, my husband is handy in the kitchen, so he'd fix dinner. We'd talk some more over dinner, and then I was back at my computer until bed. I worked every evening and just about all weekend long on my "side jobs."

Finally one day after many, many months of this, my husband yelled out from the other side of the house, "Hey! PC junkie! Can I make an appointment to see you?"

Damn. That's bad. He never saw me even though we were in the same house. He said I was worse than a teenager because I'd just come to the kitchen when I was called for dinner, and then go straight back to my office to work some more.

That's not a fun way to live. And that's definitely not how to nourish an important relationship. So, during our meeting of the minds, we discussed quality time and expectations. It was the beginning of setting personal priorities and targets.

GOAL

Before putting a single work obligation on your calendar, block off time for your personal priorities. Put yourself and your family first, before work.

TACTICS

Use a time planner of your own, or download my template at www.Helene Segura.com/30tactics. (Yes, this is the same time journal template you downloaded in the previous chapter.)

Note: This activity should not be a onetime occurrence. You'll most likely complete multiple drafts before coming up with a schedule that works for you. I also recommend that you revisit this template a minimum of once per quarter to make adjustments as necessary.

1. Brainstorm a list of all the personal tasks you complete.
2. Review all the priorities you listed in the priorities exercise in chapter 2 and the personal targets you listed in the target exercise in chapter 3, in part 1, "Create Clarity."
3. Put a star next to all the personal tasks in your brainstorm that support your personal priorities and targets.
4. On the time chart, block off the time you want to go to bed.
5. Block off at least 30 minutes before that for decompression time and no electronics.
6. Choose a wake-up time that is approximately seven to eight hours after the time you go to bed. (If you already know the amount of sleep you personally need — way to go! — use that number.)
7. Block off when you'll have dinner each evening.
8. Block off when you'll have breakfast each morning. (Lunch is important, but scheduling that will come into play when we look at your work tasks.)
9. Fill in the time chart with the personal tasks you need to complete to support your own priorities:
   Exercise?
   Meditation or prayer?

Blow-off-steam time? (a.k.a. fun!)

What else?

10. Fill in the planner template with the personal tasks you need to complete to support your other personal priorities:

Significant other / spouse?

Kids?

Parents?

Good friends?

Household maintenance?

Who or what else?

Notice that I have not asked you to schedule volunteer work, social media, chatting/texting away on the phone, and watching television. Yet these are activities that often take up much of our time without our realizing it. I'm not telling you to cut these out of your life completely. However, don't put them on your schedule yet — unless they truly feed your soul and are a necessary part of your self-care.

By this time, you should have quite a few boxes filled in on your planning template tool. If this is becoming worrisome to you, pause for a few deep breaths. Stick with me on this one. This planning-schmanning stuff may not seem fun to you, but working through this template will do wonders for your brain. It will help your brain see how to better structure your time and will give you the ability to go with the flow. You can get everything done that you *truly need to get done* — and still have time for some fun. This exercise will help you to realize how precious your time is and how protective you should be of it.

STRATEGY

What personal tasks do you complete?

You know you do a lot, but what exactly is it that you're doing? Knowing what all these tasks are will help you to prioritize which are more important and need to be done sooner rather than later. Having a list of tasks will also help you when it comes time to ask for help, which you'll learn how to do in part 3, "Assemble Your Team."

Here are some sample personal tasks:

Cooking

Cleaning

Laundry

Child care

Shopping

Home maintenance

Errands

Email/phone/texting

What else do you do? What else do you perceive you're responsible for doing?

It's all about me.

Do you remember the L'Oréal television commercials? They always featured a gorgeous model or actress gushing about the benefits of using L'Oréal makeup or hair color. Each commercial ended with the beauty saying, "Because I'm worth it."

That's the same belief you need to have when you create your schedule. If you don't put on *your* oxygen mask first, you won't be able to help everyone else around you. You're worth it. It's all about you. You come first.

> Time is the coin of your life. You spend it. Do not allow others to spend it for you.
>
> — *Carl Sandburg*

When I ask my clients to show me how they plan their days, they always start with work. I definitely understand how important your job or your business is. Bills need to be paid. You need a roof over your head, food on the table, and utilities to keep you warm (or cool).

But if you don't make time to nourish your body, your mind, and your soul, you won't be able to give it your all in your career. That's why we're beginning your scheduling lesson with your personal needs. We'll eventually build your work schedule into this when you move to the next chapters.

Don't fret if you already use another paper or digital calendar that you absolutely love. I'm not asking you to replace your current tool with my time chart. Instead, I want you to use my template as a learning and planning tool. Also keep in mind that you're not promising to complete these exact tasks at these exact times. What you're doing is learning how much time you need to devote to these priorities and targets so that you can Implement Structure *and* Flow — be structured, yet adjust your schedule as necessary, based on the amount of time you know you need. Practicing your schedule here will help you to internalize the top priorities and targets you need to schedule around.

Every day of your calendar should be scheduled based on the thought processes you experience in this exercise. By knowing how much time you need to properly care for yourself and nurture the important relationships in your life, you will be able to create more realistic to-do lists and make better decisions about how you use your time in your work and personal lives.

It will be important to review your calendar on a daily basis to ensure that you're allowing enough time for the tasks you need to complete to meet your personal and work targets and support your life priorities.

NEXT STEPS

Like the typical go-getter, I was absolutely driven to make my new career a success. But at what cost? When the adrenaline gets flowing, that's not something you think about...until you train your brain to think about it.

In addition to not taking care of my marriage, I wasn't taking care of myself. I had no life outside of working. I had no hobbies. I wasn't reading for fun. I wasn't feeding my soul. All I had was my work, my dogs, and this guy with whom I was cohabiting.

In the long talks I had with my husband after his attempt to make an appointment with me, I realized that I was chasing the idea of being my own boss, but I had not set specific goals and targets. "Make a lot of money so that I can quit my day job" is not specific. I thought I was moving forward, but really I was just searching for my next hit to feed my adrenaline craving. What project could I work on next? A brochure? A new landing page on my website? A different product? A press release? I was haphazardly scooting along, driving toward nowhere specific but picking up hitchhiker tasks along the way. It was all tactical, with no strategy.

Another realization I had during these conversations was that I was really good at project management. If there was something that needed to get done in my business, I could figure out how to do it and "git 'er done." I needed to take this strength and apply it to my personal life. My personal priorities weren't things that could just happen by accident. They were projects that needed to be managed and completed.

Priority: Marriage.

Target: Breakfast every morning together, dinner every evening together, at least one hour of evening downtime together Monday–Friday, at least five hours together on Saturday and Sunday each.

Project management: Schedule these into time slots each week to make sure that they happen; plan for weekend house maintenance or fun during evening downtime.

I needed to apply this same strategy to my own self-care because I was not practicing the level of self-care that I should be.

Forcing myself to go through the same exercise I'm asking you to do in this chapter transformed how I think about time and helped me to create time for the work life and personal life I want to have. It helped me to become more protective of the time I have on this earth.

If you are tired of working too many hours and not having a balance between your work life and personal life, start scheduling around your priorities: personal first, then work.

Ⅲ➡ PLOT YOUR NEXT STEPS

- How does the draft you just created differ from what you're currently doing?
- Which of the personal tasks you listed could possibly be completed by someone else?
- How will viewing your priorities and targets on a daily basis help support the strategies and tactics in this chapter for protecting your time?
- How does it feel knowing that you're on your way to building a schedule that supports your work yet allows you to have a life outside of it?

23 Determine Your High-Value Work Responsibilities

Terri worked for a powerful financial firm, and she set a very lofty goal for herself. She wanted to build up a client portfolio worth $5 million. She was currently at the $2 million mark. She was also working 14-hour days, and while she wanted to meet her goal, she also wanted to work fewer hours. She wanted to do more than just catch glimpses of her family.

We did a brainstorm of all the tasks she completed for work, similar to the brainstorm you did for your personal tasks in the previous chapter. She was doing a heck of a lot! This is just a partial list:

Invoicing
Accounts receivable
Coaching buddy/mentor to others in the firm
Prospecting
Proposal preparation
Prospective client meetings
Annual review preparation
Current client annual review meetings
Speaking engagements
Networking
Client dinners, lunches
Continuing Education Units (CEUs)
Helping with colleagues' projects

Email

Phone calls

In my assessment of her work habits, I found that she also had the challenges of easy distractibility, task switching, multitasking, and yes-ing.

If she was willing to work toward change, I knew I could help her with those challenges and knock off at least two hours a day of lost time. The problem was, she was working 14-hour days. Sure, we could knock it down to 12 based on her current workload, but her goal was to work "only" 10-hour days so that she could spend time with her family. And her goal was also to more than double her portfolio.

Hmmm...We needed to figure out her options.

> Definiteness of purpose is the starting point of all achievement, and its lack is the stumbling block... simply because [unsuccessful people] never really define their goals and start toward them.
>
> *— Napoleon Hill*

GOAL

Know what your top three high-value/revenue-generating activities are and what your top three work tasks are that only you can complete.

TACTICS

1. Brainstorm a list of all the work tasks you complete — on a daily, weekly, monthly, quarterly, or yearly basis. What tasks do you complete in order to do your job or run your business?

2. On printer paper, on chart paper on a wall, or on your laptop or tablet, create four areas where you can post these categories:

   - I must do.

   - Maybe I, maybe someone else.

   - Someone else definitely could do.

   - Does this really need to be done?

3. Dissect each task:

   - How much money does this task bring in directly to the company?

   - If you're not in sales and the task isn't a direct moneymaker, how integral is this task to the functioning of the company? (How many customers does this task help, keep, or acquire? Or how many products can be developed because of the task? And so on.)

- How much expertise is required to make it happen?
- If someone else did this task and screwed up once or twice, how big would the fallout be?
- Which tasks do I love the most?
- Which tasks do I dislike the most?

4. Determine your high-value tasks.
5. Use your high-value-task list to help you better schedule your day.

STRATEGY

Determine your high-value tasks.

Terri is very visual, so we put four giant sticky notes up on the wall:

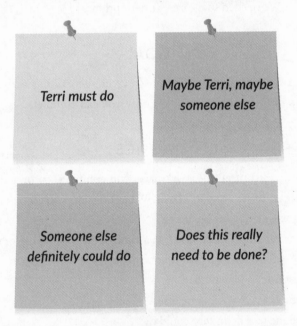

Terri must do

Maybe Terri, maybe someone else

Someone else definitely could do

Does this really need to be done?

Next, we took her task-list brainstorm and started dissecting each task:

How much money does this task bring in directly?

Technically, everything you do at work should bring in something, but if one specific task definitely brings in $1,000 and another task might bring in

$100, or if one task could bring in one new customer and another might bring in 10 new customers, you can see that there's a big difference in the value of the task.

How much expertise is required to make it happen?

Was Terri the only person with the brainpower, knowledge, and/or credentials to do the task, or could someone else be trained? What about in your situation?

If someone else did this task and screwed up once or twice, how big would the fallout be?

Let's face it — we're not perfect. So we know that any coworker or colleague to whom we can hand off our work or anyone we hire definitely won't be. What's the risk of damage from a mistake? If a complicated transfer of funds goes awry, it could cost a great deal of money and possibly lose the client. That's a big risk to take. However, if someone used the wrong font or color on presentation slides, that's not exactly the end of the world.

Which tasks do you love the most?

When we have more passion about something, we'll try harder and finish faster.

Which tasks do you dislike the most?

Tasks we don't enjoy tend not to get completed as quickly, and they quite often lead to procrastination. Neither of these helps in trying to save time.

After about an hour, our sticky-notes wall looked like this:

Terri must do

- **Prospective client meetings** — She needed to make a personal connection with each client, and her skill was in winning people over. This task had the highest dollar value because it brought in new business and added revenue to the portfolio. She loved the thrill of these meetings.
- **Current client annual review meetings** — Clients came onboard because of her, so she needed to communicate with them in order to retain

them. This was her next-highest-dollar-value task because it kept the revenue in the portfolio. She had begun to dread these meetings because she didn't have time to properly prepare. With proper prep time, she felt she would love them again.

- **Client dinners, lunches** — These were becoming tiresome to her because in the back of her mind she was thinking about everything she still had to do. However, she felt that she made stronger connections with her clients and retained more of them this way. She'd schedule these at the six-month mark so that her clients saw her one-on-one at least twice each year — at this meal, as well as at the annual review.
- **CEUs** — No exceptions, she has to take classes to obtain continuing education units; otherwise, she loses her licensing.

Maybe Terri, maybe someone else

- **Prospecting** — Someone else could drum up names, email addresses, and phone numbers for making contacts. With the proper training, this person could make the cold calls as well.
- **Networking** — This is one of Terri's best skills. But she was going to so many different events. She could scale back to the most profitable events and send team members to the others. Or nobody goes to the less profitable events, and they focus their time on the more profitable ones.
- **Email** — Terri does have to handle certain emails. However, there are some ways to cut down inefficiency on this. See chapters 14 through 17, on "Electronic Communication," for those tips.
- **Phone calls** — Terri does have to handle certain phone calls. However, there are some ways to cut down on this. See the "Electronic Communication" chapters for those tips.

Someone else definitely could do

- **Invoicing** — Someone in admin or accounting could do this.
- **Accounts receivable** — It sounds funny to say that invoicing and accounts receivable don't directly bring in money. They are admin tasks that collect money once it's been earned. If no money is earned, there's

nothing to collect. Terri's time should be spent on making the money, not collecting it.

- **Proposal preparation** — With proper training and a good template, Terri isn't needed for this.
- **Annual review preparation** — With proper training and a good template, Terri isn't needed for this either.

Does this really need to be done?

- **Coaching buddy / mentor to others in the firm** — According to the politics of her firm, it's expected that everyone who has hopes of advancement should be a mentor to someone else. So she does need to do this. To save time, we established boundaries and expectations for her mentor/buddy relationship so that it wouldn't take up an inordinate amount of time.
- **Speaking engagements** — Through polite interrogation (ha-ha!), I discovered that Terri acquired more potential clients through speaking engagements than through networking events. However, speaking engagements took time to prepare for (approximately five hours of prep time plus two hours of event time for Terri), whereas networking events did not. We calculated, however, that her seven hours of time spent on a speaking engagement yielded a greater proportion of revenue than her two hours at a networking event. So we eventually moved this task into the Terri Only category and scaled back on her networking events.
- **Helping on colleagues' projects** — Because of her firm's environment, this was a political question. So we came up with a way to address those who approach her with these requests because she can't give a flat-out no. See chapter 42, "I'd Love to Control My Time, but I Don't Know What to Say to People," for those moves.

NEXT STEPS

We narrowed down Terri's options to three choices:

Option 1 — Work on my recommended strategies to lower your hours from 14 per day to 10 per day, and keep your goal at the $2 million mark.

Option 2 — Work on my recommended strategies to lower your hours from 14 per day to 10 per day. Reconfigure the department or hire staff to complete your admin tasks so that you can focus on your high-value tasks. Set Year 1 goal for $3 million and Year 2 goal for $5 million.

Option 3 — Find a different job. This is no joke. If your work life is unbearable and your employer refuses to implement your wisely thought-out proposals for change, do you want to choose to stay miserable, or do you want to move to a company where you might make less money, but where you'll be happy?

She decided on Option 2. She wanted the $5 mil to happen instantly, but when I explained that habits take a little time to change (and we'd be changing quite a few to shave four hours off her days), and reconfiguring a department or hiring the right staff and training them also takes some time, she agreed that it was better to set realistic timelines for her goals.

So we had a strategy: tighten up the efficiency belt, restructure staff, delegate.

But now we had to decide whom to hand off tasks to and/or whom to hire. How do you know who needs to do what? You have to understand what job responsibilities that person or those people need to have. How do you know what job responsibilities they should have?

You first have to know what job responsibilities *you* should have, which is the purpose of this chapter. When you know what your high-value work responsibilities are, you'll make better decisions about how you use your time — and better decisions about what you delegate to others. If you don't have the option of reconfiguring within your department or hiring staff to complete the "someone else can do" tasks, you'll want to pay special attention in part 3, "Assemble Your Team."

You now have a much better idea of what your high-value work tasks are. Armed with this information, you'll be better able to schedule your workday, which is what we'll be doing in the next chapter. Knowing where the majority of your time should be spent will help you to make better decisions about how you use your time.

⫸ PLOT YOUR NEXT STEPS

- What are your highest-value work tasks? In other words, what are the three tasks that bring your company the most money (or customers or high ratings, etc.) that no one else — only you — can do?
- You just determined what your high-value tasks are. How much time have you been spending on these?
- Which of the work tasks you listed could possibly be completed by someone else?
- Can any tasks be dropped because they're of little to no value?
- How does it feel knowing that you're on your way to building a schedule that supports your work yet allows you to have a life outside of it?

24 Schedule around Your Work Priorities and Targets

When I first started my professional organizing career, I accepted as clients anyone and everyone at any time on any day. I was afraid of saying no. They might not like me if I say no. I might not make enough money if I say no. Yikes! I worked during the standard workday, as well as any evening someone requested and on weekends. If a client asked if I was available on Saturday morning from 8 to 11 AM, I hurriedly (but not enthusiastically) said, "Yes!"

While I was grateful for the income, I realized that my passion for consulting was beginning to take a nosedive because my life revolved around saying yes to the next client. My efficiency also suffered because I didn't have a schedule for how I'd spend my nonclient hours.

I had not set my priorities or targets. My focus instead was only on how many dollars I could bring in. And, as crazy as this may sound, that is a most unproductive way to manage a career.

GOAL

Schedule your high-value work tasks first — around your personal priorities — and spend at least 50 percent of your workday on them.

There *is* time in the day to do *what truly needs* to get done.

166

TACTICS

Note: This activity should not be a onetime occurrence. You'll most likely complete multiple drafts before figuring out the amount of time you should concentrate on your high-value tasks. I also recommend that you revisit this exercise a minimum of once per quarter to make adjustments as necessary.

1. Review all the work priorities you listed in the priorities exercise in chapter 2 and the business targets you listed in the target exercise in chapter 3, in part 1, "Create Clarity."
2. Review the value/revenue ratings you gave your tasks in the previous chapter.
3. If you're employed by a company, find out if you're permitted to adjust your work schedule as needed. If so (and definitely if you own your own business), decide on your work hours.
4. On your time chart where you've already filled in your personal priorities, block off at least 50 percent of your work hours for your high-value tasks.
5. Block off the amount of time you want to invest in each of these high-value tasks.
6. Block off when you'll have lunch each day. If it can be at the same time each day, this is wonderful. But most likely this will probably vary from day to day, depending on your meeting schedule.
7. Until you decide to delegate to others (coworkers, contractors, or employees), you'll have to complete the next most important tasks on your own. Use the other 50 percent of your time for these lower-value tasks.
8. Block off the amount of time you want to invest in each of these lower-value tasks.
9. Move your time blocks around as necessary.
10. If there's too much to do to fit on your schedule, don't panic. You'll be gaining back time as you implement the strategies and tactics in this book. Plus, in part 3, "Assemble Your Team," we'll talk about how others can help you to get everything done.

Shazam! Your brain has been flexing its scheduling muscle. The more it practices, the more it understands the need to focus during your work hours, the need to concentrate on your high-value tasks, and the need to invest blocks of time in what needs to get done. Your brain is practicing how to make better decisions about how to use your time. Your scheduling muscle is what will help you with your time protection.

Now that you've scheduled around your personal priorities and work priorities, you can look to see how much time you have for volunteer work, social media, watching television, and all those other activities that are never scheduled and are not a part of your priorities yet somehow take up a lot of time in people's lives.

STRATEGY

Increasing efficiency and, therefore, productivity involves developing processes. These processes are your standard operating procedures (SOP) — an operations manual, if you will, for running your workday and your life. Creating this SOP manual requires understanding what tasks are necessary to support your priorities and reach your targets. You brainstormed and determined those important tasks in the previous chapters and have already scheduled your personal tasks. Now it's time to get the work tasks scheduled so that you have a structure — and can understand how to flow when necessary.

Understanding your overall work and personal operations will help you to schedule your project timelines even more efficiently and create an even more lethal 3+3 at the end of each day. Lethal for lost time, that is.

Schedule around your work priorities and targets.

You'll need to decide on your work hours. I do understand that you can't be completely black-and-white and draw a line in the sand between work and personal. But if you blend too much and don't have a focus for at least a small amount of time, you won't excel in either the work or personal components of your life.

My clients who work for someone else usually are told what hours they must work. But if they are allowed to present any type of proposal for flex work hours, we use the tactics in this chapter to come up with the information for that proposal. If you can't work the schedule of your choice, you can still choose how to structure your days to get work done, so you still need to schedule your work priorities and targets. You can choose which tasks to complete at which times.

If you own your own company, however, you are the boss, and you set your hours. I have my business-owner clients build their schedules around their spouses and/or children. They may want to be home (and not working) at the same time. Or they may want to be at home (working) at different times and split the child-care schedule. If you work for a company and telecommute, you may be in this same situation.

Do you want to work straight through a large block of time? For example, you might set your office hours from 8 AM to 6 PM, Saturday through Wednesday. Now, does that mean you'll work for a solid 10 hours each day? No. As I mentioned earlier, it's impossible to be completely black-and-white and divide your day that rigidly. You'll take a few breaks, have lunch, maybe make a personal online purchase and perhaps a personal phone call or two. But, by setting office hours, you know that the majority of that time block should be focused on work. With that type of laser focus, you will be much more productive.

Or perhaps you can't work for that long of a stretch — because of your attention span, your physical condition, your kids' schedule, or any other reason. Do you instead need to work in chunks around your personal priorities? For example, you might set your office hours from 6 to 6:45 AM, 9 AM to 3 PM, and 8 PM to 10 PM, Monday through Friday.

By the way, you are allowed to change your office hours as your and your family's needs change. That's why scheduling should never be on autopilot. You'll want to examine your schedule at least once a quarter and make adjustments as necessary.

Structure: Schedule time for your high-value tasks.

Once you choose your office hours, take a look at your high-value tasks from the previous chapter. At least half of your time should be spent on bringing in the bucks or the customers or the positive reviews — whatever your big job responsibility is. Later, feel free to increase that percentage of time, but to start with, it should be at least half.

If you work for a company and just discovered that you spend more than half of your time on low-value tasks, it will be critical for you to begin implementing the various strategies and tactics throughout this handbook. You'll be more efficient with your time, which will give you the time you need to focus more on those high-value tasks.

If you're a business owner spending more than half

> Lose no Time.
> Be always employ'd in something useful.
> Cut off all unnecessary actions.
> – *Benjamin Franklin*

of your time on low-value tasks, that's like paying someone $100 an hour to do a $20-per-hour job. Yes, I know you're gifted in your field, and you're the only one who truly understands what needs to be done and how. But if you spend your time on low-level stuff, you will never have enough time in the day. Period. Now please don't fret about this. We'll address getting help with your low-value tasks in part 3, "Assemble Your Team." Besides, if you're following the other strategies and tactics in the various chapters, you'll start saving enough time so that you won't feel like you have to hire someone right this minute, which will instantly help relieve some of your pressure.

Based on the time journal you completed in chapter 21, "Know Where Your Time Goes, So That You Can Tell Your Time What to Do," you will have an idea of how long your tasks should take. You can use these estimates when you complete the tactics in this chapter. I recommend that you pad in at least 30 percent extra time so that you don't feel like you're rushed all day long. For example, if you think a particular task should take you 45 minutes, plan for one hour. If you finish early, great! You'll have some extra break time, or you can get ahead on your next task. But if something goes haywire (like your server goes down or your website "breaks" or something went wrong with a customer's order), you have time to take care of those uh-ohs — or, as some people refer to it, time for putting out fires.

Flow: Shift time blocks as necessary.

As you go through the tactics and add your work tasks around your personal tasks, you might need to do some rearranging of the time blocks. This is totally okay. The purpose of the exercises in these "Time Protection" chapters is to help you begin to see how much time you need to allot to the most important parts of your life. You're not signing in blood that you're going to stick to these same exact times on these exact days, week in and week out, forever and ever, "to infinity and beyond." Instead, you're learning about how much time you'd like to invest in each of these vital areas. With this knowledge, you'll be able to make better decisions about how you use your time. You'll have much stronger motivation to not immediately say yes to every request you receive and to check your calendar first to see how much time you have for those requests. And you'll be able to flip-flop these task time blocks around as needed. Kind of like Tetris. (Remember that video game from the eighties in which you had to slide blocks around? Who knew that would come in handy in adulthood?) Your day may not end up playing out in the original order you'd scheduled, but you'll still be able to complete your most critical tasks that support your top personal and work priorities.

Implement Structure *and* Flow.

NEXT STEPS

If you work for a company, you most likely will not have the flexibility to decide when you show up to work and leave, whether to accept a particular customer account, and whether to restructure or hire within your department to help with the workload. But you do have total control over whether you will lose time through procrastination, distractions, looking for lost items, or not planning your 3+3. Unless your boss tells you specifically what you must do each minute of the day, you are in control of your schedule too, which means you have control over how much time you devote to your high- and low-value tasks. This will make a tremendous impact on how much time you save. As you gain confidence in being able to create structure and flow and protect your time, you will also gain the confidence to communicate more assertively, as well as make suggestions to your coworkers and supervisors, which will improve your work life that much more.

If you're a business owner, you have the luxury of determining your schedule. Your clients don't set your schedule. *You* set your schedule, and you accept clients who fit into your schedule. It's a scary concept to grasp — whether you're first starting out or you've been doing this for decades and are afraid of not making enough money to survive. But once you command your time, you will find that not only will your fear subside, but also you'll be more productive and make just as much — or more — money.

As you become more successful and, therefore, busier, you will encounter more and more requests for in-person meetings, phone meetings, project participation, and then some. While you should be flattered by the requests because it means that folks have heard about how great you are, you must be careful about what you accept because you have only so much time in the day to get everything done — and complete it all at high quality levels.

Instead of asking when clients wanted to see me, I instead began to protect my time and present my available hours. Did prospective clients ever decide not to work with me because of my available hours? Yes. In fact, one gentleman screamed at my assistant and hung up when she told him that I don't have Saturday appointments. And that's okay. Because there are plenty of other folks out there who will see me on my schedule. Besides, if that's his attitude, is that who I really want to spend my time with away from my family?

Take a look at what you recorded for your work priorities and targets. These are what should always be scheduled first on your calendar. Your priorities and targets are also what you should examine before accepting an appointment or project or agreeing to someone else's timeline. Know your high-value tasks. And schedule around them.

ⅢⅢ➡ PLOT YOUR NEXT STEPS

- How does the draft you just created differ from what you're currently doing?
- How will viewing your priorities and targets on a daily basis help support the strategies and tactics for protecting your time?
- What time blocks from your current draft do you need to be prepared to flip-flop around?
- What will you do to stay focused on your high-value tasks, instead of choosing to allow low-value tasks to creep into and take over — sabotage — your day?

25 Scheduling for Road Warriors

Jack is a pharmaceutical rep. He has to report to his company's office two to four times per month. The rest of the time, he works out of his home office and car. His days are spent driving from doctors' offices to clinics to hospitals. He overbooks appointments at each location in case doctors have emergencies and can't see him. On some days, he's running around like a chicken with its head cut off to squeeze in everyone and not be too late, sometimes not having enough documents or the right samples to leave behind because he's forgotten to check what they needed and reload. On other days, he's twiddling his thumbs in a waiting room because half of his appointments canceled. He used to love the rush of zipping around, but lately he's grown weary of it — perhaps because he stays up until 1 AM to finish paperwork after his kids go to bed.

GOAL

Increase your productivity and efficiency by *not* packing in your road appointments.

TACTICS

1. Schedule fewer client appointments in a single day.
2. Pad your appointments with extra time.
3. Make a daily appointment with *yourself* at the end of each day to process.
4. Always have a Plan B.

STRATEGY

Our wireless devices allow us to work and meet in multiple places each day. But with this freedom of mobility comes the need to properly manage a schedule in order to stay efficient and productive while mobile.

My clients who are out and about multiple times per week tend to have these two major challenges:

- How to keep track of supplies and files in up to three different locations — home, work, and car
- How to squeeze in as many client appointments as possible without being late and without having to do paperwork at all hours of the night

We covered the former in chapter 13, "Create a Go-Bag and Mobile Office for Road Warriors." The latter takes a little bit of a mind shift, but here's how you can begin to manage those challenges and increase your productivity.

Schedule fewer client appointments in a single day.

Huh? That's right. Less is more when it comes to possessions and when it comes to clients too. The more rushing around you do, the more mistakes and miscommunication will happen, and the less time you'll have to nurture your client relationships. Depending on which marketing guru you listen to, it takes anywhere from three to eight times more time and money to capture a new client than to take care of a current one. Even if you don't believe those stats, wouldn't focusing on serving fewer clients better and purposefully filling your pipeline — rather than serving a ton of clients in a mediocre fashion and losing many of them — lead you to more income? Arriving unfocused and breathless to each client, combined with lower brain function from sleep deprivation, makes for a less-than-stellar experience for your customers. Give yourself more time in your workday to arrive safely, spend quality time during your appointments, and finish your paperwork before the end of the workday.

> Never confuse movement with action.
>
> – *Ernest Hemingway*

Pad your appointments with extra time.

Block off time on your calendar for traveling to your appointment, plus 20 percent extra for traffic delays and five minutes for centering yourself before you walk in. Block off time for your appointment plus 20 percent extra in case your client runs late or your appointment goes so well that you should spend additional time chatting instead of just running out. Block off 15 minutes following the appointment to document whatever notes you need to record while they're still fresh in your brain. This includes: summary of the appointment for your client file, adding the next appointment to your calendar before it's forgotten or double-booked, and setting reminders for the next actions you need to take. Padding all this time to be more efficient will mean that you'll see fewer clients in a day. But see the previous tip for why that's a great thing.

Make a daily appointment with yourself at the end of each day.

Once you decide what you want your work hours to be, save the last 30 minutes of each day for reviewing what's happened that day:

- Did you record everything that needed to be recorded?
- Did you send the client all the information they requested during that day's appointment?
- Did you set your reminders for next actions and client follow-up?
- Did you file or scan any new incoming papers?
- What's on tap for tomorrow?
- What supplies need to be packed in your go-bag and trunk office?

Always have a Plan B.

In a perfect world, things would always be, well, perfect. But alas, we don't live in a perfect world, so that's why we need to Implement Structure *and* Flow. A client may cancel at the last minute, leaving you with an extra gap in your day. If something like this happens, what project could you work on during this time gap that would make the next day or next week that much easier for you? Or maybe the stars have aligned, and you have an awesome day. You get to an appointment on time, it's successful in record time, and you end up way ahead of schedule — and with a gap before your next appointment. After a quick celebration (self high-five!), travel to your next location and work on a Plan B project while you wait for your next appointment to begin. Your 3+3 list can help guide you with your Plan B.

Increasing your productivity and lowering your stress levels will happen as you gradually implement these strategies. It may seem counterintuitive to slow things down and take your time, but doing so will give your brain clarity and allow you to better focus on what you need to get done. When your brain is focused, you'll make better decisions and produce higher-quality work. And every client of yours will love that!

NEXT STEPS

Jack initially could not wrap his head around the strategy of seeing fewer people each day. He thought his sales would nosedive for sure. He was pleasantly surprised that at the end of his first week of using these tactics, he was able to go to sleep earlier because his paperwork was completed. He'd arrived on time in a relaxed fashion, fully focused and prepped for each client. He'd been able to review his notes from his prior meetings and arrive with the ideal brochures, explanations, and samples (and goodies) for each doctor's office. With those personal touches — in addition to no longer looking scatterbrained and discombobulated — he was able to secure the same sales revenue even with seeing fewer clients and working fewer hours. By protecting his time and scheduling purposefully, he became a much more successful — and happier — man.

ⅢⅢ➡ PLOT YOUR NEXT STEPS

- How are your road warrior days currently scheduled?
- Which tactics from this chapter are you already implementing, and will you keep doing so?
- Which tactics from this chapter will you add to your tool bag to help you improve your efficiency?
- If your job takes you out of town, how will you modify the strategies and tactics in this chapter to be successful on the road and have time to catch up and regroup when you get back home?

PART 3

ASSEMBLE YOUR TEAM

*Life and Work
Are Not Solo Missions*

26 It's All in Your Head: It Takes a Village

Have you ever watched a James Bond movie or read one of the books by Ian Fleming that started it all? James Bond is a stud. Agent 007 can shoot any gun that lands in his hands. He can fly any plane. He can operate any car or machine he requires for a hurried exit. He can outrun bullets and exploding bombs. Men want to be like him and women want to do things to him.

Literary scholar Thomas A. Shippey describes James Bond as being "omni-competent." He can do anything and everything — which explains the attraction that so many of us have to this fictional character. We wish we could be that.

But we're not fictional. We live in reality. And reality doesn't allow us to be omni-competent, which is why assembling a team is critical to our success in business and our success in life. And, by the way, even the fictional *mucho macho* James Bond — "Mr. Omni-Competent" himself — has a team behind him. Though he's the star of the show, he often gets out of sticky situations because his boss, M, has provided resources, or his gadget guru, Q, has supplied him with, well, gadgets. And the rest of the gang back at MI6 is on standby to support the mission.

If you work for a company, your team — if you're not already assigned to one — can be a cubicle neighbor, members of your department, or colleagues on a different floor.

If you're a solopreneur, you might be thinking that you need to hire employees. Maybe. Or perhaps you can barter out your skills with fellow solopreneurs whose skills you need. Or contract out the services you need.

Whether you work for yourself or for a boss, you will also need a second team — your personal team. You need support in both aspects of your life: work and personal.

No matter how fiercely independent you are, be prepared to create and interact with your team. The most successful people surround themselves not with yes-men but with people who will help them rise to the top of whatever mountain they're trying to climb.

If you're applying what you learned in the **C** of CIA — **C**reate Clarity — your mind is freeing up space to allow your brain to make better decisions about how you use your time.

If you're applying what you learned in the **I** of CIA — **I**mplement Structure *and* Flow — you're implementing the strategies and tactics that will allow you to control the five key components of your workday and tell your time what to do.

And now, it's time to recruit the operatives who will give you the support you need to obtain and continue your success, to complete your mission.

In this part, we'll examine the **A** in CIA — **A**ssemble Your Team. You'll learn how to

- structure your personal team
- structure your work team
- communicate and interact with your team

Let's go on a hunt for your recruits.

27 Assemble Your Personal Team

It was a beautiful, warm Southern California day with the sun shining brightly. The people in the bleachers at a kids' soccer game were getting in a bit of tanning time while watching their children play. Brian was holding his baby boy, who'd been dressed by his wife that morning. The child was in a beautiful turtleneck onesie, complete with matching pants and socks.

As the game progressed, the baby started crying and wouldn't stop. He'd just eaten. He'd recently napped. What was the problem? "How can I get him to be quiet?" gritted Brian, the ultimate dad, through his teeth.

A woman who was seated under a canopy at the top of the bleachers called down to him, "Sir, why don't you bring your baby up here and sit in the shade?"

"No thanks. We're okay down here."

"Sir, it's really not a problem. I think you'd be more comfortable up here where it's cooler."

"No, really, it's okay. I'm not sure what's wrong, but I'll get him to stop crying."

But the baby kept on crying. Daddy was trying to figure out how to make him hush so as not to disturb everyone around them.

Finally, the woman called down, "Sir, if your baby could talk, he'd tell you, 'Get this frickin' outfit off me! It's too damn hot to be wearing it!'"

A roar of laughter went through the crowd, and the man took his baby up into the shade. The crying stopped.

GOAL

Create, maintain, and communicate with a team of at least two other people who will be your auditors and advisers (and part-time butt-kickers) for your personal life.

TACTICS

1. Recruit your household members.
2. Share with them your personal priorities and targets.
3. Recruit at least one person outside your household.
4. If you don't have household members, choose at least two people from outside your household.
5. Update them at least once per quarter on your progress.
6. Offer them the same kind of support.

STRATEGY

Sometimes we're so buried in a situation that we look only at the symptoms instead of the causes. We often don't see the whole picture, much like the gentleman in the bleachers in the beginning of this chapter.

Can you step outside yourself to look at your situation the way someone else might view it? Or do you keep your blinders on and keep doing the same old thing? It's human nature to do the latter. That's why it's important to make a conscious effort to do the former, or bring in someone who will help you to look at your situation from a different perspective.

This is where your team comes in. Having people in your inner circle who understand your priorities and targets, who support you yet aren't afraid to question your reasoning, who will stand by your side through thick and thin, is of utmost importance. Your personal team will help you to stay focused and be successful with your Time Management Revolution.

Recruit your household members.

The people you live with must be your biggest supporters. If they're not willing to do this, kick them out.

Okay, so maybe you can't kick them out, but you'll have to get their buy-in. And they must have yours. Relationships are a two-way street, so the support you expect from them is the same amount of support they expect from you.

If you have an infant or toddler, you probably don't have to worry about getting his or her buy-in...yet. But anyone in your household who is capable of communicating using at least sentence fragments will need to be a part of your team meetings.

Share with them your personal priorities and targets.

The best time to have a household meeting is on a full stomach, so that means after a terrific dinner — perhaps during dessert. This is when people are happiest. When's the worst time to have a team meeting? First thing in the morning or right before dinner, when everyone is tired, cranky, and experiencing low blood sugar levels. Another terrible time to have this meeting is when you're ticked off. Nothing will get accomplished if you're upset and snapping at people.

> Improvement usually means doing something that we have never done before.
> — *Shigeo Shingo*

Even though this meeting is all about you, everyone must feel like it's also about them. So this means everyone gets to state what their priorities and targets are, why they've chosen those goals, and how much this means to them. Everyone gets to ask for the type of support they'd like to have. And everyone gets to answer with what kind of support they're willing to give.

All meeting participants must agree to receive constructive criticism. The key word is *constructive*. You would not want your child to say to you, "Gee, you really sucked this month on your target of attending my games." A better phrasing might be, "I know your target this month was to attend at least one game per week. You made it to one game this month. Can we talk about how to meet your target?"

You must do the same for them. If the support you receive from them is not reciprocated, then you don't have a strong team. And their support will wane. And then you'll have no team.

This is also the time during which you ask for help with completing personal tasks. Everyone who lives in a household and walks upright should be pitching in and helping to complete household tasks, as age appropriate. During the team meeting — armed with your brainstorm of your personal tasks — you can ask your spouse, "Is there any way you can help? Would you like to help me complete Task X or Task Y?" By giving your spouse a choice, he or she will take ownership and won't feel put upon. By choosing which tasks to get help with, you're controlling which low-value tasks you're removing from your plate. In addition to your spouse, you can ask your kids for help.

Recruit at least one person outside your household.

It's important to have an outsider's perspective. This doesn't mean that you don't trust your household. It simply means that you're getting a third-party perspective to keep things in check — like the lady under the shade in the bleachers at the beginning of this chapter. You'll have the same type of support system with this person as you do with those in your household.

Update the team at least once per quarter on your progress.

Ideally, you'll have a household dinner at least once per week, during which everyone can state their priorities and goals, give their updates, and ask for support. But not everyone is comfortable with this frequency. Perhaps your family will prefer once per month, especially if you have teenagers who think this kind of meeting is helpful but so uncool. At a minimum, your household should gather once per quarter to reflect with power on accomplishments and plan for the future.

And when I say "meet" or "share" with your team, I mean in person. (Or via Skype or FaceTime if your nonhousehold member is not in your city.) Texting, emailing, and posting or messaging through Facebook don't count. You need true communication — looking into their eyes, hearing their tone, viewing their body language.

ⅢⅢ➡ PLOT YOUR NEXT STEPS

- Who will be on your personal team?
- What support do you want from them?
- What support will you give to them?
- How often will you meet?
- How will implementing the strategies and tactics in this chapter benefit you?

28   Assemble Your Work Team

Tim, a financial planner, spent a lot of time helping others — his clients, his colleagues, his bosses, the community...He came to the rescue of anyone and everyone. But *he* never asked for help.

He began to realize that the more help he gave to others, the more he dropped everything in an instant, and the more he allowed other people's emergencies to become his emergencies, the less work he got done, even for others. And the work he did complete did not meet his standard of high quality because he had rushed to get it done and move on to the next item on his plate.

He wanted to remain a nice guy, but there had to be a more efficient way to help his colleagues. And he finally realized that he needed help and support as well.

GOAL

Create, maintain, and communicate with a team of at least two other people who will be your auditors and advisers (and part-time butt-kickers) for your work life.

TACTICS

1. Recruit at least one person who works in your industry.
2. Recruit at least one person who works outside your industry.

3. If you work for a company, recruit at least two people from your department.
4. Share with them your work priorities and targets.
5. If you own a company, your team also consists of your managers, employees, and/or contractors.
6. Update them at least once per quarter on your progress.
7. Offer them the same kind of support.

STRATEGY

Sometimes we're so buried in a situation that we only look at bits and pieces without connecting the dots.

Can you step outside yourself to look at your situation the way someone else might view it? Or do you stay in your comfort zone and avoid change — even though your said comfort zone can get pretty stressful? It's human nature to keep doing the same ol', same ol'. That's why it's important to make a conscious effort to do the former, or bring in someone who will help you to look at your situation from a different perspective.

> Only your real friends will tell you when your face is dirty.
>
> *– Sicilian proverb*

This is where your team comes in. Having people who understand your career, who comprehend your priorities and targets, who will help you to see the pathway you need to take, who will give you a kick in the pants when you need it — is of upmost importance. Your work team will help you to stay focused and on track.

Recruit at least one person who works in your industry.

While technically you might be competitors, it's helpful to have a team member who understands the ins and outs of your industry, who can offer insight that others outside of your industry won't have, and who stays up-to-date on trends and research. You might be able to team up on projects and split the work.

Recruit at least one person who works outside your industry.

You also need the opposite. Having an outsider's perspective helps keep your intake of information fresh and objective. You can gather ideas from the outsider's industry and apply them to yours. Being able to synthesize information from a variety of sources both in and out of your industry will make your actions stronger.

If you work for a company, recruit at least two people from your department.

The first two tactics are essential for entrepreneurs and independent consultants. If you work for a company, you may not have access to those types of individuals. Whether you do or not, it's important that you have fellow department members on your team. Even if you're not in a supervisory position, you can still create your own team by simply asking those who you feel would be a good support system to join up. Ideally, you'd approach your supervisor about creating these teams, but not everyone works for a boss who's open-minded and willing to listen to employees' suggestions.

Share with the team your work priorities and targets.

Just as with your personal team, you and your work team will support each other in working toward your priorities and targets. Celebrate your wins. Ask for help with your challenges. Troubleshoot and bounce ideas around with your think tank. If you feel that your work friends and colleagues are not quite enough — or perhaps you'd like to add to the tremendous support you already receive — consider retaining a coach for six months, someone who is professionally trained to guide you to success with whatever challenges you face.

If you own a company, your team also consists of your managers, employees, and/or contractors.

You'll most likely have different relationships with your employees and contractors compared with those you have with colleagues or mentors. But it's still important to share with them your vision of the company and the targets you want to reach. How will you reach these targets as a team? Additionally, these good folks will be running the operation while you're out of town working or on vacation, so they need to be empowered with the knowledge of the business plan so that they'll make stellar decisions while you're gone.

Update them at least once per quarter on your progress.

I recommend to my entrepreneur and independent consultant clients that they meet with their think tank teams at least once per month. If they have employees or subcontractors who work remotely, I recommend that they meet with their "staff" at least twice per month to make sure that everything is firing on all cylinders and everyone is on the same page. If you work for a company, this meeting could happen as often as once per week. Yes, you heard me right! Once per week. (We'll talk about that in the next chapter.) At a bare minimum, your team should meet quarterly.

Offer them the same kind of support.

I'm sure we've all experienced people who just take, take, take. They dump all their problems on you, then bail out when you're in need. We don't want to be that person, right? So be sure to offer reciprocal support to your team.

NEXT STEPS

Tim created his personal team and different work teams. As a coach, I was initially a member of both his personal and work teams to help him get started until his teams were built up.

He established one work team that consisted of two of his colleagues on his floor. All three of them were experienced and advancing in the field, so they could help each other out. By setting up a communication structure, they no longer interrupted one another throughout the day with questions and brain picking.

He had a second team made up of his mentees — those new advisers who always sought his help. They created a structure for how "the help" would work so that Tim wasn't interrupted or overburdened. This allowed him to develop more meaningful relationships with rising stars who eventually took some of his handoffs when he got super-busy. Score! He was able to help them, delegate some of his workload, and earn a small commission for being the originator.

He also created a third team, his power team. This consisted of a man and a woman outside of his industry. They discussed best practices in their fields and brainstormed for solutions to challenges that faced them. They also became referral partners, so that they would pass business to each other. Another win!

IIII➡ PLOT YOUR NEXT STEPS

- Would you prefer to meet with your team in person, or are you comfortable with Skype or FaceTime? (This helps you narrow down the geographic location of your team members.)
- At this point in time, what kind of support do you need?
- Who in your industry would be ideal for your work team?
- Who outside of your industry would be ideal for your work team?
- Who within your company would be ideal for your work team?
- When and where would you be able to meet with your team(s)?
- How will implementing the strategies and tactics in this chapter benefit you?

29 Facilitate Productive Team Meetings

Back in my teaching days, I was voluntold to be on a committee. This committee was supposed to meet every other week in order to develop the District Improvement Plan. You can bet I had fun with the acronym for that committee name!

Teachers from across grade levels and across schools met to create this "dynamic, living document." I knew this committee had existed the previous year, so I asked where that document was.

Nothin'.

I asked about when the document we were creating would get implemented and how everything we proposed would get funded.

Nothin'.

Each meeting consisted of introductions, setting the next meeting date and time, rehashing what we had discussed in the last two meetings for those who had missed them, taking a look at what we needed to create for the plan, and then leaving without clarified outcomes or next steps.

Bloody hell, those meetings were a horrendous waste of time! So much so that nearly 20 years later, I still roll my eyes into the back of my head about how much time I lost!

According to surveys, the majority of workers find meetings to be stupid and a huge waste of time. I couldn't agree more — unless you run them the following way.

GOAL

Make sure that any meeting you attend has a clear objective, an agenda, and resulting actions. If it doesn't, give (covertly, if necessary) the meeting coordinator a copy of this book, with this chapter bookmarked. If you're in charge, implement these tactics.

TACTICS

1. Choose at least one clear goal to accomplish at the meeting.
2. Determine which questions or discussions will lead to the accomplishment of this goal.
3. Create an agenda with time blocks.
4. Email the agenda at least two business days prior to the meeting (earlier if possible).
5. Clarify expectations ahead of time.
6. Collect RSVPs.
7. Ensure that all language needs will be addressed.

STRATEGY

It's extremely important not to waste the time of your personal and work teams. It's important to meet with them, but those meetings should be meaningful — and not just a meeting to say that you had a meeting.

We've all been to them — meetings that drag on forever, yet nothing is accomplished. Or, my personal favorite, having a meeting to decide when the next one will be.

When I work with companies, I advise them to have weekly department meetings.

Whaaaaaat?

Yes, weekly department meetings. I know what you're thinking — here I've been complaining about how meetings can be a waste of time, yet I tell clients to have weekly meetings? This is why:

> Good business leaders create a vision, articulate the vision, passionately own the vision, and relentlessly drive it to completion.
>
> — Jack Welch

Many of our interruptions at work come from our coworkers or employees asking questions.

By having a weekly team meeting within a specific time frame and with a specific agenda, you hold everyone accountable for finishing what they were supposed to during the week, planning for the next week, and getting their questions answered without taking time away from anyone else. Spending these 30 minutes each week saves hours the following week. There are fewer intrusions, plus many times this is where you catch duplicate work or tasks that would have fallen through the cracks if they'd been missed — *if* the meetings are run the way I recommend.

By the way, did you know that Friday afternoon is the least productive time in America? What a perfect time to have a team meeting — when no one else is working! If you're in retail, and Friday is your busiest day, obviously this won't work. Pick a day and time that typically are not as busy for your store...mid-morning on Tuesdays, perhaps?

There's nothing I detest more than worthless meetings, so here are some strategies to ensure that you are never the facilitator of a waste of time.

Choose at least one clear goal to accomplish at the meeting.

What do you want to accomplish at this meeting? Is this a meeting to discuss a specific project? Is this your check-in meeting with your team? If you don't know what you want to accomplish, don't bother scheduling a meeting.

Determine which questions or discussions will lead to the accomplishment of this goal.

You can't just walk into a meeting, slap a goal on a PowerPoint slide or whiteboard, and hope that everyone has an instant idea. The point of scheduling a meeting is to have everyone in the room use their brainpower to bounce ideas off one another. Create at least a few questions to get the brains churning. Better yet, list those questions on the agenda so that the thinking cells are already lubricated before everyone arrives.

Create an agenda.

Depending on the nature of the meeting, you might divide up your agenda into topics that need to be discussed, or list each person who will give a report. No matter how you decide to organize your meeting, be sure to create a timeline for how long each topic or person will be given. This will keep everyone on their toes during the meeting and make sure that all necessary topics are covered by the time you want to end your meeting. (Translation: There's no time for people who just like to hear themselves talk.)

If this meeting is your weekly department check-in, consider this sample agenda for a team of 10:

High-Achiever Department — Weekly Team Meeting
Friday, April 29, 2:00–2:30 PM (snacks available beginning at 1:45)
2nd-floor conference room

2:00–2:05 PM
Round 1: Share your accomplishments for the week. (30 seconds each)

2:06–2:11 PM
Round 2: Announce the steps/tasks from the projects you'll be working on for the next week (two weeks would be fabulous!), along with any deadlines. (30 seconds each)

2:12–2:25 PM
Round 3: Announce what resources (supplies, conference line, meeting room, information from others) you need or questions you have. Receive the answers. (1.25 minutes each)

2:26–2:28 PM
Round 4: Announce your best interruption time and/or worst interruption time for the upcoming week. Everyone has fair warning. (15 seconds each)

2:29–2:30 PM
Round 5: Cheer each other on. Ready? Break!

This type of structure requires the attendees to have project timelines and understand what their 3+3s are. That means the attendees — your coworkers, employees, or department — must be organized. Having more-organized colleagues cuts down on their interrupting you with questions and also reduces the number of last-minute "emergencies" for which they'll ask you for help. That is how your team members can help themselves — and you — to become more efficient.

If your meeting follows this format, this is also how your department might begin to see duplication of work, tasks falling through the cracks, and/or a division of labor that is not based on brain types or task strengths. All of these cause lost time, so catching these inefficiencies during the meeting and correcting through restructuring or rerouting delegation will improve the work flow.

You may wish to allow 60 minutes for the first few meetings, especially if your department is not yet a well-oiled machine. Eventually, you can cut back to 45 minutes and then 30 minutes, unless you're truly maximizing all of the time (or if you have more than 10 people). I also wouldn't make this monthly. People can't plan that far out with so many variables. Stick to weekly. You want this short, focused, and to the point. No wasted time. Don't worry about this seeming impersonal. Folks can socialize before or after, if they'd like.

Email the agenda at least two business days prior to the meeting.

If this is not a weekly team meeting and, therefore, requires a different type of preparation, ideally you want to send out the agenda at least one week beforehand. But the minimum is two business days. Emailing the agenda early lets everybody know that you are organized, have it together, and mean business. It also gives attendees time to start thinking about what they'd like to say and perhaps even gather research or examples of ideas that they want to express.

Even if your weekly team meetings are the same routine, you should have agendas to make sure that everyone stays on track. Go-getters can post their questions ahead of time on the agenda so that their colleagues arrive with better ideas and solutions.

Clarify expectations ahead of time.

This should be included in the agenda. Everyone should know what the expected results of the meeting are. If you want attendees to bring specific materials, indicate that in the agenda. If attendees must perform an action — for example, they must bring monetary contributions or they'll leave with funds that they'll be expected to account for — specify that in the agenda so that there are no surprises.

Collect RSVPs.

It's important to know who will be present and who won't. Those who won't be present should be expected to send their information/submissions ahead of time to other attendees. It should also be made clear to them that they're expected to study the minutes to learn the tasks and roles for which they will be responsible.

Ensure that all language needs will be addressed.

As businesses become global, meeting languages sometimes expand beyond English. Be sure that you know the primary language of each attendee, and ensure that you or they provide interpreters for the meeting itself as well as for the meeting minutes to prevent any misunderstandings and miscommunication.

If you implement all these steps, you will become known for running efficient and productive meetings. People will show up prepared and will get to the point because they know that you won't let meetings drag on endlessly and pointlessly. And everybody loves that guy or gal.

NEXT STEPS

After about four meetings of the committee that I mentioned at the beginning of this chapter, I stopped going. I was called into my principal's office and asked why I wasn't participating. Being a wise guy (er, gal), I asked, "Participating in what?" I could tell by the look on his face that he didn't appreciate cynicism the way I did, so I stated, "Sir, I'm asked to go to a meeting for which there is no goal and at which there is nothing accomplished. I would rather use my time to create outstanding lessons for my students." His eyes narrowed. I waited for the admonishment, but how could he counter that? He didn't. I was excused from the committee.

To this day, when I'm invited to attend a meeting, I ask for a copy of the agenda. If there isn't one, I'll conveniently have a conflicting appointment and be unable to attend. (That appointment may be with an actual client, or it may be an appointment with myself to work on a high-value task or project. The host only needs to know that you have "an appointment.") Unfortunately, we can't always skip out of worthless meetings. If it's one of those "you must attend or else" meetings, and they don't provide an agenda, then I bring blank paper for capturing thoughts about any upcoming projects while a conversation full of nothingness spins around me. Instead of losing that time, I'm still managing to make progress in another area.

Ⅲ➡ PLOT YOUR NEXT STEPS

- Are there any meetings that are a waste of your time that you should no longer attend?
- If you are absolutely required to attend the above meetings, how can you make them more beneficial to yourself and everyone else there?
- How much time do you lose each week to coworkers, employees, or contractors interrupting you with questions or requests to help with their tasks or "emergencies"?
- What type of agenda would you like to have at your work team meetings?
- What type of agenda would you like to have at your personal team meetings? (These don't have to be as rigidly structured as your work team meetings, but your family still needs to arrive prepared.)

30 Delegate the Right Stuff to the Right People

My client Julie and I were in her office discussing all the different tasks that were pulling her brain away from what she does best — working billable client hours. Her gift helps her clients, her clients are happy, and she generates revenue, which makes her bank account and household happy.

But she had more "task hours" on her calendar than billable hours because she wouldn't farm out some of the work that needed to get done.

Suddenly, we were interrupted by a knock on the office door. A tree-trimming crew was cruising the area looking for jobs. She asked how much they would charge to trim every tree on the lot. She did not bat an eyelash when they said $2,300, and she immediately got out her checkbook.

She did not know them or their reputation or whether they even knew what they were doing. But she hired them on the spot.

When she returned to her chair, we continued our chat.

"How did it feel to get that task off your plate?" I asked her.

"Great!" exclaimed she.

"What made you decide to delegate that task?"

"Well, can you see me hanging off a ladder with a chain saw? I'd probably chop off one of my arms! Besides its being dangerous, I have no business using my time for that."

"I see you value your life and limb."

"Ha! Pun intended?"

"I see you value your time when it comes to delegating tasks that require heavy physical output or sweating."

"Yeah! Who wants to do that dirty stuff?"

"Do you value your mind the same way?"

Silence.

GOAL

Tell the control freak inside you to step aside. Tell the cheapskate inside you to put a lid on it. Take your task lists from your brainstorms in previous chapters and delegate your low-value work and/or personal tasks to others.

TACTICS

1. Grab your brainstorm and task lists from the exercises in previous chapters.
2. Determine which tasks absolutely need to get done, but not necessarily by you.
3. Categorize each of these tasks by the type of brain or personality that would be great at handling it.
4. For the work tasks, create job descriptions and responsibilities based on this division of labor.
5. Hire contractors or employees based on this, or create proposals for your employer based on this, or ask for help (delegate!) during your personal and work team meetings.

STRATEGY

You may tend to take what's in your brain for granted. You need to put a value on your intellect and your gifts. You know you're perfectly capable of completing almost every task necessary in your business — because it's your business — but is that the best use of your time? Delegate your chain saw and paper-pushing tasks so that you can use your genius for more important objectives — like growing your business and earning a comfortable living.

If you work for a company, your delegating may happen through restructuring tasks within your department or company or teaming up with a coworker to plow through projects more efficiently, based on the open communication during your company's staff or department meetings. If your company chooses not to implement these meetings, you can still work together with your appointed work team.

Additionally, whether you work for someone else or yourself, there's always room for saving yourself time by restructuring tasks and delegating on the *home* front.

My client Julie had a hard time wrapping her brain around delegating to other people. She had difficulty trusting people after getting burned on a few occasions. She had extremely high standards and was rarely satisfied with the quality of work — especially her own — so she was afraid of letting *someone else* do the work. She felt that no one could complete things the way she could. She also didn't want to spend time training someone because it was just easier to do it herself. She had no problem dropping some dollars on an outfit or a nice meal out or tree trimmers, but those purse strings would seal up like an oyster when it came to hiring someone for her business. She didn't want to shell out money for what she was capable of doing.

At the same time, Julie was spending money (and time) on doctors for:

her insomnia: she couldn't sleep from all her stress

her anxiety: she occasionally experienced anxiety attacks

her depression: she'd get down on herself because she'd freeze when she was overwhelmed and not getting anything done

her marriage: it was starting to crack from the pressure of her workaholic hours

Julie needed to get responsibilities off her plate if she was going to stay married... and sane.

Grab your brainstorm and task lists from the exercises in prior chapters.

From these brainstorms, you've discovered those high-value tasks on which you truly should be focused. By all means, add to and edit these as necessary before moving through the following strategies and tactics.

Determine which tasks absolutely need to get done,
but not necessarily by you.

Given the aforementioned brainstorms, what you've read in this book, and what you've been experiencing in your work life and personal life as you've been reading this book, you have probably come to the realization that not all ideas and projects on your "someday" list need to get done in order for you to have a successful career. They can remain on your someday list or get tossed.

But what about those low-value tasks (like inputting receipts into your accounting software) that must get done but are a waste of your precious billable client hours? In chapter 23, "Determine Your High-Value Work Responsibilities," you already separated these out. Revisit your list, and see if any revisions or additions need to be made.

Categorize each of these tasks by the type of brain or personality that would be great at handling it.

Many times my clients want to hire one half-time or full-time person who will do it all for them. The problem with that is we go back to the issue of expecting someone (this time, another person instead of yourself) to be omni-competent, as I discussed in chapter 26, "It's All in Your Head: It Takes a Village." Those folks are a rare find, one in a million, which are incredible odds against finding that one person who will take care of everything you need. That's why it's essential to categorize the tasks based on the talent, knowledge, and skills that a person needs, so you can match the tasks to the right person.

For example, you might need to hire for these various components:

Accounting: Inputting receipts, paying bills, running payroll, preparing numbers to hand over to your CPA at tax time, etc.

Marketing: Designing graphics and collateral for whatever campaigns you want to run — online, radio, print, trade shows, etc.

Website: Search engine optimization, security/anti-hacking, troubleshooting, etc.

Customer service: Answering incoming "first touch" phone calls and emails, giving overviews of company services, scheduling, etc.

Create job descriptions and responsibilities based on this division of labor.

You'll need to do more than create a job title. In order for you to hire the best person for the job, you'll need to develop an accurate job description, listing the type of work and deadlines that the hire would be responsible for meeting, as well as the characteristics that the person must have in order to represent your company. This is not something that is created in only 15 minutes. You want to think deeply about this. There's a saying, "Hire slow. Fire fast." Doing your research about the type of person you want to hire (along with good interviewing tactics and background checks) will help you avoid hiring a dud. Work on this project as you continue through the book.

Hire contractors or employees based on what you've just developed.

You'll need to consult with your tax and legal advisers to find out what is best for your specific situation. In an oversimplified nutshell, an employee must procedurally do everything you say and follow your operations manual. Contractors, on the other hand, are given a project and deadline and can complete it as they see fit. Many of my clients hire a combination — some part-time employees, some ongoing contractors, and some as-needed contractors for projects that pop up.

If you're a solopreneur and wish you had employees to delegate to so that you could go out of town on vacation without worries, consider hiring a temporary answering service or barter with a colleague (you'll take turns covering each other's incoming sales calls and emails while the other is out of town). This is the same idea as contracting out for projects that pop up.

If you're not self-employed, and you have no power within your company to make a hiring decision, you can use this chapter to help your department divvy up skills by brains and talents. If this division of labor still does not meet all your needs, you can work with your department colleagues on a proposal for your supervisor detailing what position/hire would streamline operations, lower stress, and increase revenue — thereby paying for the position itself. And if no one will listen to your genius about a more efficient division of labor or creating a hiring proposal, consider teaming up with an individual on your work team. Divide up tasks among yourselves, and help each other get through what needs to get done.

You can also use this same methodology on the home front. You can ask your family members for assistance with (delegate) tasks, or you might decide to hire out certain services. For example, a teacher client of mine was able to recruit her young children to clean up after themselves and straighten up their own rooms, which saved her time because she no longer picked up after them. She also decided to hire a cleaning lady to come every other Saturday. She had to tighten her purse strings a bit in order to pay for that service, but having two hours of time to grade her papers while her kids and the cleaning lady took care of the house afforded her uninterrupted relaxation time later in the day with her children. That was a worthwhile investment in her well-being.

NEXT STEPS

Julie and I discussed the basics of this chapter during two of our sessions, but the rest she completed as homework. She was able to figure out that she needed to hire the following:

Nanny/house manager: an employee who would handle child transportation, child care, and basic household pickup/straightening up from 8 AM to 5 PM. This would give Julie focus time so that she could be fully present with her kids and husband in the evening instead of only halfway paying attention to them and trying to squeeze in work here and there.

Home repair/maintenance: a contractor who would maintain the yard and pool and do basic home repairs as necessary.

Yes, this is a business productivity book. But Julie's first hires were related to her personal life because all those tasks were constantly interrupting her throughout the day as she tried to work in her home office. That's part of the reason why she never got anything done. Then she'd try to catch up with work in the evenings and would end up ignoring her family. With these two hires, she was able to set true work hours, focus on her business, and get things done — which allowed her to devote 100 percent of her attention to her family on evenings and weekends.

> I am not a product of my circumstances.
> I am a product of my decisions.
> *— Stephen Covey*

When those two positions were settled in, she was able to figure out whom she needed to hire for her business:

Bookkeeper (contracted through her CPA): She wasn't good with numbers, so even though she didn't have a lot of receipts and billing, it took up quite a bit of her time.

Graphic designer (contracted as needed): She would spend hours trying to perfect graphics for her articles and presentations. While she had an exquisite eye for art, her strength was in creating the content, not the graphics.

Once these folks were onboard, she determined how often team meetings were necessary. Her team meetings were actually one-on-ones with the individual hires, since it was rare that they'd all be working on the same project.

We agreed that she'd monitor the number of prospective clients who called or emailed to ask for information. If those numbers increased, or if her administrative task load increased, she would look into hiring an assistant. The added bonus of having an assistant was that there'd be somebody trained to handle things when she was gone — on vacation, out of town at a conference, or at her kids' games.

Because Julie was willing to invest time and money into finding the right work team to delegate to and train, she was able to cut back tremendously on the time and money spent going to her doctors, since she was no longer operating in a stress-filled vacuum. Yes, it takes time to hire the right people and train them. But Julie realized that she wasn't losing time on these steps; she was investing in her well-being.

While her expenses increased from needing to pay people, her *profit* increased because she was able to cut back on medical expenses, plus she was able to work more billable hours. That's music to my ears!

By the way, a fabulous book to help you navigate through the hiring process is *How to Choose the Right Person for the Right Job Every Time*, by Lori Davila and Louise Kursmark (McGraw-Hill Education, 2004). A colleague of mine, Erin Elizabeth Wells, told me about the book, and I refer my clients to it, if their company doesn't have a full-time HR department.

ⅢⅢ➤ PLOT YOUR NEXT STEPS

- How much time will you be able to save by removing unnecessary tasks from your life?
- How much time will you be able to save by delegating necessary but low-value tasks to others?
- Once you have the job description and characteristics hashed out, do you want to go through the hiring process on your own, or should you contract out to a company to do this for you?
- Keeping in mind that it can take several weeks to develop a job description, many more weeks to hire, and usually one to two months to train, what type of realistic timeline would you like to set for your hiring needs?
- If you work for a company, how will you apply the tactics from this chapter to help your colleagues restructure tasks and work more efficiently together on projects?
- Instead of, or in addition to, the previous question, how will you apply the tactics from this chapter to create a hiring proposal for your supervisor?

PART 4

SITUATIONAL SOLUTIONS

31

I Multitask, but I Still Can't Finish Everything

A few years back, shortly after my computer hard drive crashed, I was a little behind in printing my checks through my accounting system for the payment cycle. One of the checks I needed to create was for BK&A Advertising, who'd invoiced me the week before, after creating an updated version of my business cards. I was pretty sure they wanted their money ASAP. To save time, I decided to answer emails while waiting for each check to go through the printer.

I saved time because while my next email was loading (I have a slow internet connection), I would shift my attention to the next step of the bill-paying process. When the email finished loading, I'd leave the bill paying and return my attention to the email. Back and forth. Back and forth. In those moments, I thought I was saving a lot of time. After all, I was doing something productive during the page loading. Looking back at it, I probably saved a total of about five minutes.

Fast-forward to the email I received a week later from BK&A when I checked my phone between client appointments:

Hi Helene,

I gave your check to our Finance team when I got back from the meeting, and they pointed out to me that the check wasn't signed.

Do you want me to mail it over to you for a signature? Do you want me to come by your office? Let me know what works for you and we will get it all worked out.

Thank you!
Ryan

Feeling like a total doofus and at that moment being only 10 minutes away from their office (and not wanting them to wait on funds any longer), I drove over there. Ten minutes to get there. A few minutes to chat with Ryan. Ten minutes back.

Total time spent: approximately 25 minutes.

Time previously saved: 5 minutes.

Total time lost: 20 minutes.

So much for saving time by multitasking.

I would love to be able to tell you that multitasking will save the day, but it will actually do the opposite. There are a few instances when it can help (I'll give examples shortly), but the majority of the time, multitasking hurts us. Just read the research on it.

GOAL

Single-task: Focus on only one task at a time, even if it's for only 15 minutes.

TACTICS

1. Build up your awareness, so that you can stop yourself before you multitask.
2. Have a plan for your day.
3. Determine your attention span.
4. Discover your best brain time.
5. Find a productive work area.
6. Clear your desk of all materials except what you need.
7. Use a timer to keep you laser-focused.
8. Post your objective in your work area.
9. Take breaks.
10. Celebrate focused time.

STRATEGY

A team of researchers from the University of Glasgow, University of Leeds, and University of Hertfordshire found that our effectiveness drops by 69 percent for women and 77 percent for men when we multitask or task-switch! It's more proof that the multitasking we were told to strive for in the 1990s is definitely not one of the time management tools we should engage.

Multitasking splits the brain in two. If there is only one task, the entire brain is used. If there are two tasks, the brain divides into two parts, and each half works on one task. If there are more than two simultaneous tasks, the brain can't work. We actually give ourselves ADD-like symptoms when we multitask!

> How can you tweet and watch the [Super Bowl] commercials at the same time? That's right, you can't.
>
> — *Greg Toohey, @gregtoohey, February 2, 2014, via Twitter*

A study at the University of California, Irvine, found that when tasks get fragmented and task switching occurs, it takes workers up to 25 minutes to return to the original task, if they return at all. Participants in the study reported that this way of working stinks.

Even scarier is the fact that many of the folks in the studies I'm referring to were self-professed "expert multitaskers." They felt that they were able to accomplish multiple tasks, could do a good job, and often enjoyed the adrenaline rush from trying to do so much at once. They didn't realize how poorly they actually performed until being shown their single-tasking results versus their multitasking results. Bottom line: We think we're good at juggling, but we're not.

I believe that humans are capable of multitasking with *low*-function brain skills. "Low-function" means that thinking is not required because there is some kind of rote action (automatic, nonthinking movements) being applied. Examples:

Painting your toenails while listening to the play-by-play of the Dallas Cowboys choking yet again

Shredding papers during commercials while watching television

Gossiping on the phone while stirring a pot of chili on the stove

If you've done it often enough, painting your nails doesn't take thought, so it can be completed while listening to something. If you have your shred pile next to your chair, shredding is a no-brainer activity you can complete while watching or listening to something. Gossiping takes some brainpower because you have to pay attention to who's doing what in the stories, but stirring is a mindless, rote action, so both can be done at the same time.

It's also easy to let a task run in the background while you concentrate on a task in the forefront. This is technically not multitasking because your brain isn't working on two things at once. I call this ghost-tasking. Examples:

Cleaning the house while a load of laundry is in the washer or dryer

Emptying dishes from the dishwasher while your oatmeal is heating up in the microwave

Filing papers while your PC takes forever (okay, five minutes) to boot up

You don't have to physically do anything or think once you've hit start on an appliance, so another task can be completed while the appliance is running. Filing papers requires concentration if you want to put them in the right spot. Waiting for your computer to warm up takes zero brainpower after you hit the start button, so a task can be worked on during this wait period.

But as the research shows, we are incapable of multitasking well when it comes to *high*-function brain operations. We cannot complete two tasks effectively at the same time or while switching back and forth. We can do both tasks at mediocre levels, but not at exceedingly good ones because we are not using our whole brain and focusing on only one task at a time. And this costs us time and causes us stress in the long run.

So what do I mean about multitasking high-brain-function activities? You shouldn't do two things at once that require thought or concentration, or switch back and forth in the midst of working on two tasks that require your brain to do some thinking — no matter how unimportant you believe the thoughts might be. Examples:

Driving and texting/emailing

Participating in an important business call while checking email

Checking email in between completing different components of bill paying or creating proposals or reports

Even if you've been driving for 50 years, driving is not a rote function. It requires split-second decisions to be made, especially if there's an idiot driving next to you. Texting — yes, even LOL IMHO — requires your brain to read what someone communicated with you, think of a response, and relay to your fingers what to type back. You can't do both well at the same time. Just ask someone who's been involved in a car accident with a driver who was using his/her smartphone.

Checking email — no matter how trivial the message might be — is a high-brain-function task because you need to read, process the information, and respond. An important business call requires thought and responses. The bill-paying process is a high-brain-function task because you need to pay the correct entity the correct amount, sign off, and make sure that the payment gets delivered to the correct place. In my earlier story, I attempted to task-switch between these high-brain-function tasks, which is why I wound up making a mistake...which cost me time later on.

Think about this: if you were to multitask and/or task-switch for one hour, according to the research, your performance would drop by 69 to 77 percent, which means that you would waste about 45 minutes of your time. That's where time disappears! *We let ourselves do this!*

If you want to lower your job performance by more than two-thirds and lose time in the process, the best way to do that is to continue to allow yourself to multitask and task-switch. But you don't want that, do you? You're here to save time and lower your stress levels. Your ghost-tasking can continue, but the multitasking and task switching need to end. Now. And you're in total control of this because it's your decision.

Here are the strategies behind the tactics.

Build up your awareness.

When you find yourself moving into multitask or task-switching mode, tell yourself to stop. Say it out loud if you need to. *"Stop!"* Choose one task to focus on for the next 15 minutes.

Have a plan for your day.

Knowing exactly what you need to accomplish that day will help you to stay focused and prevent multitasking. See chapter 9, "Get It All Done in 24 Hours: Turn To-Do Lists into *Done* Lists," for how to create a plan and your 3+3.

Determine your attention span.

Whether you have ADD, ADHD, or Squirrel! (the humorous tag — possibly originating from the 2009 movie *Up* — used by many to denote the affliction of those who are easily distracted), we all have shorter attention spans nowadays — especially if we're working on something that isn't fun. Start timing how long you're able to work on a single task. Having an estimated number will help you establish your work flow. (My attention span is only nine minutes on boring tasks.)

Discover your best brain time.

Our brains tend to function at high levels during some parts of the day and lower levels at other times. It's during these low times that our brains tend to go into multitask mode because they're too tired to stay focused. Avoid working on your most critical tasks during your low-brain times of the day.

Find a productive work area.

Sometimes we accidentally task-switch because we get distracted. (Squirrel!) When you have an important project to work on, find a space without visual (striking art pieces, piles of clutter, computer screen) or auditory distractions (talking, music, message indicator on your phone or computer).

Clear your desk of all materials except what you need.

You might have multiple projects due, but you can work effectively on only one at a time. Put away the materials for all other projects, and keep visible on your desk only the materials that apply to the single project on which you'll focus during this work period.

Use a timer to keep you laser-focused.

You can pick a random number like 8 or 15 minutes. Better yet, if you know your attention span, set the timer to that number. The timer is a visual reminder that you're supposed to be working on something. It's also your fail-safe. If you have wandered away, the timer will rein you back in when it goes off.

Post your objective in your work area.

In addition to or instead of a timer, consider posting your task objective so that each time you look up to allow your brain to wander, your posted objective reminds you of what you're supposed to be working on.

Take breaks.

Everyone's brain tires at a different rate. When you feel your brainpower start to go downhill (less energy, harder to concentrate), your brain will become more susceptible to making not-so-great decisions about your time. So give your brain a break once every hour or two. Go for a short walk, do some deep breathing, go have some fun. But set your timer for when it's time to return!

Celebrate focused time.

Reflect on how powerful your brain was while you were concentrating. Celebrate by smiling, throwing your hands in the air like you just don't care, or even doing a little happy dance. This will create endorphins. The body craves endorphins. When the brain associates your focus with celebration and endorphins, it will crave more focus. Get addicted to focus!

If you find yourself moving into multitasking or task switching because:

- **your ideas distract you,** flip over to chapter 33
- **of interruptions,** hop over to chapter 34
- **you're doing busywork to avoid something else,** head on over to chapter 36
- **you never develop a plan for each day,** reread chapters 8 through 10, "Assignment and Task Completion"

NEXT STEPS

I almost fell out of my chair laughing when I read the following quote in an article in the *Philadelphia Business Journal* ("Tinder for Friends: Penn Students Ditch School for Startup," by Lauren Hertzler) about a group of four University of Pennsylvania students who were in the midst of starting up a company called Down to Chill. Michael Powell, one of the students, told the reporter:

> Between classes, exams, clubs, teams and performing arts groups, it would be impossible to optimize our performance in both [school activities and starting up a business]; there would necessarily have to be sacrifices.... For us, it was obvious that if we wanted to see how far this startup could go, we would have to free up our commitments. Why half-ass a bunch of things when you can whole-ass one?

He nailed it! Why half-ass? Why not whole-ass one task at a time? Amen, brother!

> Why half-ass a bunch of things when you can whole-ass one?
>
> — Michael Powell

From here on out, we're whole-assing. Single-tasking. One task at a time, even if that focus is for only 15 minutes. Fifteen minutes of laser focus is far better than one hour of multitasking and task switching, during which we'd lose about 45 minutes. Hey! You could laser-focus for 15 minutes, then knock off or exercise or take a nap for the other 45 instead! It's the same amount of time, but you can get so much more done when you make the decision to single-task.

ⅢⅢ➤ PLOT YOUR NEXT STEPS

- If you multitask or task-switch, what are the common causes?
- How long is your attention span?
- When is your best brain time?
- Where is your most productive work area?
- What steps will you take to cut back on multitasking and task switching?
- How will implementing the strategies and tactics in this chapter benefit you?

32 My Brain Is Constantly in Overdrive

Which describes you?

Type A: You're driven.

Type A/O: You're beyond driven. You're constantly going, going, going… but not necessarily going forward and getting things done.

If you're type A/O, you're type A on overdrive. You cannot shut off your brain when it comes to your job. You live it, eat it, breathe it.

Have you ever noticed signs on fast-food establishments and corner stores that are open for business 24/7?

Always Open

That pretty much sums up a typical go-getter's brain. It's your blessing and your curse.

GOAL

Realize that spending time on work constantly throughout the day and night prevents your brain from fully functioning. Be willing to create a life outside of work.

TACTICS

1. Set business hours for your brain.
2. Schedule break times.
3. Schedule play days.
4. Come up with nonbusiness conversation topics.
5. Develop a second obsession — but one that is not business related.
6. If it applies, get help with relationship challenges.
7. If it applies, deal with the condition of your home.

STRATEGY

If you're a go-getter and head over heels into what you do for a living, your job is your baby, so you're always thinking about how to take better care of it, how to nurture it and help it grow, how to make it better. In the evenings before bed, you might grab your laptop and work "for just a few more minutes." Before you know it, it's the wee hours of the morning.

You bring your laptop or tablet on vacation to finish up a project, or catch up on work, or get ahead of the game.

In extreme cases, all you talk about with people is business. All you read about is business. When your friend or significant other is attempting to have a conversation with you about another topic, you somehow bring it back to business.

Our obsession with work can drive others away, especially those closest to us with whom we feel like we can share everything. Our addiction to running and growing our business or advancing our career can prevent us from making a better life with our loved ones — the very reason why many people decide to start a business or climb the corporate ladder in the first place.

Outside of brain overdrive, one other reason I've found as to why clients operate 24/7 is that work allows them to avoid problems at home. This could be an issue with their spouse or significant other, the condition of their house, or a situation with their child, a parent, a roommate, or another individual occupying space in their home. As the problem has gotten worse, their work hours have increased. They dread discussing the problem because they want to avoid any possibility of confrontation. But in the meantime, this lack of communication allows the problem to grow exponentially. If this rings even remotely true in your case, please do seek help as soon as possible.

Set business hours for your brain.

My husband used to call me a PC junkie. You might remember from chapter 22, "Schedule around Your Personal Priorities and Targets," that he was upset because I'd just come to the kitchen when I was called for dinner, and then go straight back to my computer to work some more. He rarely saw me even though we were in the same house. That's not a fun way to live. So business hours were set.

Your brain will focus on business from X-time to Y-time. I use X and Y because not everyone works from eight to five. You'll have to decide what hours you'll work. If you're on carpool patrol for your kids, your business brain time might be spread throughout the day.

Schedule break times.

Cardiologists will tell you that you need to get up and walk around at least once each hour in order to keep your circulatory system healthy. Similarly, your brain needs some downtime in order to stay functional. Research shows that taking a 5- to 10-minute break each hour helps the brain stay fit and productive.

If you can work for 50 minutes straight, take a break for the last 10 minutes of the hour. If you can't maintain focus for that long, work for 25 minutes, then break for 5. Or work for 12 and break for 3. Seriously.

Schedule play days.

Americans are known around the world for being work-aholics. There's nothing wrong with working hard, but your brain will benefit from vacation days. Why do you come up with your best ideas when you're sitting on the toilet or taking a shower? Because your brain is not thinking about anything. It's relaxed. Can you imagine what creativity you could experience if you allowed your brain to relax for a *whole day*? Or what about a whole *week*? Heck, what about a whole *month*?

All right, all right. I know we can't take an entire month off from work (orrrrrrr maybe we can, but that's later, after we take back control of our days); however, for the sake of healthy brain functioning, we do need

> Rest is not idleness, and to lie sometimes on the grass under the trees on a summer's day, listening to the murmur of water, or watching the clouds float across the blue sky, is by no means a waste of time.
>
> — *John Lubbock, "Recreation," The Use of Life, 1894*

to allow our brains to take time away from work for more than five minutes at a time. Our brains need to be able to relax so that they will be able to come up with the next great thing for work.

In the meantime, start toying with the idea of taking a half day for play time! Not only will your brain thank you, but you'll feel empowered because you made it happen.

Come up with nonbusiness conversation topics.

It might be hard at first to turn your business brain off, so it's helpful to have three topics on standby to help you get through conversations. If you get stuck, try these three:

- What kind of day did you have?
- Who's the most interesting person you've ever met?
- What's on your bucket list?

Develop a second obsession — but one that is not business related.

What might a second obsession be? Well, what do you enjoy doing?

Cooking?
Watching movies?
Skydiving?
Working out?
Tasting wines?
Reading?
Spending time with your significant other?
Spending time with your children?

I'll bet that if you think long and hard, you'll find at least one activity in which you can participate when it's time to give your work brain a rest.

NEXT STEPS

Ironically, by obsessing over our jobs for 24 hours per day, we don't allow our brains to take a break and recharge, so it actually takes us longer to finally hit on a new idea or come up with a solution for a challenge. To be more effective, we need to slow down our brains.

ⅢⅢ➤ PLOT YOUR NEXT STEPS

- What are your work hours?
- What are your possible work/break times?
- When is your first possible play day (or half day)?
- What are some nonbusiness conversation topics you can have on standby?
- What are some possible future nonwork obsessions?
- How will implementing the strategies and tactics in this chapter benefit you?

33 I've Got Brainus Interruptus and Ideas Overload

Imagine this scenario: You and a potential client are sitting at a neutral location — a local coffee shop. You've researched every possible facet about this person, the company she works for, and the project she —

I need to create a follow-up system for my customers once per month so that I can keep track of their needs plus keep them engaged in —

What was it that I needed to add to my grocery list? Was it something for a salad, or was it for —

I totally forgot to call back Dolores. Man, she is going to be so upset! She'll think I'm a flake if I don't —

Egad!

One word that's become synonymous with this condition is *Squirrel!* While I dislike tree rats because of the damage they did when breaking and entering my house and eventually becoming squatters in my attic, I do have to defend those plague-carrying vermin. Have you ever watched a squirrel focus on acquiring, then eating, a nut? It's pretty impressive.

But I digress. Squirrel!

Go-getters are blessed and cursed with ideas that constantly pop into the brain. This brainus interruptus prevents us from achieving our best.

GOAL

Make focusing on the present your priority. Be prepared to capture the random thoughts that pop into your head, and get back to living and working in the present.

TACTICS

1. Focus on one task at a time.
2. Complete a Mind Liberation.
3. Arm yourself with your brainus interruptus deflector shield.

STRATEGY

When your brain tries to store too much information, it starts swirling around all those tidbits. Your brain is afraid that you'll forget something because you haven't captured it in another location. So it'll throw that idea to the forefront while you're trying to work on something else. It's kind of like having a puppy. Your puppy will come over and try to jump in your lap as if to say, "Hi! I'm here! Don't forget about me!" You acknowledge her, and then set her down and get back to what you were doing. Then 10 minutes later, she'll come back again to remind you, "I'm still here! Don't forget about me!"

> Control your own destiny or somebody else will.
>
> — Jack Welch

When you have a number of irons in multiple fires, your brain may not understand which iron goes in which fire, so it brings out all sorts of irons, which becomes confusing. So if you're working on project A for client B and proposal C for client D while also juggling event E for colleague F, your brain can become a tangled mess.

Add in the fact that if you don't have a trustworthy system for remembering to do things or remembering ideas, your brain will continue to bombard you with thoughts and ideas. Like that puppy, your brain thinks it's doing a good thing by constantly trying to remind you of what you've got going on. The problem is that when it keeps doing this, you can't get anything done. And you forget things because the mental tornado just spins faster and faster. And because you forget things, your brain spits out even more at you in hopes that the faster it spits, the less you'll forget. But it doesn't work that way. Instead, your brain overheats, and you shut down. Then nothing gets done.

When you try to work on whatever task that pops into your brain at the time, you end up doing a haphazard job. Since your brain isn't fully focused, it continues to throw more thoughts and ideas at you, thereby prolonging brainus interruptus.

An overall goal is to keep your head as empty as possible. By getting all the stuff out of your head and onto paper or your computer, you'll cut back on the brainus interruptus. If you do this at the end of each day, you'll also sleep better.

How should you deal with brainus interruptus?

Focus on one task at a time.

Even if it's for only 10 minutes, 10 focused minutes are far better than 50 brain-spinning minutes. Hmmm...but how can you make your brain stop spinning to make this happen? You can...

Complete a Mind Liberation.

You're a big dreamer. Successful businesspeople make those dreams happen. How can you manage what's going on up in that brain of yours in order to be productive and blaze a trail? How can you create the mind clarity to make better decisions? Complete a Mind Liberation. A great time to do this is during your 3+3 time.

Unload all your worries, projects, and to-do's onto a sheet of paper or into your phone, tablet, or computer. Liberate your mind! You'll want to do this on a daily basis, or at the very least at the end of the week. (But I reeeeeally encourage you to do it daily because this will clear out more space in your brain more often.) Use your Mind Liberations to help you with your 3+3 for the next day, or set reminders for longer-term projects and task ideas.

Arm yourself with your brainus interruptus deflector shield.

Let's say that brainus interruptus kicks in before your evening Mind Liberation takes place. Or you get a grand idea during your nonbusiness hours because your brain is experiencing clarity and, therefore, creates magic from out of the blue. In a perfect world, your brain would realize that you don't want it interrupted, so it would file away that thought until Mind Liberation time. But it's not a perfect world. And you're a go-getter with go-getter brain, so it's unrealistic to hope that your brain will stop making ideas while you're alive.

You'll need a place to park your random and not-so-random thoughts until it's time to address that particular topic. Therefore, it will be important for you to find a brainus interruptus deflector shield. This is a tool you will use to capture your thoughts, ideas, and musings...whatever pops into your head when you're supposed to be working on or doing something else.

There's no perfect deflector shield, so you'll need to choose a thought-capture mechanism that works best for you and is in your possession at all times. You can use apps on your mobile device or software on your computer. If you prefer nondigital tools, notebooks, spirals, or sticky notes will work. See chapter 20, "Take Notes Anytime, Anywhere — and Never Lose Them," for a list of tools. If necessary, grab scrap papers if there's nothing else around.

I use a combination. For short thoughts, I email myself from my phone. For longer thoughts, I'm not particularly adept at typing on my phone, so I carry an old-school three-by-four-inch spiral notebook. When I'm chillin' on my back porch enjoying a gin and tonic, I might remember that I need to call a client. So I reach over to my pen and notebook, jot down my thought, and go back to chillin'. I'm off the clock, so I need to focus on relaxation. In situations where it would be inappropriate to have a device out, I use the spiral. If I'm in the middle of a meeting with a client and genius hits me, I practice the same concept. I might be on the clock, but I owe that person in front of me my respect and my full attention, so I capture the key words of the thought within a few seconds and then give my complete attention to the person in front of me. On vacation, same thing. While hiking the Camino de Santiago in Spain, I came up with the topic for my previous book. I quickly jotted down the thought and then turned my focus back to enjoying the beauty in front of me. During my note-processing time, I gather up these musings and farm them out to my CRM system, calendar, or reminder system.

NEXT STEPS

As long as you're a go-getter, you'll always have some type of thoughts. As you work through the strategies and tactics in this book, eventually the rate at which your brain tosses out these thought spears at you will slow down. It's not that your brain won't work anymore. No, it's even better. Your brain will eventually learn how to calm down and think things through — filter out the extemporaneous stuff that might throw off quality thoughts — and deliver fewer but higher-quality thoughts for you to capture.

⦚⦚⦚➤ PLOT YOUR NEXT STEPS

- How often do random thoughts or ideas interrupt your train of thought?
- Often we stay on autopilot and don't realize that we've completely switched tasks and are now working on that new thought or idea. How will you recognize that this interruption is occurring?
- What capture mechanism will you use for your brainus interruptus deflector shield?
- How will implementing the strategies and tactics in this chapter benefit you?

34 | I Am Constantly Interrupted or Distracted

One Saturday morning many moons ago, I was creating a draft for an article I was asked to contribute to a women's empowerment blog. My husband kept coming into the room to ask questions; or he'd thought of something he'd forgotten to tell me earlier, and he needed to share it before he forgot again. While I love seeing him, I got nothing done because of the constant interruptions.

Factor in that I had all sorts of ideas popping into my head and thoughts about other things I needed to do, and I was distracted throughout the entire morning.

My husband is an English teacher, so every few weeks he has 150 essays to grade. Those essays come home with him in the evening or on the weekend, and he gets them done within a few days. That particular Saturday afternoon, he dove headfirst into one of his grading projects. I had chucked my writing to the side, since I hadn't accomplished anything all morning.

I came into the room often to ask him questions or to tell him something I'd thought of that I'd forgotten to tell him earlier, and I needed to share it with him before I forgot again. He was able to finish grading only a small fraction of the essays because of all the interruptions.

I wasn't intentionally trying to sabotage him. I was just operating based on my needs and my schedule, not his. He did the same in the morning. And neither of us communicated with the other to stop.

GOAL

Set boundaries for when interruptions cannot occur, and clearly communicate this to your teams.

TACTICS

Minimize Self-Interruptions

1. Turn off all indicators on your phone.
2. Turn off all indicators on your tablet.
3. Turn off all indicators on your computer.
4. Set times for when you'll check communications.
5. Remove visual distractions from your work area.
6. Remove auditory distractions from your work area.
7. Choose your idea-capture tool.
8. Post your 3+3 for the day.
9. Post your personal priorities and targets.
10. Post your work priorities and targets.
11. Set your timer for 10 minutes at a time of focused work.
12. Schedule in hourly breaks.

Minimize External Interruptions

1. Clearly state your work hours to all involved parties.
2. Post your office hours on your door.
3. Ask those who interrupt you anyway to come back during your office hours.

STRATEGY

Googling "research on interruptions at work" will bring up studies that show the following:

- The average adult receives 110 phone notifications per day.
- Checking our smartphones is addictive and equivalent to receiving a hit of dopamine.
- We lose an average of one minute every time we switch from one task to another.
- It can take up to 25 minutes to hunker back down into a project after an interruption.

When you stop to think about how many times we allow interruptions to occur, it's truly mind-boggling. And because we can control so much of this, it is an area of our lives in which we can instantly win back time.

Those of us who allow our phones to chime, whistle, or vibrate with every incoming call or message are taking our focus away from our task. We lose an average of one minute of brain re-start time with every occurrence. If the average person receives 110 phone notifications per day, and if you're allowing your phone to tell you when these occur, then you're losing 110 minutes per day just in brain-restart time. Holy stop-loss, Batman! That's over an hour and a half each day down the drain!

Because we receive that hit of dopamine each time we check, we've basically turned ourselves into junkies. Would you allow your best friend to go out and buy heroin so that she or he could feel that high? Of course not! Your friends would flush their money down the toilet on the drugs. They would lose track of time and start being less responsible. They would increase the risk of doing themselves bodily harm with each use. But we do the same thing to ourselves by letting our gadgets run our day. We lose time and money by spending hours with our noses buried in our devices. This loss of time and money causes us stress when we realize at the end of the day that we haven't done everything we were supposed to. This stress does us bodily harm in a variety of ways. Say no to drugs. Say no to this self-allowed interruption.

And that's just gadget interruptions! What about people? We let our colleagues, friends, family members, and coworkers interrupt us all the time. We also get distracted by the thoughts and ideas swirling around in our heads. But that, ladies and gentlemen, is about to change.

Distractions are caused by two types of interruptions: self-interruptions and external interruptions. Let's first take a look at the mind-set we need for dealing with the self-interruptions.

Minimize Self-Interruptions

Disruptive Devices

If you want to instantly save 90-plus minutes per day, you'll turn off all indicators on your phone, tablet, and computer. That's right. No more little dings, rings, whistles, or vibrations when emails, texts, phone calls, or social media posts arrive. Egad! Will you be able to survive this? Yes. Because instead of getting your highs from looking at that tech gadget, you'll get your highs from finishing your task lists! High five!

Now, am I telling you never to check? Absolutely not. Simply check when your brain is focused and prepared to accept and deal with the communications coming in. You might be able to get away with checking only twice a day — early morning and end of day. Or you might have a job that requires you to check once per hour. The whole idea is to check when you are ready, not when you're interrupted.

The same rings true for phone time. (*Rings true!* Get it?) When you ask someone to call you, give him or her a specific time when you'll be by your phone to accept the call. If you pick up the phone every time it rings, that's no different than leaving your email indicator on.

Unconducive Work Environment

Clutter can be a huge distraction. If we know there is a pile sitting there that needs our attention — and we've let it sit for weeks — subconsciously, our brains get distracted by the guilt or worry and lose focus on the task at hand. We lose time when we do this.

We can also lose time by daydreaming while staring at all the mementos, photos, inspirational quotes, and other items we use to decorate our work areas. You don't want naked walls because that's boring and uninspiring, but you also don't want the opposite — where every spot on a wall or shelf is filled with decor. Make sure you can see open wall space, open desk space, and open shelf space. Our brains sense opportunity when we see open spaces and tend to think better when they're in that mode.

Likewise, the sounds in our work environment can also affect how efficiently we use our time. Our favorite talk shows may slow us down because we spend more time listening than working. Pay attention to how focused you are when certain sounds are present. You might need to cut back on piping in music or talk radio, or you might find that you need to wear earbuds or headphones the whole day to keep other distracting sounds out.

Objectives Not in Our Consciousness

One reason we procrastinate or let ourselves get interrupted is because we're not sure what we're supposed to work on next. Even if you have a million things you know need to get done, that overwhelm from so much to do might prevent your brain from logically pulling out the next step to complete. This is why it's important to post your daily objectives. If you know what you need to get done by when, you're less likely to allow the interruption to occur. Planning your 3+3 will help you with this.

Priorities and Targets Not in Our Consciousness

When you have posted right in front of you your priorities and targets, it's a reminder of what the big picture is — what you're working toward. When you start to allow an interruption to take place, you'll be able to look at your priorities and targets list and ask yourself, "Will allowing this interruption to happen help support me in my quest to achieve _____?"

Mental Tornado

Even if you don't have ADD or ADHD, it can be tough to focus. We can have a lot of stuff swirling around up there. Having a place where we can capture these seemingly random thoughts and ideas will help us return to focus more quickly. (See previous chapter for details.) Having a timer will help us narrow our vision to the task at hand because we're working against the clock. Set your timer for 10 minutes at a time. Ten minutes of focused time is far better than an hour of haphazard work. When you feel that your attention span is increasing, you can set the timer for longer. Laser focus and working against the clock will help you to block out tempting interruptions.

Fried Brains

We're humans, not mechanical creatures or robots. We need to take breaks. In a perfect world, you'd take a break at least once per hour. Cardiologists would be happy if you walked for five minutes per hour to maintain good circulation. Nutritionists would be happy if you drank water once each hour to stay hydrated. Neuroscientists would be happy if you let your brain charge once per hour by taking these breaks. So, if you can, schedule a break once per hour.

Since we don't live in a perfect world, you might not be able to schedule breaks at exact times. So perhaps you can recharge after you check each item off your list. Or, if you feel some procrastination or interruptions coming on, and it's been a while since you took a break, then turn the interruption into a break.

Obviously, you can't do this 10 times per hour, but if you've had your head buried for an hour, your brain probably needs to recharge.

Minimize External Interruptions

Phones and Computers

While technically the gadgets we work with are external to our minds and bodies, the interruptions they perpetrate are allowed by us, so that makes them self-interruptions. See the previous section in this chapter about how to control those interruptions.

Work Environment

As with the phones, computers, and gadgets, while technically the environment in which we work is external to our minds and bodies, the distractions that crop up are allowed by us, so that makes them self-interruptions. See the previous section in this chapter about how to control those interruptions.

People at Home

During that Saturday I described in the beginning of this chapter, my husband and I initially were irritated with each other since we'd accomplished next to nothing during an entire day. But then we realized, how is one person supposed to know not to bother the other?

Since then, we've agreed that we'll tell each other our schedules of when we're doing concentrated brainwork and can't be interrupted. Any questions or comments we have get written down and saved until the agreed-upon break time.

If you own your own business or telecommute, it's very tempting for everyone in the house to think they can waltz right into your home office whenever they have a question. After all, you're in your sweats in the comfort of your home. The key is to set business hours — and let your family know about it. Remind them when you see them in the morning what your work (a.k.a. do-not-disturb) schedule is, and post it on your door as well. Set expectations for what constitutes an emergency, for which interruption is allowable. *The house is on fire?* Yes, that's an emergency. *You need $20 for gas?* That is not an emergency. It's their responsibility to plan ahead.

Better yet, have a powwow / team meeting with your family each day or evening in order to find out what everyone needs to get done the next day. You can devise a schedule during which there's uninterrupted work time for everyone at the same time, so that no one is bothering anyone.

Even one hour — just one hour — of uninterrupted time will yield you monumental productivity. You'll get more done in one hour of concentration than you will in three hours of constant interruptions. If you truly value your time, you will guard this hour. Then you'll have two extra hours to play. Yeah, baby!

People at Work

Do the same thing as at home. Set your work hours. Remind your coworkers or employees each morning what time you'll need uninterrupted, complex brain time, and post this on your office door or cubicle wall. If you can swing three or four hours, terrific! But swing at least one hour of a no-interruption zone. Your fully functioning brain and lowered stress levels will thank you. Set expectations for what constitutes an emergency, for which interruption is allowable. Let everyone know when you'll have your open-door office hour (or two) to answer whatever questions came up during the day.

Better yet, have a powwow / team meeting with your crew one day per week to find out what everyone needs to get done in the next several days. You can devise a schedule during which there's uninterrupted work time for everyone at the same time, so that no one is bothering anyone — if this is feasible. If not, at least everyone knows each other's do-not-disturb times. Taking 30 minutes to have this team meeting once per week will save you hours during the following week because you won't have so many doggone interruptions. See chapter 29, "Facilitate Productive Team Meetings," for a sample agenda for these types of team meetings.

What to Do with People Who Insist on Interrupting You

If they were present at your meeting during which you announced when your do-not-disturb time was, you can say politely, "Sign on the door. Stated at the meeting. Do not disturb, please. Come back at x:oo."

If you hear the word "But," look up immediately and say, "We discussed what constitutes an emergency. Did X happen? Did Y happen? No? Please come back at x:oo."

Will this conversation take longer than it probably would to answer their questions? Yes. But you should have to do it only once or twice, and then they'll realize that you're extremely serious about this crazy "do not disturb" thing. If you do answer them, you're teaching them that what you say doesn't matter and you are glad to be interrupted at any time.

Now, if you need to have this "come back later" conversation with them more than twice, you'll need to make an appointment with them to come back later to discuss their language barrier. Seriously. You need to get to the bottom of their lack of understanding; otherwise, they'll continue to interrupt you. And if they continue to interrupt you and are allowed to get away with it, others will start to interrupt you, too. Then you'll be back to where you started.

At this point, if you're saying to yourself, "Jiminy Christmas! Do I really have to be such a stickler to have just one uninterrupted hour of work each day?"

The answer is no, you don't, if you want to continue to be interrupted and stressed and overworked.

What to Do with People Who Don't Know about Your Office Hours

Maybe they're new on the scene and were never at your initial meeting, during which you explained that you were saving time and becoming more productive by reducing interruptions.

Ask if you can talk to them later, and explain your productivity practice. If you don't feel this approach will fly with the individual, set your timer for five minutes and meet them at the door to explain things. If you let them sit in your office, they might not leave for a long time. Gently explain something to the effect of this:

"I've learned some life lessons along the way, and I realize how important it is to _____ (fill in the blank: spend time with family, take care of my health, etc.). In order for me to do this, I have to become more efficient at work. I discovered that interruptions were taking up a lot of my time, so I set aside one hour a day of uninterrupted work time to get more done. I'd really love your help with this. Would you mind coming back at x:00 so that I can improve my health?"

Dude! Who would back-talk you if you said that? And if they did, do you really want to spend time with that type of person?

⟫➤ PLOT YOUR NEXT STEPS

- How much time can you gain back daily just by cutting down on interruptions?
- How does allowing constant interruptions support your progress toward your priorities and targets? (That's right! It's a trick question!)
- What constitutes a true emergency at home? (Think life or death.)
- What constitutes a true emergency at work? (Think life or death for your job.)
- If someone tells you that this focused-work stuff is stupid, what is something you can say to get him or her out of your hair?

35 When Crap Happens, I Go into a Tailspin

One fine, sunny day, I experienced a trifecta crap storm.

I was informed by a potential long-term corporate client that she had decided to go with someone uncertified, less experienced, and cheaper.

My husband found out that his PSA (a measurement taken in a prostate cancer screening) had gone from .01 to over 5.0 in one year. (The PSA should be under 5 and certainly not jump by this much.) Given the history of three men in his immediate family who'd been diagnosed with prostate cancer, this was alarming.

We had to unexpectedly put one of our dogs to sleep.

Yeah, it was one of those days. But it's not the news that determines how you'll fare. It's your reaction to these situations that determines what will happen.

GOAL

When the unexpected happens, face it with positivity and blunt-force decision making.

TACTICS

1. Review your personal priorities.
2. Review your personal targets.

3. Review your work priorities.
4. Review your work targets.
5. Acknowledge that what's just happened is not what you wanted. Give yourself 30 minutes of venting and tantrum time.
6. Figure out how much control you have over the situation, and adjust your anger/anxiety/pissiness accordingly.
7. Decide what outcome you'd like to change it to.
8. Map out the steps to make it happen.
9. Determine what resources you'll need to make it happen.
10. Readjust your time blocks if necessary.

STRATEGY

I was initially super-disappointed about losing the client contract. But I've learned that folks who look at price only and not the quality of the person end up being disappointed with their choice. I had no control over her decision making, so I needed to let that go. I cussed out the world for a few minutes, and then dropped the subject.

My husband's PSA results sent my stress levels skyrocketing. His father, oldest brother, and uncle all battled prostate cancer. (Uncle Dave succumbed to the disease in January 2014.) Did my husband have it? What would happen if he did? Where did we go from here? We decided to spend one Saturday morning doing research. That's it. No dwelling on it and prolonging the misery. We'd collect information (in addition to what we had from our family members) and stop worrying, since stress inhibits the body from fighting cancer. And if my husband had cancer, we needed his body to fight it. We had no control over the upcoming appointment and test results, so we decided that we'd schedule our worry time for when the urologist laid out all our options. You heard me right. We *scheduled* our worry time.

And then there was Deus. Deus Ex Machina, our beloved boy dog. (If you want to read the full story, visit bit.ly/deusboy.) Losing him unexpectedly was very traumatic. Dog lovers will understand this. If you're not a dog lover, you may not understand, but hopefully you'll empathize. To make matters worse, we unexpectedly had to put his big sister to sleep four days later (bit.ly/georgiegirl). My husband and I were a mess.

We are so fortunate that we've surrounded ourselves with wonderful personal and work teams. My husband's coworkers know that he never misses school (he's a teacher) or deadlines, so they covered his classes and told him to go do what he needed to do. Because I'd learned over the years to accept only kindhearted clients (instead of accepting anyone and everyone — even the richest but biggest jerks in the world), they were totally fine with my showing up with puffy red eyes. Handshakes were replaced by hugs.

Our schedules didn't go as originally planned, but because we understood our priorities and targets, we were able to make decisions about what needed to get done now and what could be delayed. Because we understood our time blocks, we were able to move tasks and appointments around and adjust our schedules — structure and flow.

We also made the decision to face this crappiness head on. We figured that we could prolong our sadness and wallow in misery, or we could shoot two middle fingers to the world and declare, "We will be just fine! *Now!*"

> To worry is to add another hazard. It retards reactions, makes one unfit.
> — *Amelia Earhart*

I pushed the cheapskate client out of my mind. It was her loss.

My husband and I rescheduled stress and anger about his PSA results to two weeks later, during his urologist appointment. We weren't suppressing our emotions; we simply realized that it was pointless to worry about something we couldn't control.

What we had left was dealing with the loss of Deus, and then Georgie Porgie Noisy le Grand. Neither of our brains could function as well during even a mild depression (and I stress-eat, which makes matters worse), so we decided to fast-forward those feelings. We threw a pity party on Wednesday, the day after we put Georgie to sleep, and five days after we put Deus to sleep. We bought pizza, chips, beer, hard cider, two types of Blue Bell ice cream...every kind of less-than-healthy food that tastes oh so good but we don't eat regularly. We pigged out and watched movies and spent time cuddling with Hildy, our third dog, who was now an only child.

On Friday, I picked up the ashes for both Deus and Georgie. More crying ensued. We held an Irish wake for them on Saturday, during which we toasted to them and celebrated their lives.

Stay strong on your mission.

When life decides to throw a few wrenches your way, it's important to hunker down and return to what makes you efficient and productive.

Take time out of your schedule to let your mind and heart absorb what's been put in front of you. Scream. Hit a punching bag. Close your door and throw a tantrum. Do what you need to in order to vent. Go primal and let it all out. Get the anger and sadness out because after that, it's time to pull up your bootstraps and kick life right back. You won't be suppressing your emotions; you simply will not be allowing them to go on for so long that they prevent you from getting your head screwed back on straight and functioning to manage what you still need to face.

Maintain your clarity by revisiting your personal priorities, personal targets, work priorities, and work targets. Doing so will remind you that even though you've hit a pothole in the road of life, you need to muster through this so that you can achieve your overall mission in life.

Sit down for a project management session. That's right. Getting through this tough time is a project. Determine what factors you truly have control over, and focus your energy on those.

Figure out what outcome you can change it to. What steps that you have control over will you need to complete in order to get the outcome you desire? Whom will you need to get onto your team? What information will you need to make progress? What resources will you need to leverage or acquire in order to move forward?

Look at your current time blocks. What will need to take a backseat in order for you to work through this project? Will you need to delegate to others or drop something completely? Will you need to complete tasks and duties in a different order, at a different time?

Sit down with your personal team and/or work team after you've done some initial individual brainstorming, and work through this together. While you'll acknowledge the crappy cards that you've been dealt, by focusing on the positive that's happening in your life and on your mission, you'll be able to soldier through.

NEXT STEPS

No matter how organized and positive you are, negative stuff will happen. To everyone.

Some people are dealt some pretty lousy hands. I do realize that everyone handles grief and pain differently. Our situation was nothing compared with what some people have to go through. But how you respond to the situation will determine how well you'll fare.

My husband's PSA tests came back negative, so we were thankful that he didn't have cancer. But the urologist told us, "It is not a matter of if, but when." There was no use stressing about that, so we once again rescheduled our worry to when his tests came back as something other than negative. Focusing on what you can control, and focusing on the positive, will help you to navigate negative situations and get through them with as much brainpower, physical might, and positivity as possible. The more positive your outlook is, the better you'll be able to deal with what's been thrown your way.

And the more you focus on the positive around you, the more clarity your brain will have. The more clarity your brain has, the better decisions you'll make about everything, including your time.

⊪➡ PLOT YOUR NEXT STEPS

- To help you keep things in perspective when bad stuff happens, what do you consider annoying versus catastrophic?
- In the event that something catastrophic happens, who in your life is patient and wise and would be willing to help you brainstorm?
- Who/what are positive people/things in your life? What positivity can you focus on in the event of a disaster?
- How will implementing the strategies and tactics in this chapter benefit you?

36 I Procrastinate…a Lot

Angela often feels stressed-out and tired because she stays up late finishing projects that are due the next day. Whether she has 24 hours or 24 days to complete a task, she puts off assignments until the last minute. Quite often she doesn't feel like thinking about the task, so she'll do other things in the meantime: work on something that was due the previous week, cruise the internet, work on low-value tasks, read at a café, or go shopping.

She always says she'll start earlier next time, but when next time comes around and she doesn't get crackin' right away, she'll say, "I work better under pressure anyway." And then the pattern repeats: stressful late-night work, followed by sleep-deprived mood swings the next day.

She is beginning to feel worn down because she's doing this more often. Her personal relationships are being affected negatively, as well as her performance at work.

GOAL

Put aside the desire to have instant pleasure (and avoid tasks) in favor of completing not-so-pleasant tasks *now*, which will make life easier and happier for you in the future.

TACTICS

Going ninja on your brain is like working with kids. Just when you think you've found the magical way to get them to listen or do their chores, the kids figure you out and stop responding to what you're doing. As the "make me happy now" part of your brain catches on to the self-regulation part of your brain, you might need to change up tactics now and then to keep this game fresh.

If you don't like doing something:

- Do it first thing in the morning so that the rest of the day is a breeze.
- Arrange for a reward (a break or some kind of treat) upon completion.
- Set a timer and race against time.
- Play your fastest-paced current favorite song, and rock out while doing the task.
- Listen to the television or a YouTube video in the background.
- Listen to an audiobook as you work.
- Drown out all distractions with word-free classical music.
- Call a friend or coworker over so that you won't be alone while you do it.
- Hire someone else to do it, or trade out with a coworker.
- Sip on a li'l sumpin' sumpin' (insert your favorite beverage here) as you work.
- Do it naked. That's exciting! (And naughty. Which makes it doubly exciting!) Note: Only do this if you work from home!
- Tell yourself that you *do* like it, and trick your brain into a positive attitude.

If you're overscheduled and overwhelmed:

- Break your tasks into smaller pieces.
- Have mini-deadlines (or "completion dates" if you don't like the word *deadline*) along the way for each of the pieces instead of one big one at the end.
- Stop adding to your calendar until further notice.
- Get over to chapter 9, "Get It All Done in 24 Hours: Turn To-Do Lists into *Done* Lists," stat. It's about time.
- Consider studying project management, which will help you plan out your timeline and necessary steps for completing projects. (See chapter 8, "Manage Long-Term Projects with Mega-efficiency," in this book and chapter 7 in my *ROAD MAP to Get Organized* book.)

If you have perfectionistic tendencies:

- Accept that "good enough" is better than "not at all."
- Do the first step in the project. Just starting will help you move past perfectionist worries.
- Get on over to the next chapter, "I May Not Be a Perfectionist, but I Want Everything Just Right," where we discuss perfectionism in more detail.

If you think, "I work better under pressure":

- Working under pressure on a daily basis is detrimental to our health and body. (Warning: It has to do with cortisol, and it is not pretty!)
- Create an earlier deadline on your calendar. The conscious part of your brain will work toward making that happen. The subconscious part of your brain won't go into stress mode, since it knows this is a false deadline and you actually have more time.

If you don't know how to do something:

- Ask for help right away.
- Back out of the project. It's better to be honest with yourself and others before the project is due, rather than apologize for doing shoddy work — or doing nothing at all.
- Hire somebody to do it, or trade out with a coworker.

If you have to make a decision about something:

- Set a due date for the decision.
- Set a maximum amount of time each day you'll spend thinking or researching.
- Research the pros and cons via the internet or speaking with a friend, colleague, or expert in that field.
- Or do all this in one day, and get it over with.

STRATEGY: A CRUTCH

No matter what our reasons are for procrastinating, if the act of procrastinating causes us to put things off and then hurry to get things done, we are placing ourselves in a stressful situation. When we get into a heightened state while cramming at the last minute to finish a task, our brains are releasing cortisol. Cortisol makes us feel like we're empowered and energized and getting a high. What we're really doing is wearing down our bodies. Cortisol has been found to cause high blood pressure, degeneration of cognitive functions, and weight gain, among other maladies. When these chemicals are released on a regular basis, it can also lead to kidney failure. We're programmed to use the chemicals to help us survive in life-or-death situations — not as a way to live life every day.

Even organized people occasionally procrastinate, so it's an unrealistic goal to say you'll never procrastinate again. The key for you is to reduce the frequency of your episodes. So how can you do that?

Procrastinate *productively*!

Yes, this entire chapter is about how *not* to procrastinate. But as I mentioned earlier, it's human nature to want to do it. We all procrastinate at some point. (Psssst. I want to do it occasionally, especially on boring tasks!) So, since we're not robots, and we will give in to task avoidance now and again, how can we make sure that we don't fall behind and still finish what we need to?

Answer: Procrastinate productively.

The most common form of procrastination is grabbing our smartphones to check email, Facebook, Twitter, Pinterest, or some other form of social media. Unless your job is social media, going down this rabbit hole for 20 minutes or an hour, or longer, won't move you ahead.

Instead, avoid one task by completing another. What else do you need to get done that's more enticing at that moment?

Wash the car?

Reconnect with your favorite client?

Write a proposal that's due next week?

Check next week's calendar and send out appointment reminders?

Go for a walk?

In the "Get It All Done in 24 Hours" chapter, we talk about my 3+3 method, and this formula will help you to procrastinate productively. You'll temporarily avoid an unsexy task, but you'll be getting something else done in the meantime. Once you feel the success of getting a task crossed off your list, the "make me happy now" part of your brain will be pleased, and you'll be more willing to dive into the original task you avoided.

Yeah, mind games.

They really do work. The next section has more that will help you to regain control of your mind and avoid procrastination as much as humanly possible.

STRATEGY

According to psychologists, procrastination is the act of wanting to feel good now. Basically, procrastination is the adult version of a three-year-old's "I don't wanna!" tantrum.

Procrastination can make life miserable. If we put off projects, phone calls, emails, or whatever the task may be, we end up working at breakneck pace in order to complete it at the eleventh hour. It's unnecessary stress that we bring upon ourselves.

What if our goal could be to get ahead for today or tomorrow, instead of living in a frazzled state from constantly playing catch-up? Or does that shot of adrenaline that you feel when you're hurrying to finish a project feel good to you?

> Procrastination is the art of keeping up with yesterday.
> — *Don Marquis*

The research shows that overcoming procrastination comes down to thought control and self-regulation. It's all about mind management. Realizing that you're dragging your feet is the first key. Once this realization occurs, you're ready to play some strategic mind games with yourself.

You can ask yourself, "Do I want to get this task/job/misery over with and avoid kidney malfunction, weight gain, brain malfunction, stressing-out later, being in a bad mood, and snapping at everyone?"

You can ask yourself, "When tomorrow rolls around, would I like to feel proud of myself for getting the job done early, relieved that it's over with already, and peaceful instead of panicked?"

You can tell yourself:

"I forgive myself for procrastinating last time. I can move forward now."

"I'll probably spend more time complaining about and avoiding this thing than it'll actually take to finish it."

"I'll pretend that I'm doing this for my best friend. I know I'd do it for her if I said I would."

Ask yourself, "How will *not* doing this right now make my life better?"

What the Research Says

Those who procrastinate seek short-term, feel-good-now benefits, but they end up suffering long-term costs.

Task avoidance (procrastination) is a strategy to avoid negative emotions like fear and anxiety.

Our decision to procrastinate sabotages all our self-regulation and decision making.

Procrastination has to do with control and self-regulation, not time management.

Procrastination causes increased secretion of cortisol, which causes bad things to happen to us, including weight gain, lowered immunity, high blood pressure, kidney failure, and impaired brain function. (Procrastination kills. For real.)

Those who forgive themselves for their last instance of procrastination have a lower likelihood of procrastinating on the same task the next go-round.

Focusing on the happiness of our future self will help us to get through the present unpleasant emotions that are trying to block us from completing the task(s) in front of us.

(For more details about the research, see my resources at www.HeleneSegura .com/30tactics.)

Types of Procrastination

Based on my consulting and coaching work, I have found that there are two types of procrastination:

Chronic

Chronic procrastinators will delay work on tasks on a daily or nearly daily basis. There may or may not be a pattern to the types of situations that spark the delays. The delays may feel like normal life to the chronic procrastinator, but this type of procrastination eventually leads to lost opportunities, lost income, damaged relationships, and problems with physical health. The chronic procrastinator outwardly displays self-deprecating humor about being a procrastinator, but internally there is a lot of pain. I've seen the anguish, witnessed the tears, and heard the heaving sobs when people in this situation are coming to terms with their current reality. They know that their procrastination is hurting them, but they feel powerless to do anything about it. They've already tried all the tactical possibilities, and nothing — short of someone sitting next to them and making them do the task — works.

If you resonate with this, I need to tell you something that you may not want to hear but that deep down inside you already know. Medical experts who subscribe to the research that finds that a lack of emotional self-regulation is the cause of procrastination recommend counseling and/or cognitive behavioral therapy. If you've honestly tried every strategy and tactic mentioned in this chapter, and your procrastination is still a major barrier to success, I encourage you to seek this type of assistance because your task avoidance goes beneath the surface of what mind management and time management tips and tricks can help you with.

Situational

Situational procrastination happens to everyone. It's human nature. We all procrastinate at one time or another. No matter how much self-control and self-regulation we have, there are times when we just don't want to do something. If we were three years old, we'd throw a tantrum. But since we're adults, the tantrums have been replaced by task avoidance — procrastination.

Why We Procrastinate

Here are some of the causes of procrastination:

We don't know how to do something. We're afraid to admit it, or we don't know where to learn how to do something, so we keep putting off the task.

We don't like doing something. "I don't wanna!"

We're overscheduled and overwhelmed. We've got so much going on that we don't know which way is up sometimes. This confuses our brains, and we don't know what to do next, or we think, "Why bother starting if I know I don't have time?" This overwhelm leads us to seek something easy to do — like checking email or going shopping.

We have to make a decision about something. For some, procrastination is a coping mechanism for difficulty with decision making. When decisions — whether earth-shattering important or completely insignificant in the grand scheme of things — are needed, taking on additional workloads, shopping, or spending too much time on tasks that don't take that long to complete are common avoidance strategies or crutches.

We've got some perfectionistic tendencies. We want everything to be exactly right. But we're not sure if what we're about to do will be perfectly right, so we avoid the task. If we don't start, then we can't screw it up.

We think, "I work better under pressure." Realize that the rush you feel when speeding through last-minute work is actually hurting your body because that rush is from cortisol. Consider a goal of replacing that rush with the feelings of relief and satisfaction you get by finishing something ahead of time. Those feelings don't cause kidney damage and obesity like cortisol does.

Make your goal to get ahead for today or tomorrow, instead of living in a frazzled state from constantly playing catch-up.

NEXT STEPS

Angela eventually cut back substantially on her procrastination. She tied her mind games to her personal priorities and targets. She was having money problems because her procrastination habit of shopping was becoming expensive, so her target was to spend only $25 per week or $100 per month on unplanned purchases. Her boyfriend was getting ready to break up with her, so she vowed to spend quality time with him every evening after 7 PM.

When she felt procrastination coming on, she'd ask herself: "Will procrastinating on this task keep me away from the stores and out of debt?" *No, procrastinating will drive me further into debt, so I need to work on this project now.*

Or, "Will procrastinating on this task support the relationship I want to have with my boyfriend?" *No, it will only drive a deeper wedge between us and cause us to break up, so I need to work on this project now.*

She used a timer and worked on unpleasant tasks for only 30 minutes at a time. Eventually, she realized that it wasn't the tasks that were so unpleasant; it was the negative by-product of procrastinating on the tasks that was so unpleasant. So, after a while, she actually looked forward to most of the projects.

IIII➤ PLOT YOUR NEXT STEPS

- If you procrastinate, what are the common causes? (This may take some digging and self-reflection to answer, but please do attempt to answer this eventually.)
- What does it feel like when you're about to procrastinate?
- When you catch yourself feeling that way, what steps will you take to cut back on procrastination?
- How much time will you save each day by cutting back on procrastination?

37 | I May Not Be a Perfectionist, but I Want Everything Just Right

Priscilla is a force of nature. She is a brilliant businesswoman with an unparalleled reputation. She is meticulous and consistently produces high-quality work.

Behind closed doors, however, she is falling to pieces. What she demands of herself she would never ask of a coworker or an employee because they'd think she was an overbearing micromanager. She will reread and redo and revamp projects countless times — sometimes in the middle of the night, even — to make sure that everything is absolutely perfect.

When she's unsure how to approach a project in a way that will result in perfection, she freezes and goes into panic mode. She's not sure where to start or how to proceed. She consistently finds the minutest errors in her work, but she seldom acknowledges the 99.5 percent part of the project that she completed impeccably. She feels she has little cause to celebrate because she always focuses on what she has left to do or what she didn't do up to par (her superhuman par, that is), instead of focusing on her outstanding accomplishments.

GOAL

Accept that there is no such thing as perfect, and chasing perfection will cause you increased stress and lost time. Accept Finished Well, instead of languishing in the hunt for Finished Exactly Right.

TACTICS

When you catch yourself stalling out on implementing one of the strategies or tactics in this book because you think that you won't be able to get it done perfectly, or you don't know where to start in order to reach perfection, use one of these mantras to help you move past the moment:

- Ninety percent is still an A. Ninety percent is still an A.
- Good enough is better than not at all. Good enough is better than not at all.
- Just do one small part first. Just do one small part first.
- In order to know whether this works for me, I need to try it for two weeks.

There is no perfect order for applying these strategies and tactics. Just try one. Just one.

If you struggle with beating yourself up about not completing tasks perfectly, set a timer for five minutes, and get the self-scolding out of your system. We will not allow success-blocking thoughts to get in your way!

STRATEGY

Perfectionism can be such an incredibly huge hindrance. If you have perfectionist tendencies, you may have experienced some of these success-blocking behaviors:

- You scrutinize every detail in a project.
- You can't look at your work only once or twice. You need to review it multiple times so that you don't overlook a mistake or you don't miss the chance to make it even better.
- Even after you submit a project, you review it to see if you could have done better.
- Or maybe you complete everything except the last step. You don't want to finish because it might not be perfect.
- Sometimes you catch yourself not wanting to take the next step because it might not be the right one.
- Everything must be perfect; otherwise, you don't do it.
- You do only the things that can be done perfectly.
- If you're not sure how to make something perfect, you freeze.
- Occasionally, you become extremely frustrated because you can't get it just right.

- "Good enough" is a cop-out to you. "Good enough" is not good enough for you.

These behaviors end up costing you more time.

To help you Create Clarity in your brain, which will save you time in the long run, here are some mind games you'll have to play with yourself:

Ninety percent is still an A! That might sound horrific to you right now, but this mantra will become your life preserver. It is possible to have high standards without demanding perfection.

You fear creating a product that is not perfect, so you never start working on it and, therefore, never reach completion. Good enough is better than not at all. "Good enough" is *not* a cop-out.

> Good enough is good enough. Perfect will make you a big fat mess every time.
>
> — *Rebecca Wells*,
> The Crowning Glory of
> Calla Lily Ponder

You fear creating a product that is not perfect, so when you do work on a project, you rework and retool it to death. You will need to catch yourself in the act of looking or doing "just one more time." You will need to divert yourself from going for the 100-plus-percent mark. Sometimes, this means telling yourself out loud to move on to something else. Leave it. Walk out of the room. Ask yourself, "Will the United States go to war if this is not 100 percent perfect? Will someone die because it's not 100 percent perfect?" If the answers are no, you will survive. Trust me. I'm still alive.

Obsessing over small details will ultimately drive you over the edge. You will eventually need to decide your priority in life: perfection or sanity. I read excerpts of Vincent van Gogh's letters to his brother and friends when I visited the mental institution where he lived in Saint-Rémy-de-Provence, France. His obsession with minutiae made him his own worst critic, and paintings were left unfinished — or sometimes not even started — because of the obsession. Granted, he did have other issues affecting his mental stability, but the pain expressed in his correspondence offers insight into a perfectionist's struggles. How many more van Gogh paintings might there be if he had been able to let go of some of those small details?

As a recovering perfectionist, I can tell you that change is difficult at first, but a life with a great deal less anxiety is the reward that awaits you. If I had let perfectionism get the best of me, I would never have published this book. There is always a better way to say something, a new factoid to learn, or yet another tip. There might even be a misspelled word or incorrect punctuation mark somewhere within these pages. But I need to stop at some point and say, "What I've completed is good enough. I am finished. I will celebrate." As with organizing systems and routines, I can always revisit this work down the road and make changes as necessary. I can publish a second edition. But in the meantime, I will cross this off my to-do list, enjoy the fruits of my labor, and rejoice!

You remain in darkness because you do not allow the light to shine on you. You focus on what's lacking instead of what has been accomplished. Just as there is never a perfect adventure (picnic, hike, museum tour, etc.) because inevitably there will be at least one or two not-so-perfect occurrences along the way, there is never a perfect project. When you recall those adventure memories, hopefully you allow the joy of the experience to outshine the minor bumps you experienced. You must do the same with your work.

NEXT STEPS

Priscilla and I focused her energy on reflecting with power. We trained her brain to shift from looking at only imperfections and unfinished work to celebrating every single success she had that day. Acknowledging what she did *right* built up her confidence. With this increased confidence, she felt more secure with what she submitted after her third or fourth go-through (instead of revisiting something 20 times before being satisfied). Her brain began to crave the celebrations, lower stress levels, and increased free time, so it became easier to step away and be satisfied.

ⅠⅠⅠⅠ➡ PLOT YOUR NEXT STEPS

- How much time do you think perfectionism costs you?
- What would you rather do with that time?
- If you fear not perfectly completing a recommendation from this book, what can you do to push past that thought and complete the recommendation?
- How will you remind yourself to not let perfectionism get in the way of what you want to accomplish?

38 I Have a Tough Time Sleeping

Many of my clients get stuck in this cycle:

You work late and finally crawl into bed absolutely wiped out. But you can't fall asleep because your mind is still racing.

Oooo! You finally do fall asleep! But then you wake up in the middle of the night. You can't go back to sleep, so you get up and work some more.

You're completely exhausted the next day, so you get cranked up on caffeine to make it through. But now you're not tired when bedtime rolls around because you've still got caffeine or energy drinks in your system, plus a ton of stuff buzzing around in your head.

"There's so much still to do!" "There's no time for a good night's sleep!" Even if you want to sleep, how can you when your brain won't turn off?

GOAL

Empty your head of thoughts, and then decompress and completely relax well before bedtime.

TACTICS

1. Complete a Mind Liberation every day.
2. Refrain from eating food or drinking nonwater liquids starting two hours before bedtime.
3. Turn off all electronics at least 30 minutes before bedtime.
4. Spend the last 30 minutes before bedtime just relaxing, not thinking about work.
5. Take 10 deep breaths before you hit the hay.

STRATEGY

What causes insomnia? According to the Mayo Clinic:

Stress

Anxiety

Depression

Change in environment or work schedule

Poor sleep habits

Caffeine, nicotine, and alcohol

Eating too much late in the evening

Note: Some types of insomnia are caused by medical conditions, so be sure to see a medical professional if there is any possibility of this.

Even if you love your job, there can be stress and anxiety at various times because of the tasks or projects you have on your plate. Emptying your brain at the end of the day will help your mind to shut down when it's time to sleep. Therefore, complete a Mind Liberation every day — preferably during your 3+3 time but, if necessary, definitely before your 30 minutes of downtime prior to going to bed.

Refrain from eating food or drinking nonwater liquids starting two hours before bedtime. Many times, what we ingest shortly before bedtime contributes to keeping us up at night. Sugar and caffeine can definitely keep us awake longer. But sometimes we're not aware of how other foods affect us — ones that also prevent us from going to sleep sooner.

Turn off all electronics at least 30 minutes before bedtime. (Some studies recommend 60.) Research shows that electronics stimulate our brains. If our brains get stimulated through watching television or checking our phone or reading a tablet right before bed, that will increase the amount of time it will take for us to fall asleep.

There should be zero decisions made or thoughts generated during this downtime. So no reading business or self-help books that give you ideas to implement. That's right, don't even read this one right before bed. I ask you to think a lot throughout this book, and that gets your brain pumped up, which is not what you want to do before bed. Even a simple game of solitaire gets the brain cranked up because you have to decide which card to play. Instead, read mindless fiction or low-brain nonfiction like biographies or celebrity gossip rags, or meditate.

Take 10 deep breaths before you hit the hay. Breathing clears your mind, slows down your pace, and calms you down.

If for any reason you still wake up in the middle of the night, do not get up to do "just a little bit of work." You most likely will not fall back asleep again because your brain will be up and running. Instead, complete another Mind Liberation. Read something low-key for a little while. Then turn off the light.

NEXT STEPS

I used to call this "entrepreneurial insomnia" because so many of the business owners I worked with suffered from this lack of sleep. But when I started working more and more with folks who were employed by companies — from admin to the C-suite — I discovered that this type of insomnia doesn't plague only entrepreneurs. It hits anybody with high levels of stress, worries, and/or ideas overload.

Relieving your mind of this burden and letting it rest are essential to being a good businessperson. When your brain has clarity, the mind is calm, and from a calm mind comes creativity and better decision making.

ⅠⅠⅠⅢ➡ PLOT YOUR NEXT STEPS

- How has a lack of sleep affected you?
- When will you complete your Mind Liberation?
- What will you do to stop drinking nonwater liquids and eating at least two hours before bedtime?
- How will you remember to turn off your electronics a minimum of 30 minutes before bedtime?
- What will you do for relaxation during those (minimum) 30 minutes?

39 I Often Am Late or Miss Appointments

Jimmy was an up-and-coming newspaper reporter. He was constantly on the go — meeting with folks, interviewing them, writing, networking…everything he needed to do to keep his job, turn out good stories, and make the powers that be happy.

One day he set an appointment with an individual who was going to help him with a project. It was tough to get this appointment because this individual, who was doing him a big favor, had a packed schedule with meetings both in and out of town. But she set aside time to meet with Jimmy because she believed in the cause they were both supporting, and she wanted to lend a hand.

This meeting was offsite from Jimmy's office, but about 20 minutes of travel time would get him there. He had the meeting on his calendar, so that he wouldn't forget.

But he didn't complete his 3+3 or check his next day's calendar the day before, so he had no idea of what was coming his way. He didn't check his calendar first thing in the morning to see what his focus was for the day.

What he did do was check email first thing in the morning and start working on addressing an issue that wasn't an emergency; the person making demands was a pain in the patootie, so he immediately buried his head in that task.

And in doing so, he completely forgot about his difficult-to-schedule meeting with someone who'd be able to help him with not only this particular project but many others in the future.

The busy woman, who had cleared her schedule to meet with Jimmy and sent him a reminder two days before the meeting, emailed him from the meeting site — five minutes after the meeting start time. "Are you okay? I'm here at the south end."

"Sorry. An editorial emergency came up, so I can't make it," Jimmy emailed back.

Jimmy missed the appointment. And he also missed out on future opportunities because his lack of respect for his time — and that of the busy woman — planted seeds of doubt and mistrust in the woman's head.

She never again agreed to meet with him.

GOAL

Use a checks-and-balances scheduling system that includes the following: capture details, confirm, block time for, and reconfirm all appointments.

TACTICS

1. During any conversation in which there's a suggestion to meet, scan your calendar for conflicts or major projects due before agreeing to meet.
2. Make sure that you hang up the phone (or end the email thread or leave the room) knowing the day, date, time, duration, and location, as well as whatever information or deliverables you need to arrive with.
3. Before you do anything else, capture this meeting information in whatever calendar system you use.
4. Send the other party a calendar invite, and/or send a confirmation email to the other party with all the details you've agreed upon.
5. Determine the amount of time you need to travel to the meeting and get centered beforehand. Set that time on your calendar.
6. Estimate how much time you need to prep for the meeting, and block that time off on your calendar.
7. Send a re-confirmation email the week before the meeting to affirm all logistics and details.
8. At the end of each day, examine your calendar for the next day while completing your 3+3. If, somehow, you have double-booked yourself, you will

be able to contact one of the double-bookings ahead of time in order to apologize and reschedule.

You may have a mind like a steel trap, but taking these precautions will not only free up space in your brain but also save you from headaches, embarrassment, and lost career opportunities in the long run.

STRATEGY

When you try to keep an awful lot of information in your head, occasionally the information about appointments will disappear from your gray matter. You might be able to slide a bit in your personal life if this is happening, but in the business world, it can be the kiss of death. If you don't show up to an appointment, you might not get a second chance with the person who was left waiting there for you.

Capture, confirm, block time, and reconfirm.

Process the proposed meeting purpose and date.

Before saying yes to any appointment, you need to determine whether you're truly needed there. Ask the meeting planner what your role is in the meeting. If you get a blank stare, you should question whether your presence is actually needed. If you are needed (or required to attend because, for instance, you're serving on a board, and it's a board meeting), scan your calendar to see what meetings, appointments, and projects you have the day before, the day of, and the day after the proposed meeting date. If you have a major project due the next day, you may not want to agree to this day, especially if it's the kind of meeting that goes for two hours without anything getting accomplished. (Eventually, you'll be able to schedule meetings the day before anything that's happening because you'll be ahead of the curve and not working at the last minute.) If you have your email inbox under control, you can also quickly scan to see if any higher-priority events have already been proposed and/or scheduled for you, so that you know to take this date off the plate.

If you're thinking to yourself, "Bloody heck! That's a lot of thinking to schedule a meeting!" why yes, it is. But "all this thinking" will save you from stress in the long run because you'll allow yourself enough time to meet with whom you need to and complete what you need to, without burning the midnight oil.

If you're being asked to schedule a meeting and you can delay an answer, simply say, "Let me check my calendar, and I'll let you know."

If you're at a meeting and need to schedule the next one while everyone is in the room, take your time going through this process right in front of them. When I'm in this position with a group, usually the group is talking, going back and forth, and I simply announce my preferences last. This gives me the time to check. If, however, I'm scheduling my next one-to-one session with a client, I let him know I need to check what's happening for that week because I don't want to reschedule on him. When I make it about not inconveniencing my clients, they're perfectly fine with waiting the 90 seconds it takes me to scan my calendar and my inbox. The silence during the wait time isn't awkward. It's empowering. Because you know that you're about to make a better decision about how you use your time.

Capture the meeting details.

No matter what situation you're in — phone, email, chat forum, or in person — be sure to get every detail possible and notate it either in your calendar or in your idea-capture tool. Really and truly. Stop for 60 seconds to capture this meeting information. What day will the meeting take place? What's the begin time and end time? Where will it be held? What are you responsible for bringing? If that information isn't readily available, who will be responsible for giving it to you at least one week before the meeting is supposed to take place? If the meeting is out of town, you'll need at least four weeks' notice, so that you can plan for travel, farm out your duties, and so on. If you can't be given this information within your requested time frame, then you probably don't want to be working with these folks, because they're disorganized and they'll cost you time (and money) in the long run.

Paper or digital?

You'll need a place to record this meeting information. If you're digitally inclined, input all the meeting information right then and there into your phone, tablet, or laptop. If you use a paper calendar, be sure to notate the meeting on your calendar, and record the details in the same spot or a designated notes page for this client or group. The 60 seconds you take to make sure that this event gets added to your calendar will prevent you from forgetting about, not preparing for, or missing this appointment. Stop and take the time to add this to your

> We are what we repeatedly do. Excellence, then, is not an act, but a habit.
>
> — Will Durant, summarizing Aristotle

calendar. Don't rely on your brain to remember to do it later. That "remember to do this" will just add to the swirl in your head and will most likely get lost in the shuffle.

At this point, most folks ask me, "Should I go paper or digital?" The question really should be, "Which type of calendar will I use both at my desk and while I'm out and about, and will I check daily?"

There is no single right answer that fits everyone. There is only a right answer for you and how your brain works. If you feel more comfortable with paper, then stick to paper. If you want to embrace technology, go digital. But no matter which you choose, you *must use it on a daily basis* to make decisions about whether to accept events on your calendar.

Like many people, I'm a hybrid; I use both. The little dots on my phone's calendar don't give me enough information. They tell me I have something I need to do, but I can't see what that is in just one glance. Or I couldn't, until I started using a Samsung Note, which has a large screen (and, therefore, won't fit into any pants pocket). But even with a large screen, I can't always see the entire description, so I do my planning based on my paper calendar. I can see a week's view at a time, and this prevents me from overscheduling and double booking. Once I make sure the appointment that's proposed fits my schedule comfortably, I write it on my paper calendar and also record it on my phone.

Using both has two benefits for me: (1) my brain relaxes because the event is in two places, so there's no way I can forget about it; (2) my assistant has access to my digital calendar, so she can also make the right decision about when to schedule my meetings. She knows to allow at least one hour in between my local clients so that I have loads of time to deal with appointments running a few minutes past schedule, traffic, and centering myself. She also knows that if it doesn't say "Available," she needs to check with me before adding anything to my calendar.

Send a confirmation.

Whether you do this immediately or when you're closing out at the end of the day, send the other party a calendar invite and/or an email confirmation. Yes, you've just agreed verbally to have this meeting, but if they're not good at managing their time or calendar, sending a meeting confirmation will make sure that this meeting doesn't fall through the cracks on their end. After all, while you'd be relieved that it was their fault and not yours for screwing up, your time would be wasted because the meeting didn't happen, and it would need to be rescheduled. If the other party beats you to it and sends you the confirmation, great! No matter who extends the first communication, make sure that all meeting details are included so that there's no confusion later on, including who is calling whom for a phone conference.

Block off travel and centering time.

One step that folks often leave off their calendars is travel time and centering time. I have many clients who are late to meetings because while they see the meeting blocked off on their calendar, they forget to build in the amount of time it takes to get there, so they run late — even when the meeting is in the same building. Figure out how much time it will take you to pack up your stuff, go to the restroom, make the trip to the meeting, take some deep breaths to center yourself, and review your notes. Add in possible delay time. Now plug this into your calendar. For example, if it will take you a total of 30 minutes to do all of the above, write on your paper calendar — or add to your digital calendar — an event title, "Leave for meeting." This will remind your brain to get you out the door in a reasonable amount of time.

Block off prep time.

If you have to show up to a meeting without any information or deliverable, you kind of have to wonder why the heck you're there. So chances are, you need to bring something or know something or be prepared for something when you walk into a meeting. How much time will you need to prepare? When will you prepare for this? Schedule this on your calendar. Why? Because if it doesn't get scheduled, and you don't set time aside for this, it will turn into one of those "Oh, crap! I've gotta do this!" tasks that take you into overtime and away from your loved ones. Whether you need 15 minutes or 15 hours to prepare, block it off on your calendar.

Reconfirm the meeting.

Send an email the week before the scheduled meeting to reconfirm all the details. If it's an out-of-town meeting, send this confirmation at least two weeks before.

The two minutes it takes to do this will help your brain focus in on the event because it knows the event is going to happen. And if the other party has forgotten or needs to back out, you'll have plenty of time to schedule another client or meeting in that time slot. This will make your brain happy because it knows that while the meeting may have fallen through, you can free up your brain to focus on other things.

Review your calendar daily.

As a part of your 3+3 at the end of each day, you will be reviewing your calendar. If you're practicing all the steps in this chapter, it's unlikely that you've double-booked yourself. But if on the very off-chance it happened, you'll have time to contact one of the other parties beforehand to let them know that you've made a mistake and need to reschedule. Why admit to a mistake? Because if you tell them that something has come up, you're telling them that they're unimportant and don't deserve your attention. They may start feeling the same way about you if this is their perception, so it's best just to fess up to making a boo-boo. Apologize. Offer to have the rescheduled meeting over lunch, your treat. Admitting to goofing will save you from the other party thinking you don't respect them, and it is worlds better than not showing up at all. The other party may be annoyed by your gaffe but will appreciate your apology and will be pleased that they still have time to schedule something else in place of your no-longer-happening appointment.

That is the mind-set to maintain and the thinking to implement in order to prevent tardiness and missed appointments.

NEXT STEPS

I love to keep things as positive as possible because I think that focusing on the negative simply leads us into more turmoil. However, it is important to learn from mistakes, so let's take that opportunity right now.

Jimmy got fired.

He felt that using all these checks and balances was just a waste of time. Because he didn't attempt to change his habits, he continued to be late to — or even flat-out miss — appointments.

He made a conscious decision to not make changes that would improve his decision-making skills, which directly affected his time management skills.

Don't be like Jimmy.

> ### Ⅲ➡ PLOT YOUR NEXT STEPS
>
> - How often are you late to appointments?
> - What do you think is causing this?
> - How often do you miss appointments completely?
> - What do you think is causing this?
> - Based on what you read in this chapter, which strategies and tactics will you apply in order to be on time to all future appointments?
> - If anyone — including the devil (or bogeyman) on your shoulder — ever gives you a hard time about implementing any of the tactics in this checks-and-balances system, what response can you have ready that explains how this process is helpful to you?

40 I Often Let Great Opportunities Turn into Big Stress

A large corporation approached Julie (my client who missed her son's first home run while her head was buried in an email) about developing a training program for them. Once she found out what all it would entail, Julie applied what she'd been learning with me and told them that she'd get back to them the next day with her decision. She calculated how much time she'd have to work on the development in order to get the program launched by their due date. She realized that she'd either have to completely ignore the clients she'd already committed to, or have to work every evening and every weekend for the next two months in order to accept this mega-dollar contract. She took a deep breath and looked at her priorities list. Then, she looked at her bank balance, which had been dwindling lately because of some emergencies around the house. She looked at her priorities again. She called the corporation by the promised deadline and told them that she couldn't do a quality job in the time frame they wanted, so she respectfully declined the project.

Could Julie have really used that income? Heck yeah! It was not easy for her to give that "no," but she was proud of herself for supporting her personal priorities. Each time in the past when she'd worked herself into a frenzy and missed so much time with her kids, she'd go into a nonproductive guilt phase, regretting not spending time with them. She was tired of those regrets, and of losing time from those down-in-the-dumps spells.

GOAL

Only allow into your life that which will support your work priorities and targets — but not at the expense of your personal priorities and targets.

Think, plan, and live by the belief that there *is* time in the day to do what *you truly need to get done.*

TACTICS

1. Refrain from immediately saying yes to anything and everything.
2. Instead, respond by saying, "I need to check my calendar. I'll get back to you by tomorrow with my timeline."
3. Determine if this task supports your personal or work priorities and targets.
   a. If no, decline the offer.
   b. If yes, list out the steps it will take to complete the request, as well as how much time each step will take.
4. Check your calendar. When will you complete each step?
5. Communicate with the requestor the timeline you will be able to implement in order to complete high-quality work and finish the project.
   a. Accept the project or task if the requestor agrees to the timeline.
   b. If the requestor does not agree to your timeline, decide what you will drop from your schedule in order to make it fit in.

STRATEGY

If you're making time to map out and schedule your long-term projects as well as create your 3+3 at the end of each day, your schedule will eventually go from overflowing to much more manageable. By following the various strategies and tactics in this book, you'll wipe out inefficiencies and win back time. You'll also learn to be much more careful about what you add to your plate.

But what about those "great opportunities" that get presented to you?

For go-getters, it's so easy to get sucked into the mentality of "I must do this task or project, or else I'll lose out!"

I'd like to remind you of what we discussed in chapter 1. What if we spun around 180 degrees and instead thought that way about our personal priorities? "I should spend time supporting my health or family or marriage, or else I'll lose out!" Will saying yes to that "next big thing" support your priorities? Viewing your personal and work priorities lists will help your brain to make better decisions about how you use your time.

Does what is being offered to you support your work priorities?

Does what is being offered to you get you one step closer to your business targets?

Can the completion of what is being offered to you happen without your sacrificing your personal priorities and targets?

If your answer is yes to all three questions, proceed to finding a place on your calendar for working on the various stages of this project.

If, however, your answer is maybe, you need to think long and hard about whether you will accept the task. You're reading this book because you want more peace in your day. Will accepting this task or project lead you to more peace, or will you keep yourself from peace again?

And if your answer is no to all three questions, your answer to the requestor should most definitely be no.

You have to take your time to save time.

What is so different about this process compared with what you may currently be doing? For starters, it requires pausing — and not giving an automatic yes just because you see dollar signs or you fear repercussions from your boss.

> The best way to predict the future is to invent it.
>
> — Alan Kay

A second difference is that I'm asking you to control your time instead of letting someone else control it. Let's examine the options I suggest you use if the requestor doesn't like the timeline you've given them or if there's no wiggle room in the timeline (such as a conference or publishing date already having been set):

- Determine if you have any lower-priority work time blocks that can be postponed to later dates so you can free up time to work on the requestor's project. *Or*

- Ask your household members for permission to cancel your "appointments" with them (quality relationship time) so that you can free up time to work on the project. *Or*
- Hire someone else to complete the tasks that are already on your calendar so that you can free up time to work on the requestor's project. *Or*
- Explain that you believe in integrity and the value of completing only your finest work, and then politely decline the project because you don't want to deliver anything less than that to the requestor.

In each of these scenarios, *you* are in total control. *You* decide how you will use your time. After all, it is *your* time. No one else can take your time away from you...unless *you* willingly let them.

A third difference is that this process requires you to maintain your laser focus on your priorities and targets, as well as think about what steps a project entails. Too many times, I've seen folks look at their phone screens to see whether they have an opening on the day that a project or presentation is due. When they don't see a little colored dot on the day and time of the request, they wholeheartedly agree to take on the client or task or project.

It's not until later that they analyze the resources and work required for the project, the time it will take to complete the project, and whether the project is a win for their career — and personal life. When this planning is done *after* saying yes, it's often too late to back out of the project because you'll look like a flake or an idiot — neither of which will be good for your business reputation.

So don't rely on colored dots on your phone's calendar. Instead:

- get as much information as possible about a prospective client or task or project,
- determine what all is required of your time and effort,
- look at your priorities and targets to see if this project will help or hinder you,
- and then give your answer of yes or no.

Opportunities are great only if they truly support what you want in life.

Only allow into your life that which will support your business priorities and targets — but not at the expense of your personal priorities and targets.

Think, plan, and live by the belief that there *is* time in the day to do what *you truly need to get done.*

What if you work for a company?

You can apply all the above strategies, except for hiring someone or saying no. This is where your negotiating skills come in. You can negotiate timelines with the requestor. If the requestor doesn't give you a chance to create the deadline, here's an example of the negotiating you can do. Scenario: It's Tuesday at 2:00. You have Project Y due for Client Loyal at 9:00 AM on Wednesday morning. Your boss drops by, and the following exchange ensues:

> *Requestor:* Client Moneybags called and wants a proposal. I need this by 5:00 today.
>
> *You:* Absolutely, ma'am. But this means I'll have to delay my work on Project Y. Don't worry, I'll get Project Y to you by Wednesday afternoon.

In a perfect world...

> *Requestor:* I'm glad you know your projects and timelines. Thank you for being so responsible. I need to give you a 10 percent raise!

In reality...

> *Requestor:* Excuse me?
>
> *You:* I care about this company, so when I'm responsible for a project, I always turn in my very best. If I put forth my absolute best on what you just gave me, then Project Y — if turned in by 9 AM tomorrow — would not be my best. I only want to submit the most outstanding work possible, so I'll get Project Y to you by Wednesday afternoon.
>
> *Requestor:* We promised both clients that we'd make it happen by a certain time, so you'd better make it happen!
>
> *You:* If I can get either client to extend the deadline without upsetting them, may I?
>
> *Requestor:* Whatever. Good luck with that. If you tick them off, you're fired. [Exits]

You: [After deciding it would be easier to ask for a postponement from the client who'd just made the request] Hello, Client Moneybags? I wanted to give you an update on your proposal. We're working on an optimal possibility for you, but we won't get confirmation until tomorrow morning that it is indeed doable. Would you allow us to spend more time researching on your behalf, and have the proposal to you by tomorrow afternoon? Great, thank you!

In part 3, "Assemble Your Team," we discussed how to keep your coworkers and supervisors aware of your schedule, which will help prevent them from doing things like this to you. It's also important to realize that sometimes there is no way out of working after hours when there's a *true* emergency. But if those situations are frequent (instead of few and far between), you'll need to have a serious conversation with yourself about whether to shift your mind-set and start loving working around the clock, or find another job in a company that might pay less but honors its employees' well-being.

NEXT STEPS

Each time Julie received a proposal request, she protected her time by going through the steps I outlined in this chapter. In a perfect world, she'd be able to say no to all but the perfect requests that aligned precisely with her schedule.

Since it's not a perfect world, and she needed income to support her family, she would have to Implement Structure *and* Flow and morph time on some occasions. In other words, she'd need to slide time blocks around, delay some lower-priority projects, or delegate out lesser tasks with deadlines to subcontractors. She occasionally would give up family time blocks, but not until after she'd had a conversation with her family members, and they'd discussed the pros and cons of her taking on the client or project.

By the way, a few of the companies that she politely declined have come back to her with proposal requests for other projects because they respected her integrity.

Generating revenue and/or making your boss happy should not come at a cost to your well-being.

⟶ PLOT YOUR NEXT STEPS

- What strategies and tactics from this chapter do you already use, and what is it about them that works for you?
- How will implementing the strategies and tactics in this chapter prevent you from getting overloaded?
- It's important to have responses ready to go — on automatic — when you are approached by someone and asked to take on a task or project. What are three different responses you can use to delay an answer to a request?
- What if they say they need an answer immediately? What are three responses you can have ready to give to delay them at least 10 minutes — long enough for you to go through the steps in this chapter at a rapid rate?
- What if you aren't given the chance to say no or set a deadline? What are some negotiating tactics you can have ready in your back pocket should the need arise?
- When can you rehearse these responses and tactics so that you don't forget them in a panic if an intimidating customer or your boss snarls at you?

41 I Have to Drop Everything When My Clients Call Me in Crisis

Rochelle is a business consultant. She works with both small and large companies around the world and helps them to develop and implement better employee training and leadership management systems.

On a growing number of occasions, she's had clients calling her in crisis. She realizes that the crisis is theirs, but she takes it upon herself to help them, and in the process she makes their crisis hers.

When she assisted clients in these types of situations a couple of times early on, she felt good about helping them, and she was able to catch up on work that had fallen by the wayside during this "crisis containment." But now that she has more clients — and more crisis calls — she can't manage both the crises and the work she's supposed to do. Her stress levels are at unbearable levels.

GOAL

Don't let someone else's emergency become yours.

TACTICS

1. Clearly state your work hours to all involved parties.
2. Define what constitutes an emergency or crisis.

3. Determine whether your job does consist of crisis containment.
4. Define whether your scope of services in the contract includes emergencies or crises that arise.
5. Develop a "red flags" assessment and communication timeline for your clients.
6. Include all this in your website and contract.

STRATEGY

I should probably start with a disclaimer. If you are a medical professional in a hospital, or an emergency responder for the police department, the fire department, or some other emergency department, I would have to say that dealing with crises is a part of your job. There's no getting around that. However, if you do not work in one of the aforementioned fields, keep reading.

Have you ever called a doctor's office and heard the following automated greeting?

"If this is an emergency, please hang up and dial 911."

If doctors' offices don't handle emergencies, you probably don't need to, either.

Clearly state your work hours to all involved parties.

There are a number of people in this world who think that the world is open 24/7, just for them. You are most likely reading this book because you don't want to be open 24/7. Once you've set your business hours, post these everywhere: website, contract, office wall, and so on. Also verbalize this to every client with whom you start a relationship. If setting office hours is a change in policy, be sure to inform all your current clients about this, along with the reasoning behind it: better quality of life for you and your employees, which leads to higher-quality work for clients during focused hours. Add your new office hours to your email signature for extra reminders. If you work for a company, your work hours should have been verified before you accepted employment. If you're unsure, verify now.

Define what constitutes an emergency or crisis.

In our personal lives, we tend to have a good idea of what an emergency is. Your spouse is having a heart attack. You just sliced your hand while chopping veggies for dinner, and you're bleeding everywhere. The house is on fire. You get the picture. But what is an emergency when it comes to work? Most professions don't have true emergencies; rather, situations evolve into so-called emergencies when someone is disorganized and forgets about something, then needs it ASAP, or they don't want to be held accountable for a problem that's cropped up.

But maybe your profession truly does have emergencies. If you're in public relations, an emergency might be that your client was arrested or died. You need to issue a statement right away. On the other hand, if your client waited until the eleventh hour to change an entire publicity campaign, that is not your emergency. Your clients should've been notified ahead of time about all deadlines and what the repercussions would be if deadlines were not met or if changes were made. They had fair warning to be responsible partners.

If you're in the website development/hosting business and a client's website gets hacked, that's an emergency. On the other hand, if your client wants to make some modifications to their website that they just thought of that morning, that is their emergency, not yours.

If you're in life insurance, an urgent situation — but not necessarily an emergency — might be that a client's spouse passed away, and you need to get the ball rolling ASAP on cashing in the policy.

You know your job best, so define the *true* emergencies in your field.

Clearly state to your customers what constitutes an emergency, or if there are no emergencies in your line of work.

Determine whether your job does consist of crisis containment.

Let's say that your client understands that you won't answer phone calls or emails in the middle of the night, but they expect you to wave a magic wand and make all their problems go away the next business day. Is crisis containment your job?

It might very well be. Or, perhaps, you love doing it because you want to feel like someone's hero. If this is the case, you'll need to leave a couple of hours' worth of time blocks in your days for crisis containment. If no crises arise that day (hooray!), you can continue working on your 3+3 and possibly even get ahead. It will also be helpful for you to develop a checklist and/or operations manual to follow in crisis containment situations so that you can ensure that all bases are covered and nothing falls through the cracks.

If, however, crisis containment is not your job, this must be clearly stated at the outset of every client relationship and detailed in your contract or any other written or verbal agreement you have with your customer.

Define whether your scope of services in the contract includes emergencies or crises that arise.

If you have decided that you want to or need to handle emergencies and crisis containment, you must decide if this is a part of your standard contract. For instance, Rochelle (from the beginning of the chapter) can spend anywhere from 2 to 20 hours mopping up a client's mess. If this time is not factored into what you or your company charges in your contract, you might end up working for only $10 an hour. So, clearly state whether "mop-ups" are included in your standard services. If they're not, the client should know ahead of time what the process is to add that service if it becomes necessary and how much that cost is.

Develop a "red flags" assessment and communication timeline for your clients.

Prevention is always the best medicine. If you see a pattern with warning signs that were evident along the way in prior client conflicts, consider developing a check-in assessment as a part of your service. At each benchmark, indicate at what point the client should call you to head off problems at the pass. If they choose to let things slide, you have documentation that they chose to ignore your communication requests and/or didn't assess the situation at necessary intervals. In other words, you're making your clients more responsible for their actions, instead of letting them use you as their bail-out system. Whether your crisis containment will be within your regular scope of services or as an add-on, be sure to specify a timeline on how quickly you will react to and assist with the situation. If clients know ahead of time that you'll acknowledge their issue within 24 hours, begin work on the issue within 72, and schedule a meeting within 7 to 10 days after that, they know up front what the expectations are, so they won't hound you for a solution *now*.

Include all this in your website and contract.

Post all your policies and procedures wherever you can: on your website (even if it's a private page to which you send prospective clients), in your agreement, in a welcome email, in a yearly check-in email...anywhere and everywhere.

NEXT STEPS

Rochelle decided that there were, indeed, a couple of emergency situations with which she should assist. She also realized that she could avoid many of these crisis calls by addressing these situations during her trainings, as well as sending monthly check-in assessments. She opted to not include crisis containment in her standard services contract, so she created a separate crisis containment contract, which she shared with clients at the time she was retained so that they had clear expectations of what she was being hired to do, and what services would require additional payment.

Simply sharing common problem scenarios with her clients during appointments helped decrease the number of emergency calls because she was giving her clients the tools to prevent crises in the first place. And when she did get a call, she knew that she didn't have to drop everything because the client had already been told what the timeline and procedures would be for crisis containment. Now, were the clients always happy about it when they were reminded? No, they were in a perceived crisis, so there was no joy. But they did acknowledge that they knew this and understood they would be taken care of.

ⅠⅠⅠ➡ PLOT YOUR NEXT STEPS

- How much time can you gain back weekly or monthly just by cutting down on fighting fires for your customer emergencies?
- How does allowing these types of interruptions support your progress toward your work priorities and targets? (That's right! It's a trick question!)
- What constitutes a true emergency for a client? (Think life or death for your business or the company for which you work.)
- Which of these emergencies, if any, are you willing to assist with?
- Which of these emergencies, if any, will be a part of your standard services, and which will require additional contracts?
- If you work for a company, and these measures are not currently in place, whom can you approach with a proposal to do this?
- Whether you work for a company or own your own business, what preventive measures could be in place to help your customers avoid crises?

42 I'd Love to Control My Time, but I Don't Know What to Say to People

When I was in high school, my dear friend Janice's aunt, Judy Chabola, was known for her choreography skills. She received high marks for her involvement with the 1984 Olympics in Los Angeles. She also was hired to work on various awards shows in Hollywood.

When we turned 16, Judy offered Janice the opportunity of a lifetime: work as a seat filler at these awards shows. The main duty was to fill the empty seats at the front of the auditorium when actors and actresses left to present awards or use the restroom or snort cocaine, so that the TV audience wouldn't see empty seats. Janice asked if I'd like to work with her, so of course I said yes! Even after we found out that it was unpaid work. (Wait, isn't that volunteering?)

Our first "job" of many was at the Emmys. I clearly remember the instructions we were given: "You do not look at or make eye contact with the celebrities. You do not talk to them. If you do so, you will be asked to leave." Sheesh! I was already intimidated by bossy adults. Now I was mortified.

I did a really great job of keeping my eyes focused on the floor, yet not bumping into anything or anyone. At one point halfway through the show, I was standing in an empty foyer. It was nice to be able to finally look up at my surroundings. When I approached the auditorium doors to go back to my position, both doors suddenly swung open toward me, and there stood the future star of *Dr. Quinn, Medicine Woman* herself, Jane Seymour. I'd seen her beauty on the screen but was absolutely captivated by it in person. Her hair was perfectly up-swept, and her deep red lipstick perfectly matched her elegant, deep red gown.

And then…I accidentally looked straight into her eyes. Oh no!

I couldn't just stand there and stare. I needed to say something. But I didn't want to get in trouble. So I whispered loudly to her from my safe, nonstalker distance:

"You look radiant!"

She smiled, looked down shyly and then back up at my eyes, and whispered to me in her beautiful English accent, "Thank you!"

She passed me by. I stood there and waited for the security guards to throw me out. They walked past me, too.

GOAL

Protect your time by saying what needs to be said — in a way that won't get you in trouble.

TACTICS

1. Know your 3+3 and time blocks.
2. Offer choices to the other party instead of waiting for choices to be given to you.
3. If negotiations are necessary, explain the choices you give as all about bene-fiting them — even though you've chosen them because they benefit you.

STRATEGY

As you become more assertive with yourself in telling your time what to do, it's also important to become more assertive with those on both your personal team and work team. If you're a nurturer, this can be a tough change because you're so used to caring for everyone else — but rarely yourself — and instantly saying yes to their every need. And ladies, many of us have an additional hurdle to clear because society has taught us that being straightforward can be a negative trait. That's why we often speak in ESP. We often don't directly say what we mean; we expect others to read between the lines and get the point we're trying to make. It's time to be more straightforward, but you can do it with soft edges so that you don't come across as an ogre.

> Do or do not.
> There is no try.
>
> — Yoda, Jedi Master

Jedi mind trick: You need to make your words sound as if it's all about the other party, even though what you're offering them will benefit you.

It's not as cagey as it sounds. I promise! In the long run, whatever benefits your work style and schedule *is* a benefit to the person you're dealing with because with your lower stress levels and clear head, you'll be able to perform better on whatever tasks he or she is asking of you.

I've given examples along the way in this handbook about how to present options to others, such as:

How to get your boss to let you rearrange deadlines — in chapter 40, "I Often Let Great Opportunities Turn into Big Stress." The focus was on making the boss look good and the clients happy, and what boss wouldn't want that? But you'd be doing it on a less stressful schedule for you.

How to get out of going to a pointless meeting — in chapter 29, "Facilitate Productive Team Meetings." The focus was on better serving the student, and what principal wouldn't want that? It would be accomplished by using time that had previously been wasted by said meetings.

The key is to state things in a way that can't get you in trouble. For example, if Jane Seymour went to the supervisor to tattle on me, imagine how it would sound:

"How dare she! Do you know what she said to me? She said I looked radiant!" She would come across as pretty silly for calling me out on that.

Now, developing this skill doesn't mean that you'll know exactly what to say in every situation of your life. I'll be the first to admit that I've uttered some cockamamie thoughts in various business meetings, in social situations, and even at a funeral. But when it comes to protecting my time, I'm armed with "all about you" templates and tactics in my back pocket, so there's less thinking to do on my feet.

How to ask for help on the home front

Have this conversation at the end of a meal, when everyone's belly is full. This is when we're at our happiest and most agreeable. Select your choices (your low-hanging fruit) ahead of time from your various brainstorm and task lists.

The template:

1. You apologize (if applicable).
2. You state your goal in a way that benefits them.
3. You state why it's important in a way that benefits them.
4. You ask for help.
5. You give them choices on what to help with.

Example:

You: I realize I've been snapping at you because I've been pretty stressed-out from everything I'm trying to do. I'm really sorry about that, and I want to stop the moodiness. When I come home, my blood pressure goes up because of the condition of the house, and how that causes us to be late or not find things. And then I just end up yelling at you. I don't want that anymore. I realize that I need your help in order to get done what needs to get done. Do you think you could help me?

Loved one(s): Okay.

You: Terrific! Here are all the things that need to get done around the house each week. I can do these 10. Which three would you like to help me with?

In your work life, you can use the same kind of template to ask for help on team projects.

How to get coworkers or business associates to conform to your schedule

The template:

1. You state what benefit the other person will receive by scheduling at your suggested time(s).
2. You offer the suggested times.
3. If the other party counters with offers, choose the offer that benefits your schedule the most.
4. Counteroffer on the other party's best offer if necessary.
5. Adjust your time blocks accordingly.

Example:

Jim Bob: We need to set up a meeting to prepare for the Big Client Gathering.

You: No problem. I can block off time for you so that we're not interrupted, so we can get more work done in less time. [Pause to look
at your calendar, which is scheduled with your work periods for
project timelines and tasks.] I can meet with you on: [start calling
out your open dates and time blocks on those dates].

Plan A:

Jim Bob: Great! Date at x:00 will work.

Plan B:

Jim Bob: Nope, none of those work. How about Monday at 9:00 or
Tuesday at 10:00?

You: [Examine your calendar to make sure this will work. If not,
counter.] Monday is a no-go. On Tuesday, I have a conflict until
10:15. Can we say Tuesday at 10:30?

Jim Bob: Sure.

NEXT STEPS

Congratulations! You now know how to negotiate in a way that protects your
time, health, and sanity. You can still be a nurturer and care about others, but now
you'll be doing so in a way that improves your efficiency and quality of work.

In the original *Star Wars* movie trilogy, Luke Skywalker did not become a
Jedi Knight overnight. It took a little bit of practice before he was able to fully
implement his Jedi mind tricks. I encourage you to practice on the home front
first, and then apply the same techniques to your work setting.

⁞⁞⁞➡ PLOT YOUR NEXT STEPS

- Which of these tactics are you already applying successfully?
- What words or actions have you used in the past that have not been suc-
  cessful?
- What will you do differently to protect your time?
- Using the templates as a guide, what phrases can you have ready to go for
  situations that crop up frequently for you?
- When will you rehearse these lines?

43 I Never Stick to My Time Management Plan

Julie is absolutely driven and pays attention to every last detail. If she has to produce a project for a client, it's a sure bet that it will be the most thorough presentation of information one has ever seen or read on the subject, and it will be issued in one of the most sleek and beautiful layouts one has ever seen. Her clients know that if she says she'll do something, boy, will she ever do it!

But when it comes to working on her time management skills for work and her personal life, the confidence that she exudes while working on her client projects completely disappears. Instead of saying, "I will," she says, "I'll try." Instead of saying, "I'll get it to work," she says, "It never works."

Instead of taking the bull by the horns as she does with her client projects — even when she's not completely sure about the subject or the deliverable that the client wants — she approaches time management with fear, trepidation, and timidity. She turns into a completely different person.

GOAL

Make a commitment to using only positive self-talk. Make a commitment to reflecting with power at least twice per month. Make a commitment to creating your 3+3 at the end of each day.

TACTICS

Remove success-blocking vocabulary from your internal dialogue:

I'll try

I can't

I never can

Repeat to yourself the following:

I need to take my time in order to save time.

I want peace in my life, so I'll do what it takes to achieve that.

I will be more present so that I can apply the strategies from this book.

I will invest the time to plan out my next day.

I will reflect with power at least twice per month.

I will be successful with my time management.

STRATEGY

The phenomenon of self-talk obstruction is split right down the middle. Fifty percent of my clients say, "Help me to create a schedule, and I'll stick to it." These are my short-term clients. They need only a few sessions to get back on track with their time management.

The other 50 percent say, "I never stick to my schedule." These are my clients who need more than my starter package. Instead of being able to dive into strategies and tactics, we have to spend time stamping out their fear and redirecting their successful approaches in other areas of their work or personal life to the arena of productivity. Once they realize that their mind-set has been the hindrance all along, they are able to get back on track. Time management is all about mind management.

Henry Ford was spot-on when he said, "Whether you believe you can do a thing or not, you are right."

If you start off by saying it won't work, it definitely won't. If you start off by saying it will work, then you just infinitely increased your likelihood of success.

Let's examine some reasons why the time management track you chose in the past might not have worked.

Were you telling yourself that you absolutely would be successful?

Were you living by the overall strategies and concepts and not just attempting to implement only the tactics?

Were you viewing your priorities and targets on a daily basis?

Were you practicing self-care?

Were you aware of exactly where your time was going?

Were you planning your schedule based on your priorities and targets?

Were you mapping out and scheduling the steps for your long-term projects?

Were you creating your 3+3 on a daily basis?

Were you controlling the five key areas of the workday (AGENT) by Implementing Structure *and* Flow?

Were you communicating with your personal and work teams?

Has your life been the same every single day, without any type of variance, change, or uh-oh?

Were you reflecting with power at the end of each week?

If you answered no to any of those questions, have no fear!

Guess what this book covers?

All that! And then some.

Here's a little secret I'll let you in on. Organized and productive people make life look easy. It's because they've had years — or perhaps even decades — of practice. It would be unfair to suggest that you can just snap your fingers and think that you'll magically be living on Easy Street. It'll take some time for you to train your brain to think about and live the strategies that we discuss in this book. You will need to be the most present you've ever been in your entire life.

Here's one more secret. Organized and productive people fall off the wagon, too. If we go on autopilot, that's when things can begin to unravel. And then we need to regroup. To stay organized and productive, we must apply these strategies and tactics on a daily basis. All day, every day.

> The dictionary is the only place where you come to SUCCESS before you get to WORK.
>
> — *Stubby Currence, "The Press Box"*

I don't tell you this to scare you off. I tell you this so that you're realistically prepared for this mission of becoming an agent of change in your Time Management Revolution. It may sound boring to have such structured days and to have to constantly think about the decisions you make about your time. But if you do, this will free up your brain for more creative thinking, and it will free up your time for living the life you want to live.

NEXT STEPS

As you read through the chapters in this book, you saw that Julie was able to turn things around. She created the life she wanted to have by practicing my CIA framework — **C**reate Clarity, **I**mplement Structure *and* Flow, and **A**ssemble Your Team. She realized that she hadn't been able to stick to her time management track in the past because she was trying to apply various tactics without understanding the strategies behind them. She learned that there wasn't a top-five list of things to do to stick to her plan. She needed to apply all the strategies and live them.

We keyed in on Julie's "no fear" mind-set that she uses successfully in her client project situations and applied it to the strategies I recommended to her. She planned, practiced, reflected, and stuck it out. There was some initial discomfort, and it did take time for these strategies to become habits, but they eventually worked because of her mind-set. She said she would do it; she said she would stick to it; she said she would be successful. She did, and she was.

It truly is all in your head.

> ⅢⅢ➡ **PLOT YOUR NEXT STEPS**
>
> - You may be familiar with many of the strategies and tactics I discuss in this book, but how many have you applied on a regular basis?
> - Which strategies and tactics have you not been using, which could be why you haven't been sticking to your time management plan?
> - How determined are you to improve your time management and productivity?
> - If any success-blocking vocabulary enters your brain, how will you eliminate it?

Conclusion

Be an Agent of Change
in Your Time Management Revolution

Congratulations on completing this phase of your mission and investing in your career, your personal relationships, and your physical and mental well-being!

You now understand why I refer to my lessons as mind-bending. Simply put, every strategy and tactic related to time management comes right down to *mind* management. Just by understanding your own self-interruptions from procrastination, distractions, lack of focus, and overwhelm, you'll be able to slash lost time from your day! And if you've never utilized your brain this way before — or if it's been quite some time — you've literally made a shift in your thinking and mind-set.

Fabulous!

It takes brainpower to make good decisions. And *it takes practice* to get your brain used to this kind of power. This may tucker you out at the beginning, but after a few months of daily implementation, your mind management will become a second-nature habit.

I hope you're eventually able to revel in working only five days a week instead of seven, or going on long holidays or short staycations instead of never taking time off. My wish is for you to experience freedom, calm, and peace on so many days during the year that when you do start to feel a little frazzled, you recognize it instantly because you're no longer used to experiencing that.

WORK-LIFE BALANCE

A few decades ago, as Americans began to feel overworked, the term *work–life balance* emerged in our vocabulary. The idea was to have these two parts of your life completely separated and level — in perfect balance each day. Spend one-third of your day on sleep, one-third at home, one-third at work. Today, that term has evolved into *work–life integration*. Some believers of this theory espouse the thought that it's impossible to separate work life from personal life, so we can expect to bounce between the two at any given time throughout the day and night.

I propose a hybrid of the two theories — a balance of the two, if you will. It's important to spend one-third of your day on sleep and rejuvenation. The other two-thirds will be split between work and personal time, but they won't necessarily be a 50–50 division. In fact, the split might vary each day: 70–30, 60–40, 50–50, 40–60, 30–70. If you telecommute, own your own company, or are a mobile warrior, you might flip-flop between work blocks of time and personal blocks of time throughout the day and evening. If you work for a company, you most likely will work in one solid block. Your line of work may have wickedly long seasonal hours and shorter hours during the rest of the year. No matter your situation, there needs to be some type of work–life separation; if not, your brain won't have a chance to recharge from either component and will never work at full capacity. It will be important to not let your work life and personal life completely integrate; otherwise, you won't know what you're living for.

REAL-LIFE BALANCE

Full disclosure: A few times a year, I go AWOL from my very own teachings and tips, and start to pile up my caseload with too much. Perhaps I skip a few workdays of doing my 3+3. Or maybe I think I can squeeze in one more task — a little adrenaline chase — since I'm ahead of the game. Perhaps I say yes to something before double-checking my priorities and targets lists because I think I know them well enough by now. I can slide for a few days or maybe a week, right? After all, I am The Inefficiency Assassin!

But then I start to feel off-balance. Since I'm used to being calm, I can literally feel my heart rate start to increase, my stress level start to creep up and tense up my body, and my brain not make the sharp decisions it normally executes — all because I chose to push the boundaries too much and leave the protection of my structure. And because I was skipping out of some of the planning, I didn't have the power to effectively shift my time blocks and go with the flow.

I share this confession with you because it's imperative for you to know that we're all human, so we'll all slip up now and then. And just because you slip up doesn't mean you're completely off track, mission aborted. You just took a temporary leave of absence, and you need to get reconnected with your Zen warrior.

It's at times like these when you need to remind yourself to step back and review your separate work priorities and targets and personal priorities and targets. Return to the strategies and tactics that I discuss in this book. Put nonurgent projects on the back burner and just focus on the more important tasks at hand. Laser in on your priorities and targets, and beat back self-interruptions and inefficiencies from your day. This is what will bring you balance.

Get back into the groove of the CIA framework:

Create Clarity
Implement Structure *and* Flow
Assemble Your Team

It's important to understand that time management is not something you can put on autopilot. Sure, you don't have to do your 3+3 on your days off or when you're on vacation, but when you're at work, when you're living your regular life, implementing my CIA framework is something you need to do consciously each day. It's this implementation that will allow you to have the time for those play days, to spend your time as you see fit, and to live the life you want to live.

It's also important to realize that the day you have absolutely nothing to do for your business or your job is the day to be very scared that you're obsolete and no longer needed. Rejoice that you do have work, but everything that you need to get done does not have to overtake your life and fill you with overwhelm, stress, and dread. Shift your mantra from "I must do this task for my business or job, or else I'll lose out!" to "I should spend time doing things that make me happy, or else I'll lose out!" Will saying yes to that "one more thing" for work support your priorities in life?

CONTROL TIME AND LIVE LIFE ON YOUR TERMS

After reading this book, you now have the weapons you need to work efficiently and obtain whatever definition of balance you seek. You can monitor the ebbs and flows of each day and adjust as necessary. After reading this book, you now understand all the strategies and tactics you can use to bring out your mind management power from deep cover and into your consciousness.

You will be an agent of change in your Time Management Revolution.

You will be productive *and* have a life outside of your business or your job.

You will work smarter, not longer.

Productivity.

Balance.

Happiness.

Success.

Peace.

Time management is all about mind-set and *mind* management.

It truly is...all in your head.

The End.

Acknowledgments

Joseph: You do everything possible to support my entrepreneur brain and crazy adventures. And you're a great cook. And travel partner. And wineaux. Happy 21+. "**A**ssemble Your Team" — you're the heart of my personal team.

Mom and Dad: Thank you for giving me a great life and for being tremendous teachers; you helped introduce me to "**C**reate Clarity."

Dean and Jill: It is so awesome to have a brother and sister-in-law who will drop everything when I visit. You work hard and are pooped at the end of the day, plus you keep your boys on a schedule, but you are willing to "**I**mplement Structure *and* Flow" when I'm in town.

This book was tough to get going because two very important loves had left my life. Two of our pups, Georgie and Deus, passed away when I first began writing a draft of this book...then stopped. They'd slept at my feet for the majority of the writing I did for my first two books. Their snoring soothed me. I miss them dearly. We are grateful that Hildy is still with us and that Freddie has joined our family.

SA Women's Power Group — my home girls, Margaret Anaglia (Al's Gourmet Nuts), Cheryl Ludwick (Koch Ranches), and Pattie Porter (Conflict Connections): Thank you for being my accountability partners and members of my work team. This book got finished because of you.

My LivingOrderSA clients: I've learned tremendously from all of you I've worked with in person, via phone, and at workshops and trainings. Thank you for being a part of my life. It brings me tremendous joy to be with you.

Jason Gardner: Thank you for championing this book.

Jeffrey Herman: Thank you for introducing me to Georgia Hughes, who assigned me to Jason and his team.

Kristen Cashman and Elissa Rabellino: Thank you for tearing apart my manuscript in order to make it better.

Munro Magruder and Monique Muhlenkamp: You and your team definitely understand timelines for long-term projects. Thank you for all your behind-the-scenes work.

Cary Corbin: Thank you for being a supportive sounding board and inviting me to events that inspire. Who knew that the National Prayer Day gathering would help The Inefficiency Assassin put the finishing touches on her book?

Lorie Marrero: Thank you for being a wonderful mentor, colleague, and friend.

Clutter Diet team — Lorie Marrero (founder), Yvette Clay, Deb Lee, Kim Oser, and Ellen Delap: I'm proud to be on a team with some of the best darn CPOs (Certified Professional Organizers) on this planet! Thank you also to the caring community members who allow us to be a part of their lives.

NSA Austin:

- Cheryl Jones: Thank you for finally getting me to attend, qualify, and join. The wonderfully supportive community of fellow speakers led me to...

- Jane Atkinson: You introduced me to Wilene Dunn, who's been sharing with meeting planners the gospel of The Inefficiency Assassin — the importance of saving time. And early on, you also helped me "Ready, Aim, Fire!" and referred me to...

- James Mapes, an NSA member she knows: You gave me the thumbs-up to listen to the folks at...

- Avanoo: This incredible start-up company invited me to create a 30-day video program. The creation of this program helped me finalize my book outline. And through Avanoo, I was introduced to and interviewed by...

- Tom Evans: Perfect timing, meeting you (a kindred spirit about time) and getting the juice to kick up writing a notch, with writing tips for the short attention span–afflicted.

- Ted Manasa: You somehow get dropped into my life (this time at an NSA meeting) whenever I'm working on a metaphor. Thank you for appearing, once again, and recommending Tony Mendez to me as I proceeded into the heart of the writing of this book.

Maribeth Likins: Thank you for being a fairy godmother–listener for prospective clients.

Bert, Skip, Heather, Jen, and Lisa of Incite Digital Marketing; Diana Turner of Turner & Cleveland; Mark and Candy Vasquez; Judy Monsees of Judy's Loft: You're part of my work team who always has my back, and I am incredibly appreciative of that.

Joe Segura: Thank you for being at my book launch events.

Joey Tellez: Thanks for pointing out the obvious.

To the soldiers and operatives I mentioned in the dedication: Gene Grabeel (former schoolteacher turned World War II code breaker), Dorothy Blum (cryptologist and computer genius), Sandy Grimes and Jeanne Vertefeuille (CIA mole hunters) — you're women who blazed a trail and protected our country from harm. Marcus Luttrell, Chris Kyle, Anthony Mendez: I read your books as I entered into the thick of writing. When I think of Luttrell, Kyle, and our nephew, Andrew Segura, holed up in some barren desert in the Middle East in the fight against terrorism, putting your lives on the line for us, or Anthony Mendez in espionage webs in Southeast Asia, Iran, and the Soviet Union, it really puts life into perspective. Time? We've got loads of it. Problems? Not compared with what you experienced. When it comes down to it, I have annoyances, not problems. And I have the freedom to write this book and say whatever I want because of you and your colleagues in the armed forces and intelligence agencies. I am forever grateful to you.

Index

About the Author

The author of two Amazon bestselling books, Helene Segura has been the featured productivity expert in more than 100 media interviews, in publications such as *U.S. News & World Report* and *Money* magazine, as well as on Fox, CBS, ABC, and NBC affiliates. Born and raised in Los Angeles, she earned her bachelor's degree from Texas A&M University (Gig 'em!) and her master's degree from the University of Texas at San Antonio.

By day, Helene presents keynotes and trainings as The Inefficiency Assassin and teaches audiences and clients how to slay wasted time. By night (and on weekends), she's a devout cheese eater, a recipe experimenter, and a travel junkie. If you blink, you might miss her sneaking adult beverages onto the lawn bowling court at her home outside of San Antonio.

For information about keynotes, workshops, and individual coaching, or to connect via social media (you're on the honor system not to procrastinate!), visit www.HeleneSegura.com.

NEW WORLD LIBRARY is dedicated to publishing books and other media that inspire and challenge us to improve the quality of our lives and the world.

We are a socially and environmentally aware company. We recognize that we have an ethical responsibility to our customers, our staff members, and our planet.

We serve our customers by creating the finest publications possible on personal growth, creativity, spirituality, wellness, and other areas of emerging importance. We serve New World Library employees with generous benefits, significant profit sharing, and constant encouragement to pursue their most expansive dreams.

As a member of the Green Press Initiative, we print an increasing number of books with soy-based ink on 100 percent postconsumer-waste recycled paper. Also, we power our offices with solar energy and contribute to non-profit organizations working to make the world a better place for us all.

Our products are available in bookstores everywhere.

www.newworldlibrary.com

At NewWorldLibrary.com you can download our catalog,
subscribe to our e-newsletter, read our blog,
and link to authors' websites, videos, and podcasts.

Find us on Facebook, follow us on Twitter, and watch us on YouTube.

Send your questions and comments our way!
You make it possible for us to do what we love to do.

Phone: 415-884-2100 or 800-972-6657
Catalog requests: Ext. 10 | Orders: Ext. 10 | Fax: 415-884-2199
escort@newworldlibrary.com

 NEW WORLD LIBRARY
publishing books that change lives   14 Pamaron Way, Novato, CA 94949